BRITISH AND AMERICAN

ENGLISH

SINCE 1900

by

Eric Partridge

and

John W. Clark

Associate Professor of English, University of Minnesota

With contributions on English in Canada, South Africa, Australia
New Zealand and India

PHILOSOPHICAL LIBRARY

NEW YORK

PUBLISHED, 1951, BY PHILOSOPHICAL LIBRARY, INC.,
15 EAST 40TH STREET, NEW YORK, 16, N.Y.

*Set in 12pt. Aldine Bembo and
Printed and made in Great Britain by
Fletcher and Son Ltd Norwich and
The Leighton-Straker Bookbinding Co Ltd London*

For

GREGORY MITCHELL
(*of Onehunga, New Zealand*)

gratefully
for much friendly assistance in Maori
and for many kind, thoughtful and generous actions
over a period of many years

ERIC PARTRIDGE

FOREWORD

THIS book constitutes an informal, not an academic, history of English since 1900. To avoid repetition, the American section is the shorter; the general themes common to both are treated in the British section, although logic demands that they be at least mentioned in the other.

By 'informal' the two authors mean neither journalistic nor arbitrary; merely that, although it will, they think, be useful to students and perhaps even to scholars, the book is addressed primarily to the general reading public—or, rather, to the intelligent members of that public.

Having agreed upon the ground to be covered and the general principles to be followed, the editors hastily assured each other that they wished to remain individuals, not to become a pair of yoke-fellows; that only in a sturdy independence could they achieve their joint purpose. Perhaps they also realized that, each refraining from indulgence in 'nasty cracks' at the English spoken or written by the other, they would avoid 'getting in each other's hair'. By a not intransigent independence and by a quite touching regard for each other's susceptibilities, they have, as excellent friends, ended a journey they began as amicable acquaintances.

Both of the partners wish to thank, very warmly, those authors and authorities who have contributed original matter or have allowed already published work to be quoted. Vague generalities soon become tedious: example is so much more helpful than precept, and so very much less boring.

ERIC PARTRIDGE
JOHN W. CLARK

CONTENTS

Part I

BRITISH ENGLISH: BY ERIC PARTRIDGE

ix

Part II

AMERICAN ENGLISH: BY JOHN W. CLARK

A GLANCE AROUND

ON being invited to contribute the volume on English to
this series of histories of British civilization in the
twentieth century, I almost simultaneously perceived
that whereas the authors of other books (Politics—Law—
Sport—etc.) could, and should, deal with the particular subject indicated by the title and remain within the terms of
reference, I could or, at least, should do nothing of the sort.

Was it to be a history of English as spoken in the British
Isles? But that would be to ignore the English spoken in
Canada, South Africa, Australia and New Zealand: and I had
no wish to perpetuate a defect far too common among English,
Scottish, Welsh and Irish philologists.

Supposing, then, I included the English spoken in the Dominions and, by implication, in the Colonies, what right had I to
ignore, as so many philologists throughout the British Empire
have so long and so successfully ignored, that branch of
English which is spoken in the United States of America?
Numerically considered in terms of its users, American English
is more important than British English. American English is
not only important in itself; it is important also because its
influence is increasing in Great Britain and Ireland—in Australia—and in Canada. These and many related facts will be
considered in their due place, some of them both by John
Clark and by myself.

Obviously I am incompetent to deal with the American
branch of English. Therefore I had to find an American authority upon the subject of American English. But not just any
authority, no matter how good he might be. In such a book as
this, designed for general reading and, incidentally, intended
rather to promote the cause of amity between two great
nations than to provide the Senior Common Rooms, whether
American or British or Dominions, with contentious matter—
in such a book the only suitable collaborator would be one
who, in addition to ranking as a good scholar, bore no grudge

against, felt no contempt for, and indeed went so far as to like Britons as well as he liked their language; one who, moreover, shared with his colleague not only the belief that *British English* and *American English* are rightly so named but also the hope that neither Americans nor Britons will come to speak of, much less to speak, *British* and *American*. Too many persons on both sides of the Atlantic have forgotten, if indeed they ever realized, that American English has had as long a history as British English and that, until the seventeenth century, the former was spoken throughout the British Isles. John Clark is not one of them.

No less obviously I have always been incompetent to speak authoritatively upon either Canadian English or South African English; although, for numerous reasons, I'm still competent to speak of Australian English, I am much less competent to speak of New Zealand English, for I left New Zealand in 1907. Something, moreover, had to be said about the position in India and Pakistan. I have therefore borrowed the eyes and ears of men far better equipped: having for many years looked about them and listened attentively, they generously contribute their findings upon these important branches of English. All five of them are healthily independent in their views; on the other hand, they do not proclaim, nor even think, that (say) Australian English is superior to the English spoken in Scotland; they go no further than to hold that it is only natural for the 'Colonial' accents to differ from the accents predominantly heard in Britain.

On glancing around at my colleagues, I notice that every one of them allows all the others the right to speak their own particular kind of English. Even Australians and Americans concede to the inhabitants of the British Isles the right to speak English as those inhabitants have learnt to speak it: and even Englishmen have been known to admit that they are entirely in the wrong when they apply to American English or Australian English or New Zealand English certain criteria that, because of tremendous climatic, geographical, historical differences, simply aren't applicable elsewhere than in England or, at most, Great Britain and Ireland.

For much the same reasons as have prompted me to seek help in America and in the Dominions, I have, for several subjects within my own branch, sought help from scholars able to write of them far more satisfactorily than ever I could.

E. P.

PART I

British English

*

CHAPTER ONE

LITERARY ENGLISH

THERE are two kinds of English, the literary and the non-literary; and each kind may be either spoken or written. That is a truism—but a truism far too often forgotten. Whereas some writers upon the English language do their best to ignore spoken English, others treat written English as merely subsidiary to spoken; and, to adopt a different classification, many writers deal solely with literary, or at least Standard, English, and ignore the rest.

Not only is nearly all spoken English non-literary and most of it not even Standard, but also more written English than not is non-literary. Since, however, the illiterate do not often write, written English suffers much less from illiteracy than spoken English suffers from it. If it were not for the constant inter-action of written and spoken English, speech being influenced by—indeed, frequently imitative of—books and newspapers, and the written word by the spoken, the gap between English written well and English spoken badly would be still greater than it is: even as it is, the gap is enormous. That is a question to be treated elsewhere, for it cannot be separated from the question of the vernacular, a subject coyly shunned by all but amazingly few scholars and by almost every professional writer.

Let us therefore consider literary English, especially in its written form. Spoken literary English differs from the written only in being less subtle, rather less formal and slightly more familiar; however familiar it may be, it remains impeccably Standard. For instance, most speakers on the Third Programme allow their scripts to be printed unchanged.

Written literary English, in some respects vastly less important than its writers suppose it to be, is in another—the traditional, the obvious—respect, the most important of all forms of
English. Rather by literary than by non-literary written
English has British civilization been judged, whether by native
or by foreign historians: the impact of English upon civilization
has come, in the main, from literature, for only historians and
other incorrigible searchers read newspapers more than a day
old, and only they read or glance at that vast mass of material
which accumulates dust in the Public Record Office and in the
county or other local archives. Luckily for British civilization!

Written literary English may conveniently, though very
loosely, be divided—as, indeed, it has long been customary to
divide it—into poetry; dramatic literature; the novel; and mis-
cellaneous or, as it is often so ineptly called, 'prose literature'.

Non-Dramatic Poetry

More clearly in poetry (especially in non-dramatic poetry)
do we see how great are the differences between the literature
of 1950 and that of 1900. Literature being inseparable from language and the manner inseparable from the matter, the style
from the thought, a brief consideration of the poetry, as of the
prose, published during the first fifty years of this century is not
merely relevant; it is unavoidable.

In 1900, poetry was in a bad way. More, it was dying on its
stilted feet. The exceedingly few examples of poetic vitality (for
instance, Kipling and Masefield) stand out like healthy men in
a land stricken by a particularly virulent and widespread form
of sleeping sickness. For the fact that poetry did not become a
dilettante hobby expressed in poems perhaps as dainty as
Tanagra figurines and certainly no less dead, we must thank
Kipling, Masefield and Hardy, who, whatever their defects in
the eyes of the moderns, were at least men, not epicenes—notably alive—generous; thank ruefully the wars of 1914-1918 and
1939-1945; thank also the poetic school of the 1930's—
Spender, Auden, Day Lewis, MacNeice, and others, most of

them fortunately still with us, with several worthy additions, especially perhaps Dylan Thomas.

Although Kipling, Masefield and Hardy were, in the main, technically conventional in their verse, yet they did invest that technique with freshness and vitality: but then, they possessed fresh, alert, observant minds and warm, undeluded hearts, and many of their themes were such as to incur many pained protests from those who were at all points conventional, who lacked that profound sense of social pity for mankind and that equally important sympathy with the lot of the eager, bewildered, striving, baffled, pathetically vulnerable men and women of their generations, which these three great writers, capable in prose and verse alike, so eminently possessed. In *The Everlasting Mercy*, 1911, Masefield gave poetic dignity to themes hitherto avoided by the poets; Kipling anticipated the poets of the 1930's and 1940's by revealing the poetry of pistons and pylons, of mechanism and motor; and Hardy showed that in a rugged beauty, a simple heart, there may be an ultimate lyricism and a spiritual nobility: all three so extended the field of poetic subjects that these subjects were now to be virtually co-extensive with life itself and its material trappings: all three so enlarged the vocabulary of poetry that it became almost co-extensive with that of prose. These three poets revived a body rapidly qualifying for the description 'corpse'.

If Kipling, Masefield and Hardy have, as poets, been traditionalists, theirs is a revolutionary traditionalism. In this, they possess much in common with T. S. Eliot, who, in religion and politics and in a regard for civilization, is essentially a traditionalist: yet look what Eliot has done for poetry—and, say his enemies, look also what he has done to it. But even what he has done to it, badly needed doing. What he has done for it can hardly yet be assessed. It is considerable. At the lowest estimate, he has completed the revivification initiated by Hardy, Kipling and Masefield.

But that would be an estimate absurdly low, for *The Waste Land*, 1922, contributed something new to English poetry—hence, soon to American poetry, a process facilitated by the fact that Eliot is an Anglo-American. Nor should his later poems be forgotten: they have reinforced the implications (he being too modest a writer to think of his implicit message as 'lessons') underlying *The Waste Land*. His passion for truth is a passion for truth in all things: only petty-minded nit-wits could accuse him of writing poetry, drama, criticism, that is either escapist or devoid of sympathy towards mankind.

Eliot's sympathies are for all mankind, not merely for one class, nor yet for one nation. To refuse to be bulldozed into thinking that a labourer working forty hours a week and envious of everyone with more brains or more guts or more ambition or wider interests is superior to a businessman whose ability creates work and wages for hundreds of employees—to a scientist working fifty or sixty hours a week in order to improve the lot of suffering men and women—to a great surgeon or a great architect—to a composer whose music brings pleasure to millions, an artist bringing a new vision to thousands, a novelist bringing either relaxation or instruction or inspiration to myriads: to fail to believe any such fantastic fairy tale is not, after all, equivalent to failing in sympathy for the working man. If working men or women lack culture or education, they nowadays should blame no one but themselves, for they have far more time at their disposal than most professional men and most business men: if they lack education and culture, they do so for the same reason that so many of the bourgeoisie lack them: they don't want them: and they don't want them, any of these people, because, not understanding these things, they think that they, the proletarian or bourgeois or aristocratic philistines, don't need them or wouldn't benefit by them. When Eliot claims that no poetry exercises any social influence whatever, he is deliberately exaggerating: he is also implying—what too many Utopians fail to realize—that the proportion of mankind interested in the things of the spirit is very small. Why, therefore, should he write down for people that, in any event, read nothing more than the newspaper or perhaps a sadistic or sexy 'thriller'?

That may, to the hasty, have appeared a digression. It isn't. Often have I heard it said that Eliot does not write for the hypothetical 'man in the street'. No poet, dramatist, novelist, scholar does write for that non-existent public: ninety per cent. of 'men (and women) in the street' or, for that matter, in the fields or the mines don't read good books, nor even good magazines. Eliot writes for those who not only can (theoretically) but also, in fact, do read; for the more intelligent of these actual and potential readers. In 1946, Stephen Spender, himself a considerable poet, remarked (*Poetry since* 1939) of Eliot that 'his may well be the greatest poetic influence in the world to-day'; now in 1951, it certainly is the greatest—by far the greatest—and probably will be for at least another decade.

Now, that is a remarkable achievement, for T. S. Eliot's poetry has, from the beginning, been rather less obvious, whether in content or in form, than (say) *Night has a thousand eyes.* That it has come, that by the end of 1923 it had already come, to exercise this great influence constitutes an extraordinary tribute to the poet's integrity, intellectual ability, spiritual worthiness, and also to the strangely compulsive appeal, aesthetic no less than mental and moral, of his highly individualized style and versification.

That literary effect, that literary influence, that merit both intrinsic and extrinsic—these facts and characteristics depend, inevitably, upon the use Eliot makes of the English language. But had he employed the effete poetic language typical of most of the poets writing in and around 1900; had he even continued the pretty-prettiness typical of the Georgian poets; he would have failed. Instead, he absorbed the sincerity, the immediacy, the unpretentiousness of Hardy, Kipling and Masefield, saw contemporary civilization as in a mirror before him, and, determined to preserve the spirit of the poets and the truth of that mirror, he set them forth in a style entirely his own, with a spirituality, a verisimilitude, an honesty and a courage frequently overlooked by those who lack the intelligence to understand and the sensitivity to respond to the subtlety, the power and the beauty of *The Waste Land.*

What sort of English, then, does T. S. Eliot employ—the varied metric, dependent upon the words, the phrases and the arrangement, lies beyond our scope—to achieve the selflessness of his aim and the radiant dignity of his purpose? For he could have achieved them only in the way he did. Already in *Prufrock*, 1917, and *Poems*, 1920, we see, maturing and indeed matured, the gifts that attained full strength in *The Waste Land* and later poems, as well as in such plays as *Murder in the Cathedral*, 1935, *The Family Reunion*, 1939, and *The Cocktail Party*, 1950; *Sweeney Agonistes*, 1932, is the fragment of an Aristophanic comedy.

To attempt to convey the effect of the language—of, say, *The Waste Land*—without quoting the entire piece, is to attempt the impossible, so inextricably interwoven are manner and matter. One can but mention a few of the features that make Eliot's poems linguistically remarkable. Long before Spender, Auden, Day Lewis and their contemporaries, Eliot showed that poetry does not require, although it may occasionally benefit from, a special vocabulary: what is good enough for prose is good enough for poetry. Yet what a poet can do with the most ordinary words is just no prose-writer's business:

> But Doris, towelled from the bath,
> Enters padding on broad feet,
> Bringing sal volatile
> And a glass of brandy neat.

Before Eliot the poets wrote occasionally in that familiar, prose-like manner; Eliot and his successors do it constantly. Whereas, before his time, this was the exception, it has, ever since 1922, been quite common. By so early as 1940, it was the rule.

The most prosaic words, or at least words entirely non-poetic in themselves, can—often do—become part of a passage eminently poetic, as in

> April is the cruellest month, breeding
> Lilacs out of the dead land, mixing
> Memory and desire, stirring
> Dull roots with spring rain.
> ....
> ....
> What are the roots that clutch, what branches grow
> Out of this stony rubbish?

Can you imagine any poet in 1900 writing the brilliant
Part V of *The Hollow Men* (1925)? This is the section ending
with the famous

> This is the way the world ends
> Not with a bang but a whimper

and containing the almost as famous, far more profound

> Between the idea
> And the reality
> Between the motion
> And the act
> Falls the Shadow
> > *For Thine is the Kingdom*

There we have an alert employment of the natural resources,
as opposed to the conventional, hence the unnecessarily restricted resources, of the English language (any language, if it
comes to that): an employment now quite usual, but in 1900
unheard-of. Into the formal moulds of thought, there has
flowed such a quicksilver of the spirit as irradiates those moulds
with an astringent yet heartening beauty, a strange, new
beauty, not facile nor glib, not obvious nor platitudinous, a
beauty of mind as much as of sense (one finds this in William
Empson too), as in 'Rhapsody on a Windy Night', beginning:

> Twelve o'clock.
> Along the reaches of the street,
> Held in a lunar synthesis,
> Whispering lunar incantations
> Dissolve the floors of memory
> And all its clear relations,
> Its divisions and precisions.

There, we listen to a new music, for there the poet has subjected us to a new thinking; there we meet with something that
constitutes a new intimation to the spirit, especially to the
spirit tremulously aware of spirituality; there the poet conveys
a new music, a new thinking, a new and pervasively refreshing

intimation, mainly because of the intellectually exquisite appre-
hension, the lovely marmoreal appreciation and arrangement,
of words no longer counters: of words with, each, its own un-
tarnished life: of words handled with reverential experimentalism.

We encounter all that—and ineffably more—in such a passage as this from *Ash Wednesday* (1930):

> And the lost heart stiffens and rejoices
> In the lost lilac and the lost sea voices
> And the weak spirit quickens to rebel
> For the bent golden-rod and the lost sea smell
> Quickens to recover
> The cry of quail and the whirling plover
> And the blind eye creates
> The empty forms between the ivory gates
> And smell renews the salt savour of the sandy earth.

Such quotations, which signally and inevitably fail to render
justice to the unforgettable eloquence of this new voice, may
nevertheless indicate something of its sweep, its power, its
profundity, its sympathy, its modernity. To quote from later
work would be interesting. It would also be unnecessary.

Another very important characteristic of T. S. Eliot's poetry
is mentioned in the following passage written by Stephen
Spender in reference to Edwin Muir's poems, *The Wheel,
The Law, The City, The Grove, The Fate*:

'In these poems Edwin Muir emphasises a tendency in
modern poetry which is more significant than the somewhat
heady and self-lacerating movement of the apocalyptics. This
is the submission of the poet, heart and soul, to the contempla-
tion of the poetry of reality, the primitive facts of the human
situation in the universe. Emotionally it is an appeal away
from the loudly proclaimed aims of human societies and individuals back to the bare facts of human existence. Poetically it
is (like Eliot's later poems) a return to the great subjects of
poetry, love, death, time—great subjects which write their own
poetry through the medium of the poet who cares more for
truth than for the expression of his own personality and the

advertisement of his own power over words.' (*Poetry since 1939*, a thoughtful and satisfying book.)

How does this tendency to universal themes affect language? The most obvious result is that, such themes being less emotional, less personal, less spontaneously springing from the maker's personality, and therefore less easy to treat, the poet has necessarily to exercise greater care with his style; has to choose his words to the best ultimate, rather than to the best immediate advantage; has to dramatize his subjects and yet avoid rendering them, in any way or degree, theatrical; has to preserve dignity amidst the arresting, perhaps even picturesque words and phrases and the effective contrasts, comparisons, juxtapositions required by those universal themes if they are not to become insipid generalities. In short, only the English best suited to the purpose will satisfy the reader. Instead of flowing tumultuously in a frenzy that is personal, although not inevitably fine, and carrying the reader along in a torrent of poetically channelled emotion, the poet must persuade him, convince him, move him with 'the inevitability of gradualness' and by all the other means in his power; means that, it should be manifest, include the lyrical no less than the logical, the particular no less than the generic, the ephemeral Eros no less than the perdurable Psyche, the individual no less than the human-racial.

In the 1930's, however, the most publicized poets (not the most prominent—a position belonging to their progenitor T. S. Eliot, a better poet than any of them) were Stephen Spender, W. H. Auden, Cecil Day Lewis, Louis MacNeice, William Empson, John Lehmann; although (much as Walter De La Mare, too elfin for imitation, had been doing ever since 1902) there were other poets working independently—for instance, Geoffrey Grigson. It is, however, of these six that Stephen Spender has so acutely written, 'In the thirties there was a group of poets who achieved a very wide reputation as a 'school' of modern poetry. They were not in a deliberate sense a literary movement; they were rather a group of friends, [approximate] contemporaries at the Universities of Oxford and Cambridge.' (William Empson was at Cambridge while

Auden was at Oxford. Auden was born in 1907; Day Lewis, 1904; Lehmann, 1907; MacNeice, 1907; Spender, 1909.) 'They had', Spender continues in that excellent pamphlet, *Poetry since 1900*, 'certain ideas in common. They consciously attempted to be modern [so, although perhaps less deliberately, had Wordsworth, Shelley, Keats, Byron, Browning, Meredith, Swinburne, Kipling, Hardy, Masefield, Eliot], choosing in their poems imagery selected from machinery [as Kipling had done much earlier], slums and the social conditions which surrounded them as [Masefield twenty, and Eliot ten-fifteen years earlier]. ... Their poetry emphasized the community, and overwhelmed as it was by the sense of communal disease, it searched for a communal cure in psychology and leftist politics. Their personal emotions…lacked finality for them…. Their approach to all problems was very intellectual. ... Their poetry often gives the impression that they stayed at the fringe of their own personalities and of the problems which obsessed them.' Nevertheless, all these poets 'are interesting because their work expresses a malaise which shows a moral conscience more sensitive than that of many of their contemporaries.'

The language of all the poets so far mentioned in this chapter is marked by the immediacy of its response to the themes: those themes are contemporary, with the topical and the particular raised to the ever-recurrent and the generic: the language differs from that of prose only in its metrical arrangement, its greater precision, its economy. No longer is there such a thing as 'poetic language', the old counters (*eve, morn, sovran*, etc.) having been discarded; language becomes poetical, not by changing the vocabulary but by processes immeasurably more fundamental.

> The nightingales are sobbing in
> The orchards of our mothers,
> And hearts that we broke long ago
> Have long been breaking others,

as Auden symbolically records. All these poets hold, as few before them and many, whether poets or others, since have held—implicitly rather than explicitly—that what is good enough for prose is good enough for verse. I have never seen the converse stated, that what is good enough for verse should be good enough for prose, with the rider that verse should employ no words, phrases, syntactical constructions inadmissible in prose; yet what prose writer would now dare to employ such words as *eftsoons* and *eke* and *wist*? There is much to be said for those who maintain that to employ a 'specialist' vocabulary peculiar to verse is to contribute to the alienation of a public already too indifferent and who also maintain that to use only the vocabulary and the constructions of prose requires a greater skill than to use both these resources and those of the old poetic convention and who further maintain that the new poetry, if lucidly written (admittedly, some of it isn't), is more consonant with the new age.

'After Auden and his contemporaries,' Stephen Spender has remarked, 'there was a reaction among a slightly younger generation of poets away from a conscious and intellectual style of writing towards the involuntary, the mysterious, the word-intoxicated, the romantic and the Celtic.' The greatest of these, perhaps, is Dylan Thomas, of whom Spender goes on to say, 'Thomas is a poet who commands the admiration of all contemporary English poets. He has influenced a number of young writers who see in him an alternative to the intellectual writing of Auden [and his fellows]. Of the poets under forty-five, he is perhaps the only one capable of exercising a literary influence as great as that of Auden'; that is no less true in 1951 than it was in 1946. (Thomas was born in 1914.)

Although not himself a regionalist, Dylan Thomas reminds us that, concerning the young Welsh poets, Vernon Watkins, Keidrych Rhys, and Alun Lewis (killed in the war), Stephen Spender, again in 1946, has noticed a rather important feature: regionalism. 'Regionalism', he said, 'is beginning to become a cultural movement (or, rather, several cultural movements) to reckon with, especially since Wales, Scotland and Ireland now have some of the most original poets writing in the British Isles. Regionalism counts as a literary movement ... because it contributes to the creation of a virile, tough poetic language. ...

The development of an international kind of European literature and a regional literature at the same time is not incompat-
ible; rather, the two kinds would be complementary.' Spender,
however, realizes that 'the question really is whether the conditions of the modern world, which seems to be feeling its way
towards a world language, admit the principle of the multi-
plication of languages for the sake of literature'. They don't;
quite other causes preserve the individualities of languages and
therefore tend to foster the cause of regionalism; economic
causes, however, tend to discourage it—indeed, to go far
towards rendering it impossible. Regionalism in literature con-
notes a degree of regionalism in language. Hence, of dialect.
Yet dialect is in a stronger position than literary regionalism
has ever been or can ever be. Here, however, we should do
well to appreciate that so long as Britons retain their sturdy
independence, they will probably retain most—or at least
some—of their dialects; as will Americans. And among the
dialects we must include Cockney, the sturdiest, the most independent of them all. But that is another story, told in another
chapter.

Literature has never existed entirely within a fixed tradition,
although in the seventeenth century in France, in the eighteenth in Britain, it went near to doing so. English literature
has, since 1914, been freer of tradition than at any time since
the Elizabethan age: and has therefore been insusceptible of
judgement by standards, whether moral, intellectual, thematic
or technical, derived from a firm, clearly defined tradition.
'But,' as Stephen Spender has cautioned us, 'modern writers
are governed by no traditional rules accepted by themselves
and their critics. What is meant by "tradition" is highly disputable, because the strength of a tradition in the arts has a certain
relation ... to its claims to present a picture of contemporary
life.' (Spender's further remarks are so pertinent, so judicious,
that to refrain from quoting them would indicate, not independence of judgement but a churlish intransigence.) 'When
life changes violently, then the tradition either becomes
academic and remote from life, and therefore loses its force and
in that sense ceases to be traditional, or else it transforms itself

and adapts itself to life, thus preserving the traditional relation‑
ship to life (which is the most living and important aspect of a
tradition). But a transformed tradition may be almost un‑
recognizable, if one attempts to judge it by the familiar appear‑
ance of past traditional literature. Thus some of the most revol‑
utionary works in modern English, such as T. S. Eliot's *The
Waste Land* [1922] and James Joyce's *Ulysses* [1922] exercise
the highest claims to be regarded as traditional. At the same
time, these claims are difficult for contemporaries to judge
because there are no academic and established standards by
which to judge them.' Spender was writing in 1946; five years
later, the position is the same, except that Eliot's position was
much strengthened by the award, in 1948, of the Nobel Prize
for Literature, as Joyce's had been dignified by his death early
in 1941. The ablest assessment of the merit of *The Waste Land*
is that made by the late R. G. Collingwood in *The Principles
of Art*, 1938.

Summing up the poetry of the six years ending in late 1945,
one of its most distinguished figures has said that 'everywhere
there is evidence of a restless mental energy, lively invention,
sincerity of feeling'; that is no less true five years later. Now, as
then, 'modern English poetry is alive. It may be struggling
through darkness towards the light' (Spender). At the least, it
struggles: and that its goal is the kingdom of light, only a blind
person (that is, a hopeless reactionary) could fail to be almost
blindingly aware. That the struggle is meeting with consider‑
able success, we see from the influence exercised by T. S. Eliot,
and by 'the Auden-Spender school', upon the themes and the
techniques of two important women poets, Ruth Ritter and
Anne Ridler, whom their male contemporaries will courte‑
ously allow me to mention to their own omission, and upon
those of several poets born during the 1890's—for instance,
Gerald Bullett.

The twentieth-century poets' secession from convention—
poets, as everyone knows, have always tended to discard con‑
vention—may sometimes have resulted in an obscurantism they
themselves would shudder at. Occasionally they have forgotten
that a genuine poet communicates far more than information

only, far more than impression only, far more than even beauty; and that, to convey these overtones and these undertones, they must first make sure that what they have to say or sing be as clear to the reader as to themselves. Occasionally they have forgotten one of the principles of all writing: that, only when the meaning has been established easily or, at least, indubitably, does the reader willingly pass to the further values of a poem. By so exhausting the reader in a grim struggle to reach the meaning, that he is quite unable to enjoy the spiritual or aesthetic rewards additional to those of apprehending the meaning, poets have, more than once, circumvented themselves. This is certainly not to say that the reader should be pampered; it is merely to say that, expecting a sustenance of beauty (whether spiritual, intellectual, or merely emotional), the reader should not be faced with an iron curtain. Literary enjoyment can be obtained at its fullest, its best, only when both the producer and the customer act their part, the customer paying a fair price and the producer offering goods worthy of purchase.

All *pro's* accounted for, all *con's* duly weighed, I find that the new attitude adopted by the poets of 1922 onwards has, in the main, exercised a beneficial influence upon not only the language of poetry but, even more importantly, the language of all writers capable of being influenced at all, hence upon that of the educated and cultured public. This modern attitude has, moreover, rendered that public a little less disinclined to think, to ponder, to meditate, and a little more tolerant of experimentalism. Manifestly, the war of 1939-1945 (far more than that of 1914-1918) has done much to prepare both the writers for their pioneering and the public for stoically 'roughing it'.

Drama

Thus we come to a notable field of experimentalism: the drama. George Bernard Shaw's attempts to convert drama from the old theory—and practice—of action shown in, and furthered by, talk to his own theory—and almost his practice—

of talk for brilliant talk's sake merely carry, to one stage further, one stage too far (as many think), a tendency already danger-ously marked in Wilde's comedies and tragi-comedies. Barrie, Galsworthy, Somerset Maugham humanized English drama; technically, they did not change it. Experimentalism does, however, characterize some of the plays written by Sean O'Casey, J. B. Priestley, James Bridie, T. S. Eliot, Denis Johnston, Christopher Fry. In 1947, Robert Speaight, actor and novelist, mentioned that 'we live in a fragmentary time, and ... [Priestley, for example] does show by the variety of his themes and the versatility of his technique that he knows we are all in the crucible' (*Drama since* 1939). What Speaight has to say of Priestley's outlook is applicable to that of several other contemporary dramatists: 'Priestley does not pretend to any of the orthodox certainties, but he is profoundly concerned about the *values* of human life.'

Notable and exciting as are the best plays of the prose play-wrights, perhaps still more notable and exciting are the best plays of the playwrights employing verse: T. S. Eliot and Christopher Fry, especially; but also Ronald Duncan, Anne Ridler, Peter Yates. A discussion of the technical merits possessed by any of these dramatists, whether they use poetry or prose, would be irrelevant here. But the medium is emin-ently relevant.

'What has poetry to say in the British Theatre? Is it worth saying and is it said well?' asks Robert Speaight, who answers thus, 'The truth is that for more than three hundred years, ever since the death of Shakespeare, poetry and drama have been steadily drifting and developing apart. Shakespeare in his later plays [and in several of the earlier], and his near-contempor-aries, had brought the poetry of the playhouse close to the prose of the ante-chamber and even to the jargon [i.e., ordinary language] of the street. The rhythm and idiom of contemporary speech were orchestrated into the complex harmonies of *King Lear* and *The Tempest* and *Antony and Cleopatra*.' This was poetry designed to appeal to ears desirous of rhetoric, yet a rhetoric bearing sufficient resemblance to the everyday speech of the times.

But then Milton 'forged a new and artificial style for blank verse. ... The links between English poetry and English vernacular speech were not so close as they had been. ... The dramatist, the man writing for the most popular medium of art, tended to [employ prose for all his plays] because it was in prose that he was most likely to catch the public ear. ... Both poetry and drama have suffered from this divorce. Poetry had tended to become academic and drama dismally prosaic. ... A new link between the author and his public had to be forged before dramatic poetry could be rescued from the doldrums'. (Robert Speaight).

It was ultimately forged. The 'smith' was T. S. Eliot, first with *Murder in the Cathedral*, 1935; then *The Family Reunion*, 1939; and, with something close to finality, *The Cocktail Party*, 1950. *Murder in the Cathedral* has been phenomenally successful, both in Britain and in the United States of America; more successful, by far, than any other verse play written in the twentieth century. Why is this?

'In the first place,' to quote the unusually authoritative Robert Speaight, 'the dramatist was telling a well-known story'—melodrama at its best. 'In the second place he told a complicated story in an intelligible fashion, stressing with great subtlety its relevance to the contemporary battle between the Church and the totalitarian state'—a relevance as urgent now as it was in 1935, the death of Hitler and Mussolini having merely removed two of the dragon's-toothèd foemen. 'In the third place, though his thought was intricate and profound, Eliot addressed us in direct and simple language. ... And fourthly, not only was the verse interrupted at two important moments by prose ... but the verse itself was extremely varied' and thus able to forestall in the listener the weariness that so often comes from hearing scene after scene in blank verse. Whereas *Murder in the Cathedral* was explicitly, *The Family Reunion* was implicitly religious.

About this time (1935), the plays of W. H. Auden in collaboration with Christopher Isherwood were proving that, if it possess 'theatrical vigour', poetic drama can deal successfully with politics, whether satirically or idealistically. *The Dog under the Skin* (1935), 'containing verse of considerable beauty and caustic wit', is much more than political only; so are the other Auden-Isherwood plays.

A comparison of their verse style with that of Eliot is instructive, the more so as the following two passages come from plays that, in 1935, rendered their authors famous. From Eliot's opening chorus:

> Since golden October declined into sombre November
> And the apples were gathered and stored, and the land became
>   brown sharp points of death in a waste of water and mud,
> The New Year waits, breathes, waits, whispers in darkness.
> While the labourer kicks off a muddy boot and stretches his
>   hand to the fire,
> The New Year waits, destiny waits for the coming.

And from the opening chorus of *The Dog beneath the Skin:*

> The Summer holds: upon its glittering lake
> Lies Europe and the islands; many rivers
> Wrinkling its surface like a ploughman's palm.
> ....
> ....
> We would show you at first an English village: you shall
>   choose its location
> Wherever your heart directs you most longingly to look; ...
> Whether north to Scots Gap and Bellingham where the black
>   rams defy the panting engine:
> Or west to the Welsh Marches; to the lilting speech and the
>   magicians' faces.

The matching of an ancient, traditional form to an entirely modern idiom is worth noting.

After Eliot and, as dramatist, probably to become no less famous and no less brilliantly competent, is Christopher Fry, whose *The Boy with a Cart*, 1939, *A Phoenix too Frequent*, 1946, *The Lady's Not for Burning*, 1949, and *Venus Observed*, 1950, are all written mainly in verse. In its adroit admixture of prose

and in its religious theme, *The Boy with a Cart* reveals the
influence of Eliot. But it was *A Phoenix too Frequent* that
brought success—'a complete success, brilliantly achieved by a
man of the theatre who is equally prepared for the exigencies
of drama and the possibilities of poetry. Mr Fry may well
develop into a really important dramatist', as Robert Speaight
prophesied in 1947.

That prophecy came true, only two years later, with *The
Lady's Not for Burning;* and *Venus Observed* confirmed a reputation for brilliance, wit, dramatic skill. All the little men dis-
trustful of brilliance and shuddering away from creativeness
as though it were public immorality now began their envious
and repellent pranks—'Too much talk, too little action'—
'Spontaneity? Well, facility perhaps'—'Metrical dexterity?
Rubbish! A conjuror's prestidigitation'—'Lay figures, not
sharply individualized persons'—and the rest of the depressing
gamut of denigration. All those belittlements are as little true
of the latest as of the earliest of Fry's poetic dramas. The truth
is that Christopher Fry's not so very numerous detractors, in
common with all the costives of this lax world, are irritated by
his ability to invest realism with spirituality, quite ordinary
words with poetry, apparently recalcitrant material with a
dazzlingly fluent metric, a brilliant wit with a rich, tolerant,
alarmingly sympathetic and profound warm-heartedness, without peevishness and without that curmudgeonly inability to
praise others which has ever been the stigma by which we may
recognize the ungenerous.

Consider briefly this passage (*The Lady's Not for Burning*) in
which the pompous, worldly little bureaucrat, Hebble Tyson,
is answered by Thomas Mendip, a discharged soldier possessed
of something akin to genius:

> *Tyson*   Who do people
>   Think they are, coming here without
>   Identity, and putting us to considerable
>   Trouble and expense to have them punished?
>   You don't deserve to be listened to.

Thomas   It's a habit.
         I've been unidentifiably
         Floundering in Flanders for the past seven years,
         Prising open ribs to let men go
         On the indefinite leave which needs no pass.
         And now all roads are uncommonly flat, and all hair
         Stands on end.

If one cannot, even from a passage so unfairly short, perceive the deftly dramatic touches, the almost inevitable sense of
theatre, the shrewd characterization, the wit and the humour,
the effect of poetry haloing the realistic, the very ordinary
words handled with a very unordinary skill, then one were
better dead: then, indeed, one already is, with all that ice chill-
ing the heart and all that ivory encasing a brain too feeble to
escape the prison of its own ineptitude.

Language, the vehicle, cannot be separated from speech and
the written word; and, above all, no attempt should be made
to separate it from its finest context, literature. (Not even a
single word means anything without a context.) For the
moment, however, let us try to concentrate rather more on the
language itself than on the dazzling and lovely, yet easily
apprehensible and earth-real thought of this passage from a
speech (again from Act I of *The Lady's Not for Burning*) gaily
cast, as a scarf from impatient shoulders, at the Lady's very
mixed auditory:

                                        I burn a sprig
         Of thyme, and time returns, a little crazy,
         The worse for burial, hazily re-enacting
         The palatial past: for instance, Helen comes,
         Brushing the maggots from her eyes,
         And, clearing her throat of several thousand years,
         She says, 'I loved—'; but cannot any longer
         Remember names. Or Alexander, wearing
         His imperial cobwebs and breastplate of shining worms,
         Wakens and looks for his glasses, to find the empire
         Which he knows he put beside his bed ...
         ....
         ....
         ....

                                        Once when the moon
Was gibbous and in a high dazed state
Of nimbus love, I shook a jonquil's dew
On to a pearl and let a cricket chirp
Three times, thinking of pale Peter:
And there Titania was, vexed by a cloud
Of pollen, using the sting of a bee to clean
Her nails and singing, as drearily as a gnat,
        'Why try to keep clean?'

It is impossible to ignore the allusiveness and the wit, the
satire and the metrical dexterity, the poetry of it all. Merely
pretend that you can. With no more than a peep at loveliness,
avert your reluctant eyes and, for a moment, apply your enchanted mind to the language—to the manner, the phrasing,
the words, rather than to the matter. Assuming your and my
inability to perform the impossible, what do we find? Here are
a few of the features and qualities and potentialities, 'considerations of space' (as they say) precluding anything better than
inadequacy:

the *thyme-time* pun that will shock those punsters who per-
petrate monstrosities of torturous improbability; a light-
hearted, careless pun of the bewitching witch possessed of an
intelligence that baffles and angers the crass officialdom with
which she is beset;

the *palatial past*, with its alliteration, with its hint of a sump-
tuous, spacious roominess, and with *maggots* bringing selective
romanticism back to the earthiness of the present—and of the
past;

Helen's great loves reduced, in a few, neatly merciless words
and with a reminiscence of *hazily*, to dilapidated and moth-
eaten memories;

Alexander the Great, who held a world in his arms by the
time he was thirty, is now festooned with cobwebs (set beside
the immemorial dust in Helen's lovely throat) and corsleted
with worms, he whose past glory is likened to a pair of spectacles and perhaps to a shabby, comfortable pair of slippers or
maybe a chamber-pot handy for old age's bane;

the moonlit world of *A Midsummer Night's Dream*, bodied

forth in such imagery as Shakespeare himself might have used
and with the same sort of modernity as characterizes so much
of Shakespeare;

not a single word, not a single phrase, not a grammatical
construction that would jar—or even be remarked upon—in
good prose, for neither Watling Street nor Wardour Street is a
path this modern would consent to tread;

even the calm, lambent, all-pervasive imagination and the
restless, coruscating fancy do not seduce the poet from such
English words and phrases and constructions as a newspaper
could theoretically use—but, manifestly, would not use in this
brilliant manner—and as a cultured, witty, original, penetrating, fearless mind would delight in using among his peers.

Set that passage beside some representative lines taken from
Stephen Phillips's *Paolo and Francesca*, published fifty years
earlier—that is, late in 1899—and produced on the stage in
1900. In a sense, Stephen Phillips was the Christopher Fry of
the late 1890's and 1900's, but without his wit and humour, his
fearlessness, his profundity, his intellectual and spiritual honesty, and also without his metrical and verbal dexterity:

> O God, Thou seest us thy creatures bound
> Together by that law which holds the stars
> In palpitating cosmic passion bright;
> By which the very sun enthrals the earth,
> And all the waves of the world faint to the moon.
> Even by such attraction we two rush
> Together through the everlasting years.
> Us, then, whose only pain can be to part,
> How wilt Thou punish? For what ecstasy
> Together to be blown about the globe!
> What rapture in perpetual fire to burn
> Together!—where we are is endless fire.

Quite apart from the egomaniac adjuration to the Deity and
the pretentious comparison of physical passion to the operations of universal laws, the scene lacks sincerity and probability:
for what lover with an attractive girl in his arms would waste
time in irrelevant and unseemly apostrophes to a third person,

even to the Inescapable Third? Compare this passage with one or two in Fry's *Venus Observed*—I have not done it here, for I am reluctant to overstate the case—and you will agree that Phillips mistook fustian for eloquence and romanticism for reality. Upon rare occasion, Phillips achieved eloquence. Upon occasion, Fry is romantic—but it is a gay, cynical, mocking romanticism, not the maudlin slaverings of a self-deluder.

However solemn or poignant, however beautiful or symbolic the scene they happen to be describing or, rather, setting in motion, Eliot, Auden-Isherwood, and Fry never forget that they are writing for men and women of their day, not for imaginary creatures either dreaming or muzzily footling their lives away in a past that, whether recent or remote, never even existed. Sharing, at least imaginatively, the fears, indecisions, turpitudes, pettinesses, no less than the hopes, fortitudes, nobilities, of the characters they accompany as men, not twitch as showmen their puppets, Eliot and Fry and several other dramatists can obtain their full effects only by using English that is contemporary; English that, although dramatically or poetically employed, remains, both in its principles and in its ingredients, the English of every day—but not the everyday language of the morons and the zombies, nor yet the half-sketched, jerky, impressionistic, often extremely ambiguous language of the average, casual conversation.

The Novel

Passing to the novel, which, for the compulsive reason that the language of most novels is much closer to that of speech, at least of educated speech, than is that of poetry and drama, and therefore requires less of distinguishing, separative treatment, will here be treated far more briefly than poetry and drama have been—passing to the novel, we need do little more than mention the names of those novelists who have exercised the greatest influence upon novel-writing in the twentieth century. Wells, Conrad, Galsworthy, Bennett, although widely

read, have exercised less influence upon the twentieth century
novel than have Thomas Hardy, who wrote no novels during
the period—than Henry James, who wrote few after 1900—
and James Joyce, who was known to few before 1918 in the
United States, where *Ulysses* began, in March of that year, to
appear in the pages of *The Little Review*, or, in Britain, before
1922, when, for the first time as a whole, it was published in
Paris. Whereas *Ulysses* consists of the events of one man's life
within the confines of a single sentient day, the second of
Joyce's two greatest books, *Finnegan's Wake*, published complete in 1939 but parts of it throughout the preceding decade,
consists of the state, the processes, the dreams and half-dreams
of one man's life, enacted during the subconsciousness of sleep
within the confines of a single night.

'From Hardy our novelists inherit a legacy of poetry and
architecture; from James a legacy of subtlety and psychological
curiosity; from Joyce a rejuvenation of language. And from all
three, many other things as well', as Henry Reed has said in
The Novel since 1939 (published in 1946). Among those 'many
other things' we should mention at least these: Hardy, in
addition to contributing a lively sense of the oddities and the
humours of country life and country people, converted the lay-
figure of Fate into the instant figure of an active protagonist,
usually hostile and frequently malignant; Henry James brought
certain subtleties of architectonics and style, cosmopolitanism,
and a respect for mind into the hitherto somewhat insular and
philistine atmosphere pervading the British Isles; besides introducing the 'interior monologue', which he may have developed
from germinal traces in Henry James and which has been so
influential on the English novel since 1922, and confirming the
practicability of the 'stream of consciousness' method in fiction
(a method perfected by Virginia Woolf, but proving to be
rather too much for inferior intellects), Joyce has, in *Ulysses*
and elsewhere, imposed upon the more serious and scrupulous
British writers a well-established consciousness of style and,
especially, of the artistic and spiritual necessity of adapting
one's style to the subject. Joyce detested the Gallionic, mildly
ironical, adolescently cynical, leisurely, gentlemanly, rather

stodgy, certainly unexciting style adopted by so many novelists during the forty years beginning at 1900. 'Unfortunately,'
remarks Henry Reed, 'many writers who have recoiled with
him have recoiled into the brawny arms of Mr Ernest Hemingway, whose tough, staccato style has had a catastrophic influence'—an influence much less noticeable in 1951 than in 1946.
To imitate Hemingway tolerably well is easy; to imitate Joyce
at all well is impossible except to writers of very considerable
talent: and therefore Joyce's stylistic influence is exercised only
upon a very small company. Yet it is a notable company.

In *Ulysses*, the plan, the structure, the composition are as
important as the style. Only the style can be exemplified here;
and only the style need be exemplified, for the other aspects do
not affect the language. It is best to take an entirely lucid example, such as this passage from Stephen's thoughts upon
Shakespeare:

'He has hidden his own name, a fair name, William, in the
plays, a super here, a clown there, as a painter of old Italy set
his face in a dark corner of the canvas. He has revealed it in the
Sonnets where there is Will in overplus. Like John O'Gaunt,
his name is dear to him, as dear as the coat of arms he toadied
for, on a bend sable a spear or steeled argent, honorificabili-
tudinitatibus, dearer than his glory of greatest Shakescene in
the country. What's in a name? That is what we ask ourselves
in childhood when we write the name that we are told is ours.
A star, a daystar, a fire drake rose at his birth. It shone by day
in the heavens alone, brighter than Venus in the night, and by
night it shone over delta in Cassiopeia, the recumbent con-
stellation which is the signature of his initials among the stars.
His eyes watched it, lowlying on the horizon, eastward of the
Bear, as he walked by the slumberous summer fields at midnight, returning from Shottery and from her arms.'

That style can be—often has been—imitated; in its entirety,
only by an erudite poet or dramatist or by an erudite prose-
author endowed with poetic or dramatic gifts. The book itself,
a masterpiece of intricate construction, can hardly be imitated.

Other writers influential upon the twentieth century novel
are Somerset Maugham, Aldous Huxley, Virginia Woolf,

E. M. Forster, Elizabeth Bowen, Rosamund Lehmann, Tennyson Jesse, Rose Macaulay, George Orwell, Grahame Greene, Joyce Cary, and, from abroad, Franz Kafka, especially the third, the fourth, and the last. Several others might be mentioned; and would be, if the subject of this book were English literature. Upon the twentieth century short story, the greatest influences have perhaps been those of Chekov, James, Leonard Merrick, Joyce, Maugham, Galsworthy, Wells, Virginia Woolf, Katherine Mansfield, Elizabeth Bowen, A. E. Coppard, H. E. Bates, Rhys Davies, James Hanley.

Upon the technique of novel and short story, the wars of 1914-1918 and 1939-1945 have exercised little influence, except that of a short-lived, febrile impressionism, which, inexcusable in the older writers, is readily excusable in the younger men— the men engaged on active service. Of the subtler, the slowly degrading and insidiously undermining effects of war, especially the effects upon the civil population, the finest portrayer is perhaps Elizabeth Bowen (Henry Reed has, in this regard, cited *The Demon Lover*); but whereas Elizabeth Bowen took the war in her artistic stride, many other novelists and short-story writers were put out of their stride by it. War tends to determine, more rapidly than any other force, or set of events, can determine, which are the securely, which the insecurely, balanced writers. Of the latter, indeed, some need only the thrust of war to send them toppling into skin-saving or San Francisco, into yoga or Yellowstone. (For the general effect of war, see the semi-historical chapter 'General Trends and Particular Influences'.)

General

If, from literature, we subtract poetry, drama, fiction, we are left with only history, biography, autobiography, and the exposition, or the criticism, of religion, philosophy, science, art; of criticism, the literary is perhaps the most important. But these things have little direct bearing upon language. In the non-scientific and the non-philosophic thinking and writing, we find the phenomenon of one who has written little yet has tremendous influence—an influence reinforced by that which he exercises as a poet. Whether as critic or as poet, T. S. Eliot has remarkable authority 'over the whole field of contemporary literature. His influence is paramount in his own generation [he was born in 1888], in its immediate successor—the generation of such writers as Auden, Spender, MacNeice, Day Lewis, and Empson—and on the young. No English writer living is more revered by his admirers or ... more respected by his critics. None, in his writing, has done more to create the climate* of thought and sensibility which has conditioned the form and content of English literature in the past quarter of a century,' as John Hayward has noted in his well-informed, well-argued *Prose Literature since* 1939: and what he said there holds good to-day. Eliot has achieved that position not only by the integrity, originality and fearlessness of his writing but also by the integrity of his character and by his strong and attractive personality.

If we regard the literature of 1900-1950 as a whole in its relation to language, and if, further, we compare the language of 1950 with that of 1900, can we point to any outstanding features? Not to say here what has to be said in Chapter VII, I draw attention merely to these facts: literary English has become more direct, less pretentious; less latinized, less gallic, less imitative of foreign languages; less polysyllabic, less lengthy of paragraph and sentence; less abstract, hence more concrete; less stiff and formal; less addicted to allegory and to other ambitious rhetorical devices; less artificial, hence more natural; rather less ponderous and much less pompous; less

---

* *Climate of opinion* (or *thought* or *belief* or ...) has become a vogue phrase of the period beginning in *ca.* 1946. The ground was partially prepared by Basil Willey, especially in his two earlier *Background* books, *The Seventeenth Century Background*, 1934, and *The Eighteenth Century Background*, 1940. Compare William James's dictum, 'The philosophic background of our time inevitably forces its own clothing upon us' (*Varieties of Religious Experience*, 1902) and John Morley's reference to a 'general mental climate' that has 'ceased to be invigorating' (*Compromise*, 1874). The phrase has descended to us from some genial seventeenth-century writer. Where once we blamed God, not by any chance ourselves—or the reigning dynasty, not its subjects—or revolution, not (of course) the revolters—or evolution, not ourselves—or complexes, instead of avoidable complications—we now blame 'climate', not ourselves, for national or world-wide catastrophe, cataclysm, catalysis.

didactic but more persuasive; less allusive; freer of circum-
locution and cumbrous euphemism; in short, simpler and
clearer, more vigorous and less verbose.

Is there anything that, in spoken English, corresponds to
literary English? Only oratory and the very best conversation
of the best conversationalists. Both that conversation and that
oratory are characterized by the same features as those we have
just been outlining. Oratory, designed for print almost as much
as for the immediate audience, now depends much less on the
long rolling period; and it employs quotation, especially from
the classics, much less than in 1900. The modern age is in too
much of a hurry to arrive nowhere in particular for it to listen
patiently to the Ciceronian or even to the Tacitean period; the
modern audience, especially in the House of Commons, lacks
the education that would enable it to appreciate quotations.
Nowadays, most people have a better education than they
would have had in 1900, yet very few people to-day are well
educated. There is far more twopenny-halfpenny, far less
sterling, education than formerly. The nation pays hopefully
and heavily for an education that, usually, turns out to be a
smattering. Luckily, comparatively few of the smatterers write
books; and, of the books they do write, very few are good.
Very few, therefore, influential.

CHAPTER TWO

NON-LITERARY ENGLISH

'Non-literary English' exactly describes what is read by quite
90 per cent., spoken by at least 95 per cent. and written by more
than 99 per cent. of the English-speaking population of the
world. (But then, much the same thing holds good of almost
every other language. The figures, as only the solemn will need
to be told, are not statistical; they are tentative, observational,
imaginative—yet not designedly provocative.) So far, however,
the implied minorities have—except during war and revolution, and during plague, famine and cataclysm—been amazingly influential in general, as also in the intellectual and the
spiritual spheres: these minorities have not only constituted,
they have also worked the leaven of civilization. Will the loaf
remain sweet, or will it turn sour? Or will the loaf merely
change to something outwardly very different, yet inwardly
wholesome?

Iconoclastes Delphicus: a fore-thought noted on 14 July 1950.

BEFORE dealing with certain kinds of non-literary English
I should like to caution the innocent reader that the kinds
are not exhaustive and that, whatever the kind, what I
shall say concerns spoken as well as written English; far too
many theorists tacitly ignore spoken English. Then, having
apparently come to the end of the selected kinds (admittedly
the more important), I shall conclude the chapter with a few
remarks upon a fascinating, because unknowable subject: the
future of English. The subject of the vernacular, however,
must be deferred; it will constitute the final section of the
chapter entitled 'General Trends and Particular Influences'.

Written Non-Literary English

By a paradox more apparent than real, this section should
logically and sensibly begin with a retrospect upon certain
kinds of predominantly or ostensibly literary English.

In 1928, Professor J. Y. T. Greig, in *Breaking Priscian's Head*, made an exceedingly provocative statement. 'Many learned and worthy persons,' he said, 'would lay it down as a strict rule' that, in his writings, an author 'ought to make the best of the existing tools. ... If, they say, he can't find the tool he needs, it is only because he hasn't looked for it long enough. ... And this, though not perhaps accepted doctrine to the leading English philologists[—in equity, it wasn't—], is accepted doctrine to most original [i.e., creative] writers, most professional critics, and most educated readers in England to-day. [They— the readers, anyway—are in 1951 a little more tolerant.] Neologisms, dialectal words, obvious colloquialisms, and slang, are frowned upon. Hence many of the attacks upon Mr James Joyce, who flouts the rule; on American writers in general and American novelists in particular, who are much less pernickety than the English about colloquial phrases and slang [these attacks, at least, are now fewer—and more forlorn than hopeful]; and on many modern French writers, ... who are said to have no "literary conscience" because they are content to take a word from anywhere if it serves their turn. Hence, too,' he concludes, 'the flatness, the dreary gentility, the wairsh [*wearish*, insipid] inkhorn flavour, the deliberate preciosity of much even of the best prose now being written in England.'

Continuing, with special reference to David Garnett as we see him writing in the novel, *The Sailor's Return*, Professor Greig continued, 'His style, which within its narrow range is nearly perfect, is as good an example as I know of the present tendency in the best prose-writers of England to shut themselves up in a hothouse and cultivate words. The result is extreme delicacy of rhythm, colour, and pattern at the expense of vigour and of that robust, windy vulgarity to be found on the tops of hills and in the mouths of common untutored folk.' And, a few pages later, 'Public School standard, when written by Mr David Garnett and Mr Edward Shanks, shows only too many signs of becoming hieratic, languid, and degenerate'— charges laid against English writers, poets included, by Richard Aldington in 1920. 'It needs to be taken out into the open air, and buffeted by trans-Atlantic winds.'

Such tendencies towards flat, nerveless, languid and effete prose—not, of course, always present, nor even predominant, in the authors named by Greig merely as examples—continued until early in the war of 1939-1945; to be irritatingly precise, until the books that began to be written from May, 1940, onwards. Writing in the latter half of 1939, Dr J. Hubert Jagger pointed, in his *English in the Future*, to the increasing number of clichés that were being used and then remarked 'The accusation that [English] is becoming unduly abstract and conventional is much more weighty, and is a real ground for uneasiness if it is a true accusation; for it is levelled at what is regarded as the most serious part of modern English literature; moreover, the accusation is that this is an organic tendency.' (That sentence itself exemplifies a fault that Arthur Quiller-Couch often deplored: the use of *is* ... *is* ... *is* where active verbs or, at the least, 'concrete' verbs would, investing a passage with life and colour, prevent that flatness, that depressive impersonalism, which a constant repetition of *is* will inevitably produce.)

Dr Jagger points out that there has arisen 'a good expository style', suitable to the reasoner but unsuitable to the creative artist, and that one of its characteristics is this tendency to abstraction. He admits that, very often, abstraction results from the laudable desire to be exact; too often, however, abstraction comes to be practised for its own sake. 'Then the writer, in emptying his sentences of all imagery, also empties them of all meaning. He creates an intellectual vacuum in which he can gesticulate without meeting any resistance, and so deceives himself and his readers into believing that he is revealing profound truths when all he is doing is to render the obvious obscure.' Sir Alan Herbert, in *What a Word!*, has quoted the sentence, 'The unity of view of the participants in the conversations has been established regarding the exceptional importance at the present time of an all-embracing collective organization of security on the basis of the indivisibility of peace', which means that 'Diplomats have agreed that the only way to ensure universal peace is for all nations to combine to defend it.'

It is not hard to see that these faults were—and still are—occurring in such writing as should have attained to the status of good literary English: they have occurred so regularly that the writing has become non-literary. There is another fault, implied by Professor Greig in the passages already quoted from *Breaking Priscian's Head*, 1928, and unequivocally attacked by him nearly twenty years later in *Keep up the Fight for English*, a far too little-known pamphlet issued in 1946 by the Witwatersrand University Press.

'*Concrete*', he says, 'is the last word to apply to a great deal of the English we suffer from to-day. If we are looking for a single word to characterize it, *invertebrate* will serve very well. Invertebrate English has become so common in the mouths and the documents of politicians, journalists, scientists, civil servants, university teachers, school teachers, town clerks, and even judges on the Bench that we have almost resigned ourselves to it and tend to forget that we have a just right to look for something better.' One feature of invertebracy is what Professor Greig has called 'elephantine writing', as in an example he himself quotes: 'A class has been regularly offered, but insufficient application has materialized to form a group', which, in his translation, means that 'We have offered a class each year, but too few students have come forward to make it worth forming'.

Professor Greig then cites the late George Orwell's trenchant article, 'Politics and the English Language', which had appeared in *Horizon*. Orwell, having examined five passages, concluded that, in addition to faults peculiar to this one or that, all had two defects in common. 'The first is staleness of imagery: the other is lack of precision. The writer either has a meaning and cannot express it, or he inadvertently says something else, or he is almost indifferent as to whether his words mean anything or not. This mixture of vagueness and sheer incompetence is the most marked characteristic of modern English prose, and especially of any kind of political writing ... Prose consists less and less of *words* chosen for the sake of their meaning, and more and more of *phrases* tacked together like the sections of a prefabricated hen-house.' This imprecision and this staleness, 'the most marked characteristics of Jungle English' (Sir Alan Herbert's phrase), are 'plain signs of incoherent thinking';

a disease more fittingly diagnosed in the chapter 'General Trends and Particular Influences'.

We can now the more easily deal with such aspects of twentieth-century English as the increasing power and popularity of journalese, officialese and commercialese—a power and a popularity obviously deriving from the increased power of journalism, officialdom and commerce.

Close to 'the hell of language, where the damned are tormented with inability to express any simple idea in a simple way', there lies, says Dr Jagger, 'the abyss of Journalese, which is the employment of a pretentious vocabulary and phraseology instead of an honest workaday diction. The practitioners of Journalese ... never use a concrete term if it has an abstract synonym. They prefer the tortuous to the direct, the periphrasis to the single word, and the long to the short. Their choice of words ... is quite unnatural. They also grasp at violent images, whose power to excite sensation they by excessive use rapidly wear out.'

Jagger recognizes that 'our own tastes mainly determine the fare that the journalist lays before us; but he is cook as well as waiter, and that is how the mischief is generally done. ... Our present preoccupation'—no less in 1950 than in 1940—'with international politics, and with social conditions and problems, is having an immense effect upon written English. Neither the politician nor the social worker is by nature a stylist. ... The commonest vices of the social worker are illiteracy and a general slipshodness of expression; those of the politician arise from his fierce determination to have a technical jargon'; that jargon is disseminated by the Press; the less critical the newspaper reader, the more powerfully affected is he by this poisonous tripe. Language infected by political and sociological jargon loses the two greatest virtues of language: clarity, which constitutes the prime virtue of language in its utilitarian aspect —that of communication; and fitness or appositeness, the prime virtue of language in its aesthetic or emotive aspect. Jargon is not so much language as a substitute for language.

Journalese is defined in *Webster's New International Dictionary* as 'English of a style featured by use of colloquialisms, superficiality of thought or reasoning, clever or sensational presentation of material, and evidences of haste in composition'—held to be, and in fact being, characteristic of newspaper writing.

Yet journalism, although necessarily topical and necessarily written in some haste, may, at its best, be hardly distinguishable from literature; the 'leaders' or editorials of, say, *The Times* or the *Manchester Guardian*, *The New Statesman* or *The Spectator*, may equal anything the best of the literary men could write on these themes and with so little time for revision. *Journalese* is a term applicable far less to the leading articles than to the staple of the newspapers and the weeklies; that is, to most of the other articles and, above all, to the reporting.

The new journalism began in England with the *Daily Mail* and the other organs of the Northcliffe Press, in which the mover, the inaugurator, the instigator was Alfred Harmsworth (1865-1922), Lord Northcliffe. On the 4th of May, 1896, the *Daily Mail* started its career—and Fleet Street acquired a different face. 'Its advent coincided with a period both of awakening popular interest in the stirring events of the world ... and also of singular inertia on the part of its older rivals.' The new daily 'completely fulfilled its purpose of presenting "all the news in the smallest space". It was comprehensive, alert, and concise. The services of a number of brilliant writers' (including G. W. Steevens) 'were enlisted. ... Leading articles were reduced to paragraphs. Immense attention was paid to what were regarded as the interests of the new reading public.' By 1899, it was firmly established. Northcliffe had seen the paramount opportunity for such a newspaper: he took that opportunity: he made the most of it. (Quotations from Geoffrey Dawson's article on Northcliffe in *The Dictionary of National Biography*: 1922-1930.)

George Warrington Steevens, who, aged thirty, died at Ladysmith at the turn of the century, neatly exemplifies both the change that took place even in the very best journalism and also the influence of the Press (especially the *Daily Mail*, which he joined very soon after its inception) upon literature. A friend of mine, Dr G. Pratt Insh, has reminded me that 'among Steevens's earlier writings was a series of articles for Blackwood's

Magazine; these imitated not only the polite irony of
Gibbon but the polished and cadenced prose of the eighteenth
century historian. When Harmsworth got hold of him he
wrote—as in his *In India* and *With Kitchener to Khartoum*—in
terse, staccato sentences for the new public that the *Daily Mail*
catered for. He was more Macaulayesque than Macaulay: but
he handled his brief sentences with more finesse than the dogmatic champion of Whiggery.' Steevens, therefore, as capably
and as clearly as any journalist we could name, shows the
transition—he largely helped to engineer that transition—
between the, by comparison, leisurely writing of the pre-
Daily Mail period (see, for instance, the articles by that extremely able journalist, William Thomas Stead (1849-1912),
in one of his most dramatic series, later a book, *If Christ Came
to Chicago*, published in 1894) and the swift hustle of the journalistic writing so deliberately introduced and encouraged by
Alfred, Lord Northcliffe. Of Steevens, Sidney Lee remarked
(*D.N.B.*) that 'It was his endeavour in journalism to present in
words with all possible vividness, frankness and terseness what
he saw, thought, and felt'. It should be added that Steevens
exhibited considerably more respect for the truth than did
many of his successors in journalism. Journalists have, throughout the twentieth century, tended to put 'the story' first, the
truth second—often a very poor second—and, apart from the
need to tell a good story, aesthetic considerations third—that is,
those who know what these mean put them third. There are
honourable exceptions; not unnaturally, these exceptions
happen to be almost identical with such journalists as have
gone nearest to ranking with 'the writers'.

Dr Insh, after some intensive research in the files of *The
Times* for the year 1905, tells me that 'between *The Times* of
that period and the journalism of to-day—leaving out the headlines, the sub-headings and other technicalities—the main
difference seems to me to resemble very closely what the
student of Latin, trained in Cicero, Livy and Caesar, finds when
he turns to ecclesiastical and medieval Latin: a great simplification of the syntax and a very great extension of the vocabulary'
(private letter of 24 June 1950—so too for the earlier quotation).

Other differences between the journalism of the decade immediately preceding the advent of the *Daily Mail* and the journalism of to-day include the rapid development of the often perverse art of the headline, with its inevitable tendency to ambiguity and its distortion of the senses of short words (e.g., *bid*) used for their typographical convenience; a disquieting increase in the number of vogue words (e.g., *target*), often grossly misused; the development of a 'snappy' style— terse, short-sentenced, often intolerably jerky—as far removed from the tenor of natural conversation, whether among ordinary people or among the witty and the cultured, as from the more pretentious, often pompous style of the 1880's and early 1890's, with its measured periods and its comfortable Victorian leisureliness, the difference being comparable to that between the Ciceronian and the Tacitean, but without the genius that prevents the latter from becoming a burlesque of itself; the abandonment of restfulness for restlessness, of the calm for the feverish, of the hansom's jog-trot for the motor car's speed; 'pictures'—formerly subordinate and truly illustrative—have become autocrats irrelevantly arrogant; the cynical encouragement of the odd belief that mediocrity is somehow preferable to merit, that brilliance smacks of dishonesty, that integrity depends not upon character but upon expediency, that the Englishman's home is the reporter's saloon bar, that private emotions are public tit-bits, that noise is infinitely desirable, that sport is more important than spirituality, that culture is a form of snobbery, that education is a matter of bursaries, that happiness depends upon money, that envy is a virtue; on the other hand, the sane and salutary conviction that the poor and the lowly, the stupid, the uneducated, the uncultured, the philistines and the barbarians should have their pleasures, their chance of happiness—that opportunity should be equal for all— that the specific interests of women (housekeeping, care of children, knitting, and so forth) are hardly less important than carpentry and gardening—that women have minds as well as bodies—that trades may be honourable, and crafts have their beauty; the increasing readability of news about trade and commerce, sociological developments and politics; the vast improvement of the general public's knowledge of foreign countries and strange lands; simplification, and a human approach, in the treatment of discoveries in science and technology; popular discussion of art, music, literature; information, much of it interesting, and most of it lucid and simple, about law and medicine; but sensationalism in the articles, sometimes even in the leaders, about disasters and national emergencies—the glorification of the cinema at the expense of the theatre, of the best-seller at the expense of true creative writing, of the ephemeral at the expense of the durable; the 'humanizing' of crime by means of chatty paragraphs about shady spivs and petty crooks, but a dangerous forgetfulness of the existence of men and women, youths and girls, incorrigibly or almost incorrigibly evil (as the police are aware)—if not overtly, then covertly or potentially; an ever more facile subscription to a facile and superficial utopianism; yet with a more realistic appreciation by journalists of their own limitations and of the limitations prescribed by the—in many instances—Moloch they serve, and with the suspicion, felt though too seldom acted on by journalists, that to sway the mob—the gullibles, constituting 90 per cent. of every nation—by appealing rather to its powerful, ill-understood emotions than to its brains—may have its charms but may also have its dangers, and that such an easy exercise of their powers is perhaps less worthy than to appeal to the reason of the intelligent, admittedly a small minority yet certainly very influential, and to the decency inherent in the vast majority of people.

If we look at journalism as a whole—both the old tradition, continued in *The Times*, *The Observer*, the *Sunday Times*, *The Daily Telegraph*, the *Manchester Guardian*, the *Yorkshire Post*, *The Scotsman* and several others; and the new tradition, inaugurated in 1896 by the *Daily Mail*, heightened by the *Daily Express*, carried to an *n*th in 'the picture papers' but diluted in the *Daily Herald*—we find that the tempo of journalistic writing has become faster; that journalistic writing is slicker yet also simpler, more homely and more personal, more intimate; and more direct.

But the sensationalism and the childishness that rather often

characterize, and have, ever since 1896, increasingly characterized, so much—by far the larger part—of the popular Press,
have not permeated the traditional and more dignified newspapers. Many unreflecting persons, speaking of 'the national
newspapers' (even 'the national Press'), think it co-extensive
with the popular Press; but *The Times*, with a circulation only
one-tenth of that of two or three of the 'popular' dailies,
exercises, not only abroad but at home, more influence than
any of those so-called 'national' newspapers, and *The Daily
Telegraph*, with a circulation midway between the two extremes, has probably as great, or nearly as great, an influence
as any of the others; the *Manchester Guardian* has an influence
out of all proportion to its circulation, much smaller than that
of *The Times*.

Enough has, I think, been said to show, or at the least to
imply quite unmistakably, that when we compare the journalism of the beginning with that of the middle of the twentieth
century, we should, to be logical, make three distinct comparisons: between the Press, in its entirety, as it was then and the
Press, in its entirety, as it is now; between the traditional Press
then and the traditional Press now; between the popular Press
then and the popular Press now. Perhaps we might also compare the traditional Press with the popular Press: but since that
is a comparison irrelevant, in the main, to the purpose of this
book, we need do no more than say that whereas the traditional
Press has become rather less traditionalistic, much less ponderous, and considerably more readable, the popular Press has
become more popular, more sensational, more 'snippety', less
dignified ('Anything for a story!'), but hardly more readable—
but then it nearly always has been eminently readable.

Most of the journalistic changes and other developments
worthy of notice have already been noticed in the foregoing
paragraphs. Yet I, for one, should feel uneasy if I did not mention several features so far either ignored or insufficiently
defined. (The list could be much extended, certainly by others
—who doubtless will—and probably by myself.) Newspapers
have become physically easier to read, because of better type,
better display, more and larger headlines, more section-titles

('Break it up!'); more personal, yet, in the British Isles at least, less libellous, and more intimate yet less scandalous; with a few notable exceptions, the popular newspapers (though not 'the picture papers') and the serious weeklies and monthlies have, since 1914, become more ideological; the serious Press has become more, the popular Press less, trustworthy in its handling of news—perhaps not quite so much in faithless transmission or in deliberate suppression, as in degree of emphasis and in other distortion and manipulation; the number of gossip columns has, both proportionately and absolutely, increased; yet, in the mass, newspapers and magazines alike have become less Social, perhaps because more Sociological; relatively to the theatre and to literature, both art and music have been gaining ground—not at the expense of the former but to the lessening of 'middles'; increasing space has had to be found, in chronological succession, for the cinema, for the radio, and for that cinema of radio, television; at first sight oddly (in view of its rapid and wonderful advances), articles whether 'popular' or erudite upon science are slightly less frequent now than they were in 1900, mainly because far fewer persons nowadays pin a desperate faith to science than there did before the wars of 1914-1918 and 1939-1945 caused them to wonder whether science was, after all, either a universal panacea or a universal solvent; on the other hand, technics have increased their popularity; psychological terms have entered the public domain; and, on an entirely different level, there seems to be, in general, more wit, but less humour.

'But what has all this to do with the history of the English language in the twentieth century?' It has a very great deal to do with the English language; journalists use the English language, some of them with great skill and great effect; although they have no right to misuse it, they misuse it much less than most of their readers; like their readers, journalists have the privilege of using it; it is one of the finest privileges of the human race. When journalists write of homely incidents, homely things, they tend to use homely words and phrases; if their subjects are technical or scientific (e.g., medical), they are almost bound to use a few technical and scientific terms. In short, not to enlarge the list, journalists now deploy a larger army of words in a greater variety of styles than the more limited range of subjects available or permissible in 1900 rendered necessary or advisable.

Not more now than then have journalists been obliged to write, all the time, in journalese; but now, even more than then, have circumstances often forced them into doing so: such circumstances as the tremendous urgency so often arising in 1914-1918 and again in 1939-1945, when editors had to print news before events had rendered it out of date, or deductions drawn from them invalid; the inadequate supplies of newsprint available from quite early in the latter war until the present day have vitiated the virtues of judicial consideration, invited the too brief judgement, and enhanced the value of facile generalizations and picturesque or violent examples.

Although, since ca. 1941, the general public has gone short of paper supplies for periodicals and books, the various Government Departments, through the Civil Servants, have not noticeably reduced either the number or the wordage of the pamphlets they put out or of the multiple forms they use or issue. But then, in a country that had, by the end of 1945, become as bureaucratic as France at her most bureaucratic and almost as totalitarian as Mussolini's Italy or Hitler's Germany or Stalin's Russia, Civil Servants now need only pretend to be servants where, as they well know, they are in fact the undeclared masters. What curb has there been on their verbosity; on their preference for a hundred words where forty would suffice and for thirty where three would have been excessive; on that tediously protracted obscurity which causes so much explanatory or cautionary official correspondence (not to dwell upon the deplorable waste of reputable citizens' time); on the drabness, the dullness, the boredom, the negativeness of so very many official documents? Almost none, until Sir Alan Herbert attacked officialese and analogous diseases; this he did, all guns firing, in that lively book, *What a Word!*, published in 1935. In *Usage and Abusage* (1942, U.S.A.; 1947, Britain) I contributed a few rounds; in *Keep up the Fight for English*, 1946, Professor J. Y. T. Greig fought a brief, very brisk engagement;

and in 1948, Sir Ernest Gowers delivered the severest and probably most effectual attack of all, for, being himself a highly
placed Civil Servant, he not only criticized, very severely,
certain types of official writing but also showed how much
there was to excuse by eloquently excusing it and how much
there was to improve by most reasonably and convincingly
improving it.

Sir Alan's attack is too well known to be mentionable, my
few rounds too sporadic to be quotable. But Professor Greig's
onslaught, more sustained than mine and more recent than
Sir Alan's, will serve very aptly. He quotes a truly delicious
example of a sort of prose just about as anaesthetic and as un-
useful as one could find:

> It will be apparent that the draining away of senior experi-
> enced men will be of such proportions for some years to come
> as to constitute a serious factor to be contended with in provid-
> ing for the adequate staffing of State departments. The diffi-
> culty in this respect is aggravated by the expansion of govern-
> mental activities which has been a feature during the last few
> years, and which seems likely to persist for some time. This
> expansion has already imposed considerable strain upon the
> personnel of the public service and, coupled with the progres-
> sive wastage in the ranks of the senior officers to which refer-
> ence has been made, tends to produce conditions which, on
> occasion, border on the acute. The Commission is giving its
> particular attention to the problems contained in and en-
> gendered by the circumstances already present and those which
> it is anticipated will develop in future.

Greig comments, 'That is one of the finest gems in my collection. If I tried to, I could not have written a better parody of
the twisted, pretentious, long-winded and down-at-heel
English called "officialese".' He rewrites it thus:

> So many senior and experienced officers will leave the
> service during the next few years that State departments will
> be short of staff; and the difficulties this will cause will be
> aggravated if, as seems possible, the State's activities continue
> to expand. The Commission is giving this matter attention.

Comment: 'It isn't elegant, certainly, my rewriting; but we're not concerned at the moment with elegance. It is English, not officialese; it says clearly in 49 words what the other scribe could only say cloudily in 146.'

Officialese, which has steadily increased in volume and volubility alike, has become proportionately an ever greater menace to English. It is read by millions; they have to read it, even although, otherwise, most of them read nothing else than a newspaper of 'the popular Press' and perhaps a comic or a western or a sexy thriller. This huge majority, lacking a literary standard and lacking even a standard of tolerable English, imitate that deleterious officialese both in their writing (a few letters) and, worse still, in any formal speaking they may have to do.

Let us, however, be fair: and listen to a Civil Servant upon this subject. Sir Ernest Gowers has had a well-deserved success with *Plain Words* ('A Guide to the Use of English'—addressed to Civil Servants), published in April, 1948. I can't say that I have noticed any improvement in official English, but that may easily be because I do not receive letters from officials writing 'at the highest levels'.

'The official,' says Sir Ernest, 'must use the written word for many different purposes—for Parliamentary Bills, Statutory Orders and other legal documents, for despatches to His Majesty's representatives abroad, for reports of commissions and committees, for circulars to Local Authorities and similar bodies, for departmental instructions, for minute writing [? minute-writing], for correspondence with other departments and with the public and for explaining the law to the millions for whom it now creates complicated personal rights and obligations, and whose daily lives it orders in countless ways.' (That formidable list may help to convince both the sceptical and the unthinking that the potentialities of official English for good—some official writing is excellent—or for bad, i.e. for the fostering, almost the inculcation, of officialese, are tremendous.) 'Whatever the purpose,' Sir Ernest Gowers continues, 'the object of the writer will be the same—to make the reader take his meaning readily and precisely. But the choice has

sometimes to be made between the simplicity that conveys
some meaning readily and the elaboration necessary'—rather,
'so often necessary'—'to convey a precise one.'

Sir Ernest rightly points out that legal language, required for
'Parliamentary Bills, Statutory Orders, and other legal documents', has peculiarities that 'are often used as a stick to beat
the official with' and that it is wholly unfair to call legal jargon
'officialese'; for one thing, it is written by lawyers, not by Civil
Servants, and for another, much legal jargon is probably unavoidable. He ends this short and excellent chapter ('A Digression on Legal English') with these admirable words, 'The
official has therefore two good defences against a charge of
failing to draft a law in literary English: one that he did not
draft it, and the other that if it had been so drafted it would not
have served its purpose'. (Sir Ernest's own English is so good
that several so-called literary men have, it is—none too authoritatively—reported, gone into the Civil Service.)

In the 'Epilogue' he loyally states, 'I should be sorry to be
thought to support the popular notion that officials write a
language of their own of a uniquely deplorable kind. Undoubtedly they have their peculiar faults of style. So have
journalists theirs. It is reasonable to attribute those of officialese
in the main to the peculiar difficulties with which official
writers have to contend. ... It is certainly wrong to imagine
that official writing, as an instrument for conveying thought, is
generally inferior to the lamentably low standard now prevalent except among professional writers. ... From some common
faults he [the Civil Servant] is comparatively free. Most
officials write grammatically correct English. Their style is un-
tainted by the silly jargon of commercialese, the catchpenny
tricks of the worst sort of journalism, the more nebulous
nebulosities of politicians, or the recondite abstractions ... in
which men of science, philosophers and economists too often
wrap their thoughts.'

But language is more than 'an instrument for conveying
thought'. The conveyance of thought merely constitutes its
chief importance in communication—the utilitarian purpose of
language. Language also constitutes the subtlest means of

expression or, as it is sometimes and needlessly called, self-expression (as if there were any other!)—the aesthetic and emotional purpose of language. Admittedly, thought enters—must enter—into expression; but in the conveyance of beauty or of emotion, thought normally takes second place to the expression of that beauty or that emotion. To say or write things clearly, to communicate clearly, is the primary need; to say or write them as best one can—this is where literature, whether actual or potential, i.e. whether written or spoken, rises above ordinary writing and ordinary speech. The ability to communicate clearly is something, not everything; to write or speak both clearly and pleasingly will not only afford far more pleasure but will also far more convincingly, because more profoundly, move or even persuade. It is not a crime to speak or to write attractively: and officials might do worse than to remember that the recipients of their conversations or of their letters will prove the more readily amenable to their advice, the more quickly understand their information (and thus, perhaps, save valuable time), if that advice or that information be conveyed not only lucidly but agreeably. It is by the spellbinders—the great orators, the eloquent talkers, the great writers—that events are the most powerfully originated and sustained.

The preceding paragraph, so far from being a digression, is needed as a complement to the many excellent things in Sir Ernest Gowers's *Plain Words*, much the best book ever written either incidentally upon officialese or, in the main, as a guide—designed for Civil Servants, Local Government staffs, and officers and others in the Services—to the writing of good English.

Nevertheless, Sir Ernest inevitably softens the blow: the members of his specific public are to be encouraged, not discouraged. He soft-pedals (nor do we blame him) the harm that has been done by officialese, the defects it has grafted upon much writing. Defects that have become alarmingly common. The increase in officialese is a fact in the history of English; another fact is the increase in the general public's knowledge of all official writing, whether good, i.e. ordinary educated

English (Standard English) as applied to official matters, or bad, i.e. officialese. In short, the influence of official English has not been entirely harmful; it has, for instance, increased the general vocabulary. But, in the main, that influence has been bad, for it has aggravated the evil of that flat, colourless, nerveless and spineless English which has become increasingly common throughout the century, at least until about 1940; since then, this flat and colourless English has, outside official circles, become rather less common. And, thanks to Sir Ernest Gowers's precept and example, it may even become noticeably less common in official circles.

It is indeed to be hoped that everywhere this negation of effective English will tend more and more to die out, for English, like every other language, cannot afford to be vitiated by the presence of language so exasperatingly cautious, so coldly reserved, so circumlocutory, so devoid of life and energy, so damnably dull and, in its very attempts to be correct, often merely inept.

Sir Ernest Gowers has alluded to journalese, which we have surveyed or at least glanced at, and to commercialese, which must now engage our attention. In *What a Word!* Sir Alan Herbert has shown up commercialese for the fungoid growth it is: ugly, useless, dangerous; but also childish and ludicrous.

Commercialese concerns us here for two reasons. It seems to have become even more general by the mid-century than it was at the beginning, though just a little less widespread in 1950 than in 1935. That slight decrease may be traced to the attacks made upon it by H. W. Fowler in *A Dictionary of Modern English Usage*, 1926, by Sir Alan in 1935 (this has been the wittiest—and the weightiest—of all the attacks made upon commercialese), by myself in *Usage and Abusage: A Guide to Good English* in 1947, and by several other critics. Precisely why commercialese should have increased during the first third of the twentieth century, it is difficult to say. One of the reasons, however, was the very considerable growth in the number and size of the Business Colleges, all spreading the doctrine and the practice of 'business English' or 'commercial

English', which, being extraordinarily wordy and horribly insincere, is most unbusinesslike, and which, being a jumble of the juvenile and the jejune, is hardly English. Such English, instead of being confined to the Vallombrosan leaves of business correspondence, where it was merely corrupting the already corrupt, wormed its way into the newspapers by the channel of advertisements, which, in the rapidly growing mail-order business and even elsewhere, assured its 'esteemed customers' or its 'distinguished clientèle' that their 'esteemed (or, valued) orders' would receive immediate attention.

The other reason for which commercialese concerns us here is that, by its very nature, it tends to add the malefic influence of sloppy ineptitude to that of the colourlessness, chilliness and verbosity of officialese and to that of the slick approximations and story-at-any-price subterfuges of journalese. Journalese, officialese, commercialese are 'fellow-travellers' in the sinister contemporary sense of that once companionable term.

If only the users of commercialese would self-critically examine the letters or advertisements they write, or permit to be written, it would soon decrease quite rapidly. Nobody with an ounce of humour would, on inspection, pass such a letter as this, quoted by Sir Alan Herbert. (I have slightly modified it to make it conform to the standard of many letters I myself have received.)

> Madam,
> We are in receipt of your esteemed favour of the 9th inst. with regard to the estimate required for the removal of your furniture and household effects from the above address to Burbleton, and will arrange for a Representative to call to make an inspection on Tuesday next, the 14th inst., before 12 noon, which we trust will be convenient to your good self, after which our quotation will at once issue.

To omit the intermediate stage, at which Sir Alan merely converts commercialese (he calls it officese) into ordinary, respectable English, I quote his final recast into good English.

Madam,

Thank you for your letter of May 9th. A man will call next Tuesday, forenoon, to see your furniture and effects, after which, without delay, we will send our estimate for their removal to Burbleton.

(35 words against the original 72; or 157 letters against 325.)

One does not need to be a master of analytical psychology to be able to perceive the dangers inherent in commercialese, nor a particularly acute observer of the currents in that stream of factors and influences which, at any period, forms the English (or any other) language, to be able to chart the current named commercialese: to see, in short, what has already resulted from its spread and what may easily happen if that spread be not continually checked.

Fortunately, commercial correspondence has comparatively little affected private correspondence, except—if the obvious may be tolerated—among those clerks and typists who are constantly subjected to commercialese and among the less educated businessmen who either propagate or permit it.

Private correspondence, being unofficial and uncommercial and non-journalistic, runs naturally, hence easily. It may be and usually is less correct, grammatically; but if it loses in correctness, it loses also in stiffness and in unreality. Positively, it gains in directness and simplicity, vividness and vigour. Free of the verbal trickery and the almost relentless slickness of journalism; of the coldness, remoteness and caution of official correspondence, and of the indirectness and dreary flatness and staleness of official instructions, minutes, reports, memoranda; free, too, of the smarmy insincerity of so much commercial letter-writing; free of these obstacles to prompt comprehension, to fair-dealing, and to the promotion of any civilization other than superficial, private correspondence is less subject to the vagaries of fashion and to the whims of coteries than are all other kinds of writing. But from the very conditions and circumstances in which private letters are written and exchanged, and then—very much later, if ever—published, one finds it exceedingly difficult to evaluate the changes, or even to determine what are the changes and developments, in letter-writing over a period so short as half a century or so.

Clearly, private letter-writing has become less and less formal, more and more natural and intimate and therefore revelatory, wider in its range, shrewder in its judgements, more sophisticated: and here we see certain results of the influence of two great wars, of the increasing influence of the popular Press, of the meteoric acceleration in the influence of cinema and radio, of rapidly growing social consciousness: all of which, along with other factors and elements, will come up for review and (so far as possible) assessment in the chapter entitled, rather vaguely, 'General Trends and Particular Influences'.

Passing from the spheres of journalism, the Civil Service and commerce, with their jargons, and from an antipodal world common or, rather, available to everybody, that of private letter-writing, we come to certain grades of English: dialect, on the one hand; colloquialism, slang and cant, on the other.

Dialect has already, in Chapter One, been mentioned in reference to modern poetry. Let us first make sure that we do know precisely what dialect is. Perhaps the best definition is that made by H. W. Fowler: 'A dialect is [that] variety of a language which prevails in a district, with local peculiarities of vocabulary, pronunciation, and phrase': for it implies the important fact that dialects are languages *within* a language.

Dialectal pronunciations exercise very little influence upon Standard English. Dialectal words and phrases, especially if vivid or picturesque, forcible or apposite, have, ever since there was such a thing as Standard English, been constantly incorporated into colloquial—into slangy—even, sooner or later, directly or ultimately, into Standard English. 'At ordinary times, the incorporation is slow and inconsiderable, but on special occasions and during intense periods, as in a war ... numerous dialectal terms become part of the common stock and some few of them pass into formal speech and into the language of literature, whether prose or poetry' (*Usage and Abusage*).

During the twentieth century, three wars have notably influenced the English language: the Boer War (1899-1902); and World War I (often called 'the Great War') and World War II (often simply 'the World War'). Countrymen, mixing freely for long periods and at very close quarters with townsmen, have richly coloured the speech, hence, soon the writing, of the latter; and men and women of one great city have mingled with those of another. The latter mixture is to be stressed, because several great cities, notably Glasgow, have a speech predominantly dialectal and one great city (London) has, at its core, a speech essentially dialectal, although fashion has elected to treat Cockney as if it were entirely sui-generic. Linguistically, Cockney is a dialect; socially it represents an enclave; psychologically it expresses the spirit of independence; and, in terms of humankind, it is 'a sheer joy', for it 'cocks a snook' at ass and authority alike, its humour being irrepressible and invincible. Cockney is so important that it receives a chapter to itself, written by someone much better informed on the subject than myself; so important, in a specific aspect, that it figures prominently in the section on the vernacular (at the end of the chapter 'General Trends and Particular Influences').

Dialect, despite damage wrought by the well-meaning and by the onset of cinema and radio, is far from moribund. For the future of English, it might be well if Standard English were to substitute for many of its effete and shop-soiled words and phrases and for its 'weary Willie and Tired Tim' attitude towards language, the fresh, forceful, vigorous words, the pithy and arresting phrases, and the natural, direct, realistic yet often strangely poetic attitude of dialect and its speakers. One has only to think of such twentieth-century masters of dialect as, in England, Eden Phillpotts and for Cockney, Edwin Pugh and Neil Lyons; J. J. Bell or Neil Munro in Scotland; any of half-a-dozen writers in Ireland; and, in the United States of America, (say) Alfred Henry Lewis, Hervey Allen, Paul Horgan, John Steinbeck, to mention a quartet merely representative of a land that has so many excellent writers of dialect: and, thinking of them, one is assailed by a mass of evidence for the realism and objectivity, the immediacy and rightness, the directness and simplicity, the sturdy manliness or the unhysterical femininity, and the remarkable sound-to-sense correspondence of their writing in comparison with the writing of the majority of those who have never come into a long or impressive or otherwise formative period of association, whether voluntary or enforced, with a dialect—or with some sort of English that, in naturalness, freshness and vigour, resembles a dialect in its impact.

There may be proportionally fewer dialect-speakers in the 1950's than in the 1900's. Those of to-day are not less tenacious of their privileges, and some of them would unaffectedly talk of their rights. The novelists and short-story writers that often, or otherwise notably, employ dialect to-day are proportionally at least as numerous as those who did so in 1900. Nor is this dialectal speaking and writing at all nostalgic or vaguely sentimental: its origination is commendable, its theory terse, its practice unaffected. We could do with more of it.

—For an example of dialect, see the brief chapter entitled 'Dialect: A Note'.—

As we have heard, dialect may pass into colloquialism. Since 'the colloquial' or 'colloquialisms' is the term applied to all that huge tract of English (correspondingly for any other language) which lies between Standard English and slang and is, at many points, only narrowly distinguishable from Familiar English (or informal Standard English) and since, as Henry Bradley—the greatest philologist ever to grace the British Isles—once remarked, 'at no period ... has the colloquial vocabulary and idiom of the English language been completely preserved in the literature' or even in the dictionaries, and, as he also remarked, 'the homely expressions of everyday intercourse ... have been but very imperfectly recorded', it is, as a result, none too easy to relate the developments in the colloquial English of even the twentieth century. Have there, indeed, been any changes worth recording? Can we differentiate between the colloquial speech current in 1950 and that current in 1900?

One can, with confidence, say that the attitude of scholars, like that of all other educated and cultured persons, has become more tolerant, both in theory and—more importantly—in practice. All such persons now employ colloquialism more freely now than in 1900; only slightly more freely in conversation, for already they employed it without constraint and with little restraint; but much more freely in writing, whether that of private correspondence or that of books. The increase in the literary employment of colloquialism forms part of the general movement away from stiffness, pomposity, pretentiousness, solemnity and portentousness. And all that vast majority of Britons who are not—and, to their credit, would not claim to be—either cultured or well-educated, all these tend to be even more colloquial than before.

They, like their 'betters', also tend to be even more slangy than was the generation that reached its prime in and around the year 1900. Estimable if rather starchy persons, who in 1900 would have shuddered away from slang and looked grimacefully at colloquialism, nowadays use colloquialisms almost freely and, greatly daring, permit themselves ('We, too, are modern') an occasional slangy term or a smart catch-phrase. Both in drama and in fiction, dialogue has become not only far more realistic, in the sense of life-like, but—except for a few omissions dictated by law—at all points faithful. Dramatists, novelists, short-story writers no longer feel a need to dignify the dialogue they invent or, as must sometimes happen, paraphrase or, seldom, report: there is no transposition of jazz into light opera, nor of light opera into opera. Along with an appreciable increase of colloquialism has inevitably gone a marked, yet not, so far, dangerous increase in the employment of slang, whether in oratory or in conversation, at no matter what level, and also in written English, whether that of private correspondence or that of journalism or that of literature.

Those two very closely related increases have been, in the main, caused by the growing consciousness of Britons, those abroad no less than those 'at home', that the entire domain of the English language is theirs to use and to enjoy: that no longer do there exist vast regions where it is illegal or illicit or, on the other hand, unsafe or unhealthy to wander: that these regions need never have existed, would never have existed had they, men priding themselves on their freedom, grasped the important, the glaringly obvious truths that language exists for mankind, not mankind for language, and that they, at no period less than the pundits and the policemen, and now in the twentieth century far more than those others, have made and are, every day and in every trade and every profession, in their games, their hobbies, their entertainments, and in the routine usualness of their daily existences, still making and will continue to make the language with which they have to live, to labour, and to create.

The preceding paragraph must not be interpreted to mean that 'the authorities' have been blind to the requirements of the general public. However sympathetic they may feel towards the public, they have a duty to perform. It is they who safeguard property: and the English language is property; the property not only of the nation as a whole but also of every individual. Immediately freedom becomes lawlessness, property tends to get destroyed by those who have none worth mentioning and who, eaten up with envy, cannot bear that anyone else should have any. Such lawlessness, issuing in destructiveness, could be as damaging to language as it is to material things. Moreover, many scholars will now assert, where once they reluctantly admitted, that slang constitutes one of the main reservoirs from which language, as thirsty as a metropolis, can draw refreshment, and one of the greatest granaries from which it can draw sustenance.

There remains one unconventional source. That of cant, or the language of the underworld. Whereas colloquialism lies at only one remove, and slang at two removes, from Standard English, cant lies, theoretically, very far, yet in practice at only three or four removes, for a cant word or phrase easily passes into low slang, then perhaps into ordinary slang, whence it may become colloquial and finally standard. *Spiv*, cant until *ca.* 1945, had, not later than 1949, become an accepted part of the most reputable English: an official classification. So vivid, apposite, realistic a terminology, and so deft a phrasing, as those of cant will probably come, to a small extent, to affect the composition of the vocabulary and the use of concrete imagery in phrase-making.

Spoken Non-Literary English

Something has inevitably been said already about spoken English. Much remains.

In 1941, William Barkley, in a pamphlet entitled *The Two Englishes*, noted that 'It is only in modern times [i.e., in Modern English—since *ca.* 1450] that the written language has assumed such importance in comparison with the spoken language'—a statement with which few would disagree—and continued thus, 'and in modern times we should give it [the written language] a modern streamlined dress'. The 'should' is unnecessary, for language rarely lags behind life. (That Barkley was leading us up the garden path to simplified spelling need not concern us here.)

Pronunciation will, in very general terms, have an organic mention at Standardization in the section 'Particular Influences' of the chapter 'General Trends'; but certain aspects cannot be fittingly treated at any point other than this. Pronunciation has not yet reached stability or, if you prefer, uniformity. The pronunciation of the uneducated is so varied, so variable, that one can hardly analyse it. For obvious reasons, too, it is better to put Dominions English on one side if, in a discussion of standard pronunciation, we wish to avoid a hopelessly complex accumulation of facts and theories.

'Considering only the speech of the educated classes, we may say that there are four main standard pronunciations for English: Public School Standard (sometimes called Southern English), Scots Standard, Irish Standard, and American Standard. Each is *received* ... within its own area or sphere of influence, and tolerated (more or less) outside. An educated Englishman who speaks with a noticeable Newcastle or Manchester or Nottingham accent is socially at a disadvantage among those who speak Public School Standard; he is required to prove his intellectual status in some other way than by his tongue before he is accepted.' Yet 'a Scotsman or Irishman or American speaking his own Standard is accepted with little or no hesitation', as J. Y. T. Greig remarks in his extremely provocative, very readable, and eminently sensible and practical *Breaking Priscian's Head*, 1928.

'Of the four,' he continues, 'only ... Public School Standard has ever put forward a claim to be the Standard, and thus to take precedence of the other three. This claim is still'—in the 1950's, let me add, as in the 1920's—'being made. It is countenanced in every dictionary published in England ...; it is tacitly assumed by nearly every writer on the language save Americans ... ; and it is recognized by teachers of English on the Continent, who drill their pupils in this, the most slovenly of all the ways of speaking English, in the fond belief that it alone is correct. It has been challenged again and again, and by writers who deserve to be listened to [footnote: 'Notably ... Dr Bridges, ... whose challenge gains in force by his admission that he still'—1928—'speaks "the bad Southern English" that he learnt "as a child and at school"], but it is still far from being overthrown'.

That remains true in the 1950's, with these modifications: the status of Scots Standard and of Irish Standard has advanced; American Standard has not advanced—being the Standard of a great, independent nation, it hasn't needed to advance, except perhaps in some hardly determinable improvement along lines of its own; such educated Englishmen and, by the way, Welshmen as do not speak Southern English have, ever since 1939 or so, adopted an attitude expressible in either of two not unconnected manners—'To hell with this assumption of superiority by people no better, no more learned, than ourselves!' and 'What sort of people do they take us for, anyway?' On the other hand, the speakers of Southern or Public School English, partly from a growing uneasiness about the impregnability of their own linguistic position and their own self-conferred award of all the prizes for virtue, and partly from an honest recognition of 'the other fellow's right' to a place in the linguistic sun and of his 'doubtless sterling qualities, what!' have begun, since the days of Dunkirk (a miracle far greater in its moral results than in its physical achievement), to suspect that a sense of spiritual values and an appreciation of 'first things first' possess an importance outweighing that of the disputable merits of a certain set of vowels (admittedly musical) and of a sword-swallowing manipulation of consonants and of the suppression, or the neutralization, of unstressed syllables.

Summing up, Professor Greig finds that, 'on nearly every count, Public School Standard must be condemned, and I for one believe it is past mending'. He then makes a counter-suggestion, all the more attractive because he himself is 'a Scotsman born abroad': 'As between Scots Standard and Irish Standard, no one who is free from national prejudice can hesitate an instant. Irish Standard, as spoken by the educated classes in Dublin, is as pure and harmonious a form of English as the heart of man could desire. Its intonation is as varied and flex-ible as that of Public School Standard, and its articulation of separate syllables as careful as the best American. Each syllable is given its proper value, vowels are clearly marked and dis-tinguished one from another without silly diphthongization, consonants are sharp ... At the same time there is none of the harshness of Scots Standard.'

The other side—the defence of Southern, or Public School, English—has been put by Dr R. W. Chapman in his Society for Pure English tract, 'Oxford' English (1932), a title referring to the fact that, not very satisfactorily, Oxford English—or rather, the Oxford accent—has been proposed by certain scholars as an alternative to Southern English. Dr Chapman, who neatly and convincingly disposes of the Oxford tag, does his able, temperate, scholarly best. That best isn't good enough. Profes-sor Greig has wittily if a trifle unkindly remarked that 'the only languages that do not change are those already dead, like San-scrit, Latin, and classical Greek. Even Public School Standard English still shows faint signs of life, despite the prayers for its early death put up by thousands of English-speakers all over the world, and despite Mr Daniel Jones's attempt to bury it in the pages of his Phonetic Dictionary.' Dr Bridges, in On British Homophones (1919), made a most damning attack on Southern English—this, by the way, in a tract published by the Society for Pure English, of which he was the founder and, until shortly before his death in 1930 at the age of eighty-five, the leading figure and a never-failing light.

Leaving that specific question, whose importance it is easy to exaggerate, we pass to several larger considerations and aspects. Both in general pronunciation and in general vocabulary, phrasing, syntax—that is, in English as a whole, throughout the British Isles and in the Dominions and Colonies—anyone with an 'observant' ear and with a mind capable of simplificatory synthesis as well as of selective analysis will have noticed one predominant fact: English has been rapidly approaching, or at least working towards, uniformity; a uniformity it will probably never attain; a uniformity still only a potentiality very far from realization. The trend is unmistakable; it is powerful; as a result of compulsory education, it is inevitable. (The Elementary Education Act was passed in 1870.) No less now than in 1928 do 'we hear complaints on every hand that children are being taught to speak a bastard tongue, which is neither Standard English nor their own local dialect but combines the faults of both' (J. Y. T. Greig).

What is the influence of spoken upon written English? Several famous writers have wished it to be greater than, in the fact, it ever has been. For instance, Montaigne once wrote, 'The language that I like is simple, the same thing on paper as on the lips'; Hazlitt, 'The master spirit of prose-writing is sensible conversation'. Admirable sentiments! Commendable aims! Nevertheless, one has to recall that although Montaigne did achieve a notably conversational effect in his writing (much as Voltaire was to do), yet many of his sentences were of a length and of a syntactical complexity far beyond the scope of conversation. One must also remember that when Hazlitt wrote 'sensible conversation' he meant either 'such conversation as you might expect of a man of great good sense and of an at least tolerable education' or, less probably, 'a man of keen and delicate perceptions and of an artist's sensitiveness'. William Barkley, the quoter of Montaigne and Hazlitt, has, so recently as 1941, iterated his belief that 'the grammatical simplicity of the spoken English language is the secret of England's greatness'. In that forgivable hyperbole, he implied this: that the more closely written English approximates to good spoken

English, the better. With the insidious influence of the cinema
and with the growing popularity of radio, the spoken word
may very strongly affect the written; clearly, however, that
influence may be bad—or it may be good.

One aspect of the influence of the spoken upon the written
word can be perceived in the novels of Henry Green, who uses
conversation as the vehicle for most of the story, many a novel
by him consisting mainly of dialogue. Dialogue startlingly
similar to the ordinary conversation of precisely the characters
he writes about: averagely well educated, averagely cultured;
civilized; not 'disgustingly rich' nor yet poor; and, most of
them, belonging to what we formerly called the upper middle
class. Here is a conversation—not, however, 'upper middle'—
from *Concluding*, 1948.

> 'But have you got the latest?' she demanded. 'Right before
> the finish, pipped at the post, one minute before the whistle,
> two seconds left for play, guess what? Liz has hooked him.
> He's buying the hoop Saturday, and they'll be married in
> September.'
> 'Who's he?'
> 'Why Sebastian, naturally, old "Cause and Effect". Or have
> you been asleep till now? Isn't it splendid for Mr Rock,
> though.' And it was plain from her voice that Moira meant
> this. 'He might be a great grandfather extraordinarily quick.
> Only nine months, and what's that in his lifetime?'
> The news was taken reflectively. Then someone asked, by
> way of fun,
> 'I wonder what Edgey'll give for a present?'

The fidelity is such that a Henry Green novel, viewed as a
whole, combines much of what is best in the novel with much
of what is best in drama of the light, witty, sophisticated kind.
Some day, these novels, stimulating now (*sauce piquante*, of an
acquired taste—a taste richly worth the acquiring), will be
treasured as records of spoken English and of manners. They
also stand out by reason of their profound, aseptic, yet sympathetic understanding of human nature.

The readers of such a book as this expect the author to prophesy. It is an unreasonable expectation. The wise man doesn't.

The situation has not vastly changed since, in 1926, Basil de Sélincourt brought out his *Pomona: or the Future of English* and, in 1928, J. Y. T. Greig his *Breaking Priscian's Head: or English as She Will be Spoke and Wrote*. The latter author had some excuse for being incensed with the former. Basil de Sélincourt's book, polished and cultured, was not hopelessly conservative, nor hopelessly conventional: it was merely conventional and conservative: its author regarded 'English' as synonymous with 'the English of the best English literature'. In the wider view, Professor Greig's book was, in the main, fully justified, for English, so far from being what the dons would like it to be or even what ninety per cent. of them say it is, happens to be what Britons all over the world and what Americans all over America make it and make of it.

A remote yet not impossible contingency is envisaged in a question posed to me by an intelligent non-alarmist. 'What will happen to English if Britain becomes the 49th State of the U.S.A.?' The 'sturdy independence of the Briton'—perhaps less sturdy than it was—would probably survive either the shock or, conceivably, the relaxation that ensues a feeling of relief; Britons would, I think, continue to speak British English; British writers would, I hope, continue to write British English. Yet, at the lowest estimate, there would be some infiltration of American English, both into the English used by officials, who might be forced to abandon the Scylla of Whitehallese for the Charybdis of Federal prose, and into the English of certain smart-Alec journalists. The Dominions would be affected in corresponding measure through the same two channels.

If the British Commonwealth of Nations remains British, and if the ostensibly well-meaning have not succeeded in discarding any more huge chunks of it and in otherwise weakening the ties that, if sincere, they would admit to be abhorrent to them, English will simply follow the course that we have seen it follow for centuries and especially in the twentieth.

Written English will become increasingly less stiff and formal; it will increasingly approximate to the rules, or the lack of rules, governing the spoken English of the educated and (we hope) the cultured; and spoken English, perhaps even among the educated and the cultured, will, though much less in the dying art of oratory and in the specialized arts of lecturing and teaching than elsewhere, slowly—probably very slowly indeed —approximate to the vernacular. This matter of the vernacular is extremely important, but, as I have already suggested, it is best left to the chapter 'General Trends and Particular Influences'.

But I should be guilty of an intolerable egotism if I were to ignore what was so ably said in 1928 by J. Y. T. Greig upon the future of English. It is as applicable now as it was then: and its urgency is perhaps greater now than then.

'Scotsmen, Irishmen, Welshmen, Englishmen who reject Public School Standard, Canadians, Australians, South Africans, and New Zealanders, may come more or less consciously to an agreement with Americans that the English language shall be maintained as an organic whole, despite dialectal differences; and that it shall be helped everywhere to develop freely in accordance with the natural laws of human speech in general, and the peculiar habits ... of English in particular. The mechanical aids to unity—newspapers, rapid transport, the telegraph, broadcasting—are not in themselves strong enough to arrest disintegration, if disintegration is willed by human beings; but if integration is willed instead, the mechanical aids to it must become more powerful every day.'

That Britons should deliberately will and then effect the disintegration of British English is perhaps even more unlikely than that Americans should deliberately disintegrate American English. Probably no less unlikely is any conscious attempt, by either Britons or Americans, to integrate the language, not because of spinelessness or apathy, but because language in general and English in particular are unamenable to regimentation. A few simplifications of accidence and syntax may— probably will—take place, and they will do so more rapidly in America than in Britain and the Dominions; yet, everywhere, the time required may be very much longer than iconoclasts dare to suppose. Reluctant to hazard a prophecy, I yet venture, tentatively and shamefacedly, to suggest that the gap between literature and the spoken language will widen, although rather more in American than in the countries speaking British English; that then, after a period of linguistic doubt, uncertainty, experimentation, the vernacular will win a considerable victory; that, to a large (yet, paradoxically, not a dangerous) extent, the vernacular will become—rather, will be—the literary language; and that the potential dangers of this identification will result in a tightening-up of the principles of clear thinking as a means to clearer writing. And I shall probably be wrong.

CHAPTER THREE

DOMINIONS ENGLISH

GENERAL

CERTAIN Englishmen—they are few, and becoming fewer —speak as if the only kind of English with a right to exist were the English spoken by those who, born in England, have spent most of their lives there. Even Scots come under their mystic suspicion; yet when, in 1921, I went to Oxford, a certain famous don told me that the best English spoken in Britain was that spoken in the cultured circles of Edinburgh. By the Little Englanders we are told that the Irish speak, not English but Anglo-Irish; yet many educated and cultured Irishmen speak and write the most admirable, if slightly old-fashioned, English. My studies, however, have shown me that without the influence of Scottish, Irish, Welsh novelists, dramatists and poets, English might now have reached just such another stage of 'ghastly good taste' and in-sipid correctitude as almost stifled it in the middle third of the eighteenth century.

As for American English! For three centuries scarcely any scholar in England admitted that it possessed great merits of its own: and even now, the English-born scholars that, consciously or sub-consciously, do not still apply the criterion of British English to American English, could be counted on the fingers (only) of one-and-a-half hands. But that is a tale that is told elsewhere.

And the Dominions? Although one feels that the linguistic nationalist movements, so far as they exist, are based upon exaggerations and misapprehensions, yet one must admit that, as retaliatory expressions of independence, they are almost justified. But Australia is the only country in which such a movement is both strong and vocal. In Canada, it is strong, not vocal, for it is hardly conscious: Canadians have a very distinct variety of English, far more different from that spoken in Britain than is the English spoken by Australians; yet Cana-dians—so imperceptibly, so constantly has the process operated —'just get on with the job'; having this very different English, they therefore do not feel the need to have it at all. In New Zealand, there is no appreciable nationalist movement: the most English of the Dominions, New Zealand does not wish to be linguistically different; except in pronunciation (determined, in the main, by climate and geography) it tries to remain at one with the mother country. South Africa, despite its intense political nationalism (in the fact, rather truculent than intransigent), has no strong linguistic nationalism—a feature caused, probably, by the fact that the small European population speaks either English or Afrikaans; many whites speak both. In India, English is by far the most favoured of the foreign languages: the 'better' (that is, the purer) the English is and the closer it is to the English spoken by educated and cultured Englishmen, the better pleased are the native inhabitants of India and Pakistan. If there is ever a world-language, it will be English, in one variety or another: and India and Pakistan will merely be taking out a very effective form of insurance if they decide that, instead of reducing the teaching of English, they will do everything in their power to promote the knowledge of English, the speaking of English, the writing of English. This argument applies with perhaps even greater cogency to the British Crown Colonies: and, by the way, to the overseas possessions of the United States. That these American possessions speak, and will speak, American English is a comparatively minor point.

There are and always will be variations in the vocabulary of each Dominion as compared with that of Britain. That is only natural. Natural, because inevitable. Different fauna and flora; an aboriginal race with its customs, implements, weapons, clothes; different geographical and topographical features; climatic differences; in short, new conditions, new needs, new activities: these require a special vocabulary, and that special vocabulary becomes part of the everyday, as well as of the cultural, life of the Dominion. Finally, the more basic and the more picturesque words and phrases work their way into the general vocabulary of British English and, indeed, constitute a major reason for our speaking of *British English* as opposed to *English*.

In this, the specifically Dominion vocabularies have been

determined by very much the same conditions, and therefore have most of the same distinctive general features, as those governing, and possessed by, American English. The pronunci-ation of the words forming these Dominion and American vocabularies is rightly decided by the colonists and, later, the citizens in the new countries. Educated or influential English-men, Scots, Welshmen, Irishmen have had a voice in that decision; it has, however, lain with the colonists as a whole, then with the American and Dominion citizens as peoples, to determine the pronunciation, which, abroad as 'at Home', may change, either in general characteristics or in particular words. The Dominion varieties of English stand, historically, in the same relation to the English spoken in Britain as does American English; and in almost the same relation geographic-ally, ethnologically and socially; culturally, the American relationship to Britain is less different from the Dominion relationships to Britain than has usually been admitted on either side of the Atlantic.

The already mentioned question of pronunciation requires a little further attention. The factors influencing Dominion pronunciations are virtually the same as those influencing American pronunciations; there are, by the way, at least as many American as there are Dominion pronunciations. Aus-tralian pronunciation differs more widely from English than do the South African and especially the New Zealand, but slightly less than does the Canadian. In addition to the influence exer-cised by physical conditions, chiefly that of climate, there is the social factor. Few educated and cultured persons went to North America, South Africa, Australia and New Zealand until the colonies in those countries were fairly well established; very few indeed to America and Australia. The inevitable and, so far from being reprehensible, entirely natural and circumstantially fitting result was that there arose, quite soon in every colony, a predominant pronunciation differing considerably from that of educated and cultured persons in England: and in pro-nunciation must be included not only vowel-value and accent, but stress and intonation and enunciation.

The difference increased. It is no less evident now than it was in (say) 1850, despite the efforts of purists and educationists. Even among the educated, especially the educated persons of culture, pronunciation in the Dominions, as in the United States, differs appreciably from that of the corresponding persons in Britain. Moreover, the Dominions differ among themselves. And the United States differs from all of them. To deprecate these differences may be human, but it is just about as effectual and, regarded dispassionately, as reasonable as Canute's traditional injunction to the waves on that historic shore. (Canute, however, knew what he was doing.)

At first, accidence and syntax suffered violence in the new, often violent lands. Among the educated, no scars remain; but the vernacular speech has never since been the same—if it ever were! All over the English-speaking world, even during Anglo-Saxon times, the vernacular has differed almost as much from the literary language as did Low (or Vulgar) from Classical Latin; that difference applies to accidence and syntax—to vocabulary—and to pronunciation. This vernacular is both more strikingly different and more widely spread in the United States than in near-by Canada and in the other British Dominions. Many well-educated Americans use it supplementarily, or even complementarily, to their usual speech; and this tendency may grow stronger in other countries, especially perhaps Canada and Australia; certainly it is already stronger in all the Dominions than it is in Britain—and all except a few ivory-towered pedants know that this vernacular is amazingly strong in Britain itself. Pronunciation is the first linguistic feature to be affected by the influence of the vernacular; in the Dominions, as in the United States, all the strong influences characteristic of new countries merge with the influence of the vernacular to increase and reinforce the divergence, whether of pronunciation or of vocabulary or of accidence and syntax.

The tempo of life, hence of speech, tends to differ in one Dominion as compared with another, and, whether collectively or individually, in all of them (as also in the United States) as compared with the tempo of life and speech in Great Britain and Ireland. Nor should one forget that the tempo of speech, as of life, is not the same in Scotland or Ireland or

Wales as in England: in this respect, however, it is permissible to generalize the four (? five) countries of Great Britain and Ireland into one. On the other hand, it should be remembered that, abroad, Scots and Irish and Welsh preserve their characteristic speech even more jealously than do the English.

To return, however, to tempo. Tempos of life result in tempos of speech: and tempos of speech vary in two ways, the one according to the country, the other according to the period —for instance, how different the tempo of speech, because how different the tempo of life, in 1950 from that in 1900! Hence, the only tempo one can safely analyse into a unit is that of a given country at a given period. One may speak of the tempo of civilization, whether civilization in the world as a whole or civilization of a race (the British, the American, and so forth) or civilization of variations (for instance, English, Canadian, Australian) within a race. Of these variations, one may fairly assert that whereas the tempo of life, hence the tempo of speech, has appreciably, although not startlingly, increased in Canada, South Africa, Australia, New Zealand and also in India, the tempo of literary English, however much that of newspaper English has accelerated, has only a little accelerated. Literary English, however, has lost much of its pomposity and solemnity and rigidity; it views the colloquial and the slangy with a much more tolerant eye.

Besides the heightened tempo of life in the Dominions (as also in the United States), there is a hitherto unmentioned factor contributing to the heightened tempo of speech in the Dominions as opposed to the mother country: and that is the much more decided laconism of Dominion conversation. Laconism in the expression of the emotions—for instance, in the expression of urgency—leads to, or rather is inseparable from, terse and pithy speech; hence to economy of time as well as of words. This laconism is less marked in South Africa and especially in New Zealand than in Canada and especially in Australia. It is perhaps a pity that, in the Dominions, this laconism has not much more profoundly affected literary English and that it has not gone even further than it already has gone in its impact on journalistic English. Compare the novels of Ruth Park with those of Kylie Tennant and you will perceive how notably laconism enhances the power of the former and how insidiously the comparative lack of it weakens the latter. Kylie Tennant is an indisputably meritorious novelist of the sociological, documentary school; Ruth Park has literary distinction—and no less sociological value, implicitly instead of explicitly expressed.

To attempt to distinguish the general character of Dominion speech and writing from that of English speech and writing would be to court disaster. Some of the specific differences will be treated by the scholars whose contributions follow this preamble. There are, however, several generic differences that may safely be mentioned. Collectively, Dominion speech and Dominion writing, as contrasted with the speech, the journalism and the literature of England, exhibit a greater independence of mind and attitude, hence less respect for authority; they are more ingenuous, though not less shrewd; they are more forthright and less sophisticated; they are less cultured; they shun the psychologically complicated and tend to shun the intellectually subtle; the alembicated, the etiolate, the highly elaborate are seldom present in the writings and almost entirely absent from the speech of the Dominions; the delicacies, the niceties and the finesses characteristic of an ancient civilization are rarely found, and, even then, mostly in the homes of Britons either recently arrived or so long established that they have formed tiny enclaves of gracious living in an atmosphere occasionally hostile, frequently envious and only rarely appreciative. (But then, such enclaves are not peculiar to British, nor yet to American, civilization: all over the world, they represent the elect, a small core of culture, education, distinction and integrity.) The Dominions will probably become increasingly cultured; certainly they have, in this respect, progressed since 1900. But they may also become more independent; certainly they are more independent now than in 1900.

All the preceding considerations gain in perspective if a few elementary dates be remembered. To prevent oneself from making wild statements and from building wild theories, one would do well to glance at—rather, to study carefully—the following table of facts and factors essential to any well-founded deduction or comparison.

DATE AND POPULATION CHART

COUNTRY	Discovered by Europeans in	Settled by Europeans in	Area (to nearest 1,000 sq. miles)	Population in 1901	Population in 1951 (estimated)
GREAT BRITAIN AND IRELAND (and islands)			121,000	41,600,000	53,000,000 (including ca. 2,960,000 in Eire)
INDIA	326 B.C. Alexander the Great ca. 1293 Marco Polo 1498 Vasco da Gama	1510 Portuguese at Goa 1612 East India Company at Surat	1,583,000	295,000,000 (Europeans: ca. 250,000)	390,000,000 (Europeans: ca. 300,000)
UNITED STATES (British colony until 1776)	1513 Ponce de Leon landed in Florida. (Columbus had discovered West Indies in 1492; Amerigo Vespucci, South America in 1499)	1565 St Augustine, Florida, founded by the Spanish 1607 Jamestown founded 1614 Dutch settle Manhattan 1620 Plymouth Colony founded. ('The Mayflower') 1628 Salem (Mass.) founded	2,977,000	76,150,000	150,000,000

CANADA (Including NEWFOUNDLAND and LABRADOR)	1497 (June 24) Newfoundland, by Cabot; Northmen rumoured discoverers in *ca.* 1000	*ca.* 1510 Newfoundland, by French, English, Spanish and Portuguese fishermen. 1608 Quebec, by the French. 1713 Nova Scotia ceded by the French to the British	3,845,000	5,600,000	14,000,000
SOUTH AFRICA (CAPE COLONY ORANGE FREE STATE TRANSVAAL NATAL)	1497 (Dec. 25) Vasco da Gama (at Port Natal —now Durban)	1652 Dutch settle in Cape of Good Hope region. 1795 Settlement captured by the British. 1836 Boer migration from Cape Colony to Transvaal	473,000	6,000,000 (approx.) including nearly 1,500,000 Europeans	12,000,000 (including *ca.* 2,250,000 Europeans) *Note.* In 1936, of 1,904,000 Europeans, 1,121,000 spoke Afrikaans, whereas only 783,000 spoke English
AUSTRALIA (including TASMANIA)	1606-07 Dutch navigators	1788 New South Wales. 1803 Tasmania. 1825 Western Australia. 1826 Queensland. 1834 Victoria. 1835 South Australia	2,975,000	3,770,000	7,750,000
NEW ZEALAND	1642 Tasman 1769-77 Cook	1840	104,000	773,000 Europeans 43,000 Maoris	1,850,000

CANADIAN ENGLISH

F. E. L. PRIESTLEY

Associate Professor of English in the University of Toronto

Canada is officially a bi-lingual country; about a third of its thirteen and a half million inhabitants are French-speaking, direct descendants of the settlers in New France. Since these Canadians have formed for over three centuries a well-knit, coherent community with a common origin, common language and faith, and well-established traditions, the last half-century has been less momentous with them than with the rest of the population. It is true that accelerated industrialism, the advent of radio, the tendency of the urban French-Canadian to acquire English, and the occasional weakening of ties with France have produced minor changes in the language, but only minor.

The Rector of Laval University recently told me of a significant experience. He was travelling in France after the war with another French-Canadian cleric, and was engaged in conversation by a Frenchman who shared their railway compartment. The Frenchman confessed that he was curious; the two priests were apparently not French, since their dress was foreign, yet their speech was unmistakably French. 'Perhaps,' said the Rector, 'you can even tell me what part of France I come from?' 'Ah yes, that is too easy,' replied the Frenchman. 'You are obviously from Normandy.' 'That is so,' said the Rector. 'But I have been for some time in Canada, and this is my first journey back to France.' 'And when did you leave France?' 'In the seventeenth century,' said the Rector. And although he was the first of his family to set foot on French soil since, he was as recognizably Norman as his ancestor. Canadian French is as stable and well-defined a language as, say, Yorkshire English. And it has a strong and well-defined literary tradition.

The rest of Canada offers nothing so simple. No English-speaking Canadian has ever returned at even one generation's remove to be told in an English railway carriage that he has preserved the accent of Wigan, Wakefield, or Stepney. No

one has so far even defined Canadian English, unless it is
included in the jocular definition of the Canadian as one who
is always mistaken for an Englishman in the United States and
for an American in England. The task of defining or describing
Canadian English accurately would be well beyond the limits
of this article and of its author. It may, however, be useful to
set down a few general observations, even though these, not
having the support of detailed facts of linguistic history, will
necessarily be somewhat tentative and cautious.

First, since the subject is primarily historical, a little relevant
history. To understand the Canadian language (or, if I may use
the term, English) in the twentieth century, we shall have to
go back to the eighteenth. Who brought the English language
to Canada? What sort of English did they speak? The first
considerable influx of English-speaking settlers was that of
Loyalists from the revolting American colonies, who formed
the original population of Ontario and of New Brunswick.
Until the war of 1812, further numbers of Americans continued to migrate to Ontario, so that the greater part of the
English-speaking population of Canada in 1815 was actually
American in origin. A notable exception was the settlement
of Highlanders started in Prince Edward Island by Lord Selkirk.
This provided a precedent for a number of Scottish colonies in
Ontario and in Manitoba, and marked the beginning of that
pervasive Caledonian influence which is such a noticeable
feature of Canadian life.

The effect of the Scots upon a country is never in simple
arithmetical ratio to their numbers; a bare tenth of the present
Canadian population avows or admits Scottish origin; but
hardly a village in the Dominion but has its Burns Night, its
Hallowe'en, its New Year's Eve Ball, or even its pipe band.
And every town of respectable size has a Highland regiment.
English Canada was, then, mainly American and Scottish by
origin, although Loyalist politically. And Canadian English
(since language is in some measure a reflection of the national
character) was not English in the limited sense. It was perhaps
already becoming Canadian.

The heavy immigration during the nineteenth century did

apparently nothing to change that character. Between 1815 and 1875, immigrants from the United Kingdom provided the bulk of the new population of Canada. At Confederation, the country had three and a half million inhabitants; one and a half million had come since 1815 from Britain. But a good many of them were not English; the hungry forties brought out thousands of Irish. Moreover, the Irish and the Scots tended to form 'colonies', Irishmen settling near Irishmen, Scots near Scots, in a restricted area, whereas the English usually dispersed and presumably took on protective colouring. The English seem to have played little part in public affairs. The leaders, George Brown, Sir Allan MacNab, Sir John A. Macdonald, Sir Alexander Galt, Lord Strathcona, Alexander Mackenzie, John Sandfield Macdonald—all were Scots; I cannot recall an English-born politician of eminence in the period. I leave the explanation to historians; if I were pressed for surmises, I should guess that educated Englishmen had become associated with the official class under the old colonial régime, and were suspect from their speech, and that the uneducated English lacked the capacity of the Scot for self-education. At any rate, Canada tended to be British but by no means English; loyal but nationalist. And so she has remained.

The mass immigrations from 1880 on, which transformed the West from a wilderness to a well-developed community of farms and towns, and brought the total population from five to ten millions in a generation, gave much of Canada an appearance of Babel. Any traveller crossing the continent even thirty years ago would have noted characteristic speech only as far west as the Great Lakes; he would have recognized in the Highland districts of Cape Breton Island and the Nova Scotia mainland the familiar pronunciation, intonation, and turn of phrase of the Gael speaking English as a second language; elsewhere in the Maritimes he would have observed a largely uniform style of speech, not harsh, but unmistakable in its vowels and consonants (it might remind him slightly of the language of Edinburgh or of Belfast, although it was less strongly marked than either); in Ontario he would have found a somewhat harsher and flatter speech, closer in pronunciation

to American, but, in the fact, close only to the speech of upper
New York State (and not identical with it); by listening closely,
he would have detected differences from American in intonation
and sentence-pitch, and perhaps lesser differences in vocabulary
and idiom. So far, if he were acute, he would have recognized
two kinds of characteristic Canadian English. From here on, he
might as well have given up. In Alberta, for example, he could
have visited towns where nearly everyone seemed to come
from Lancashire; others where English, if spoken at all, had to
work its way through a thick accent, which might be Ukrain-
ian, German, Esthonian, Finnish, Norwegian, Swedish, or
Czech. Other communities would have been almost entirely
made up of Americans from the Mid-west, like the large
Mormon townships in the south of the province. He would
soon have realized that the first question one asked in the West
was 'Where are you from?' and that the only mark of Canadian
English west of Winnipeg was its heterogeneity.

If our traveller could repeat his journey now, he would be
struck first of all by the comparative stabilizing of the population, and consequently of the language. He would, to be sure,
find traces in pronunciation and in syntax here and there that
suggested foreign-language parentage or grand-parentage, but
on the whole he would find that the speech of young Canadians from Halifax to Victoria tended to be far more uniform
than that of young Englishmen brought up twenty miles apart,
or of young Americans from, say, New York and Washington
(let alone Vermont and Georgia). In short, the most surprising
thing about the English currently spoken in Canada is its homo-
geneity. Regional differences exist, but they are subtle, and are
perhaps not much greater than mere individual peculiarities.

Now, it is possible for a linguistic expert in the United States
to place a speaker, from his reading of a few chosen sentences,
quite definitely within one of the forty-eight states, and often
within a narrow section of it. One such expert carried on a
successful radio programme, astounding his audiences by telling
New Yorkers what suburb they lived in, or even by defining
those areas in which the speaker must have lived at various
periods in his life. I doubt very much whether any such speech

atlas could be compiled for Canada, except perhaps for the
Maritimes and Ontario. I met one young American research
student who was trying to map British Columbia; when he
played some of his records to me I had no trouble in identifying
voices from Lancashire and Devonshire, and one from Somerset—but he had no records of native Canadians. It is certain
that no Ontario Canadian, meeting another Canadian, can
tell whether he comes from Manitoba, Saskatchewan, Alberta,
or British Columbia,—or even Ontario, unless he asks. But
almost any American can detect a Canadian in a few minutes'
talk; and a Canadian can recognize most Americans. This
emergence within fifty years of a predominantly homogeneous
speech over a three-thousand-mile-long geographical area
seems to me most unusual.

It is also significant that Canadian speech has tended to preserve a national identity. The great majority of Canadians live
within a hundred miles of the United States border. They
listen to American radio stations, see mainly American films,
read American magazines and fiction. But strong as American
influence is, it has its limits. The most important limit is perhaps that set by growing national self-confidence in Canada.
Since the Imperial Conference in 1926, the recognition that
Canada is no longer threatened with 'colonialism' has tended
to become so thoroughly established that it can be accepted
unself-consciously. The Liberal party has always taken the lead
in asserting Canadian nationalism; it is consequently worth
noting that, in 1950, Liberal M.P.s spoke strongly in Parliament against any weakening of Commonwealth ties, and
helped defeat a bill to change Dominion Day into Canada
Day. The leaning away from Britain in the past often meant a
leaning towards the United States (although never far enough
to entertain the notion of absorption); the industrial power and
the importance in world trade achieved by Canada in the last
quarter of a century have given Canadians a calm conviction
that they need be neither English nor American, but Canadian.
This conviction acts as a persistent and effective limit to that
wholesale imitation of American modes of thought and speech
which one might expect or fear.

The developments in radio will serve as illustration. The Canadian Broadcasting Corporation was established as a nationally-owned network; (it did not displace, but has supplemented the private stations). Since it was not wholly commercial, it could devote a good deal of its efforts to producing Canadian programmes: musical, dramatic, and documentary. This it has done with considerable success: one of its dramatic series, presenting radio plays written or adapted by Canadian playwrights, and acted by Canadian actors, has been awarded a prize as the best programme of its kind on the continent. This single series alone has done a great deal to develop a mature school of Canadian drama, and with it a Canadian style of writing and of acting. The maturing of the C.B.C. drama and of C.B.C. commentaries has brought with it some tendency to establish a national standard of speech; and anyone wishing to know what Canadian English is like when purged of individual peculiarities and accidentals would be well advised to listen to the best C.B.C. announcers and to C.B.C. drama. These offer something which is not a copy of British English, nor yet of American English.

The motion pictures, of course, and the American radio, have a strong influence in Canada as in England; and the type of youth in both countries which takes the Hollywood gangster or spiv as his ideal will naturally become as un-Canadian or as un-English in appearance, manner, and language as his circumstances permit. But in neither country does this type form a majority, and the forces of education and of adult disapproval win some victories. For if the Canadian youth is constantly exposed to American films and radio, he is as constantly badgered at school to learn the mother-tongue and its masterpieces. Even in spelling, he is allowed to stray only a short way into the American fold: he may spell *tire* and *wagon*, but must be faithful to *woollen* and, in most Provinces, *honour*. He is also subjected to a persistent (if unavailing) campaign to induce him to use *shall* in the right places; he seldom learns, since the whole continent is as stubborn as the legendary Welshman on this point; but at least he is taught that English usage is the 'correct' one.

In school, he reads the classics of English literature, and is taught to admire the great masters of English prose and poetry; if he grows up at all literary, his tastes are likely to be rather more conservative than those of his American counterpart. Nevertheless, when he writes a novel or a short story, since the American market is a large and profitable one, he is strongly tempted to write in the American idiom. But if he is not primarily commercial, he is perhaps more inclined to try to achieve something naturally Canadian, using as a rule a traditional rather than experimental technique and style. On the whole, he is reluctant to confuse the colloquial and the literary. If he is not interested in writing, of course, he may be unaware that the colloquial and the literary are not identical, since he hears more than he reads. This, however, is a failing the Canadian has no monopoly in. It must with sorrow be admitted that the failing extends higher in the scale of education in North America than in Britain; a difference which the Canadian educator laments, and which he hopes is temporary. He sometimes speculates maliciously on the possible effect of opening the British universities more widely to the uncultured.

Some counter-balance to American influence has also been provided by Canadian participation in the two wars. During these, a million and a half young Canadians served for various periods, almost always alongside troops from the United Kingdom. Most of them spent some time in Britain. They usually brought back a much widened appreciation of Britain and of things British; they also brought back a rich vocabulary of English idiom and slang. As a result, Canadian colloquial speech draws on American and English sources with a fine impartiality; and thousands of young Canadians are bilingual in an unofficial sense. English comedians have lately been packing houses in Canada; if there ever was any truth in the legend that *Punch* was unintelligible abroad without explanatory notes there is certainly none now. And Gracie Fields' aspidistra is as well known in Toronto as in Rochdale.

The half-century has, I believe, brought about the emergence of a distinct Canadian national character, and a distinct Canadian language. Neither is as fully developed or as clearly defined as it is likely to become, but both are there—very much there. Sir Basil Brooke, in a B.B.C. talk on his return from North America recently, made a very happy comparison. Canadian neckties, he observed, might look startling to the English, but to Americans they seemed to verge on the dowdy. The Canadian likes to think that in all things he observes this happy compromise. He would also, I believe, insist that a closer examination of the neckwear would reveal something of an exclusive Canadian pattern.

ENGLISH IN SOUTH AFRICA

A. G. HOOPER

Professor of English in the University of Stellenbosch

The position of English in South Africa is very different from that of English in any of the other Dominions, for in South Africa English is the language of a minority of the white population, which is itself a minority in the Union as a whole. And the history of English in South Africa since 1900, and its prospects in the future, are those of the gradually decreasing influence of a language that was overwhelmingly important in 1900.

To understand the changes that have taken place since 1900, the present status and possible future of English in South Africa, one needs to remember the political background. At the beginning of the century the Boers were a defeated people, many of whose men had been killed or were in exile, many of whose women and children had died in concentration camps. In 1950 they were represented by a Nationalist government that has acquired power by democratic and constitutional means. It has been a triumph of not always quiet persistency.

At the turn of the century the Victoria College of Stellenbosch, for example, had many English-speaking members of staff and probably most classes were given in English. The student magazines sounded like their counterparts at many a British school; there were reports of societies, youthful verses (in English by Afrikaners, including one J. C. Smuts), and characteristic comments on members of the cricket and rugby teams: "Hofmeyr, a good bat, but must brush up his fielding'. A first impression is that it was just another little outpost of Empire. In 1950 the University of Stellenbosch has an almost exclusively Afrikaans-speaking staff, and in May of the same year the Stellenbosch University Debating Society with an overwhelming majority carried the motion that 'The English language has no chance of survival'. A hope, and premature perhaps, but another symptom of the urge of Afrikaners to reinstate themselves, evidence of which is to be seen everywhere, from the high birth-rate* to commerce and industry, where English has long been and still is at present supreme.

The English-speaking population is of course concentrated in the few, surprisingly few, cities and large towns. But the influence of English in the towns is great in proportion to the financial and commercial power of the speakers of English rather than to their numbers.† Even at the 1936 census the population figures did not show a very large majority of English-speaking people in the towns (Town: English 52.61 per cent., Afrikaans 40.96 per cent.; Country: English 13.67 per cent., Afrikaans 84.03 per cent.), and since then there has been a steady flow of Afrikaans speakers from the country to the towns (1946: Town: English 48.48 per cent., Afrikaans 47.78 per cent.).

All this implies an increasingly strong influence of Afrikaans upon English.‡ It usually means that in the country and smaller towns the English-speaking children are bilingual, and in the larger towns the Afrikaans-speaking children have the better chance of being really bilingual. In the country and smaller towns the teachers are almost all Afrikaans-speaking. And since the teaching profession does not carry the prestige among the English-speaking section of the people that it still does among the Afrikaans-speaking, chiefly because it is as poorly paid in South Africa as elsewhere, it attracts very few English-speaking men and not enough women. This means that even in some of the larger towns too the class teachers in English-medium schools, and even the teachers of English to English-speaking pupils, are now not English-speaking them-selves, i.e. are people whose first or home language is not English. They are frequently, but not always, very fluent in

*	1936	1941	1946	1946 (ages 7-20)	1946 (under 27)
English speaking	39.08%	39.94%	39.35%	33.21%	32.72%
Afrik. speaking	55.93	55.94	57.30	63.98	65.11
English-speaking population	783,071	875,541	933,821	201,434	120,434
Afrik. speaking population	1,120,770	1,226,382	1,359,705	388,513	239,627
Afrik. majority	337,699	350,841	425,884	—	—

† When a separate commercial broadcasting programme was started in 1950 it was criticized because, it was alleged, 90 per cent. was in English.

‡ By comparison, the influence of all other languages, e.g. native languages, American English, since 1900 is negligible.

English, and many are good teachers, but the pronunciation of most is strongly influenced by Afrikaans.

Hence the strong and increasing influence of Afrikaans on the English of those born and brought up in South Africa, not only in vocabulary, but in idiom and pronunciation.

The influence of Dutch and Afrikaans on the vocabulary has been fairly fully recorded in *O.E.D.* and such works as Pettman's *Africanderisms*, and varies from names of physical features of the country, familiar now to readers in England, such as *veld*, *kloof*, *kopje*, to more recent introductions such as the political slogan of the Nationalist party in 1948: *apartheid* (racial segregation).

The degree to which expression is affected naturally depends on the degree of contact with Afrikaans speakers. But since, even in 1936, Johannesburg, the largest city in the Union, was listed as one in which 25 to 50 per cent. of the population was Afrikaans-speaking, it follows that in most of the smaller centres the influence of Afrikaans will be even stronger. And expressions such as 'Are you coming with?' (a direct translation of Afrikaans) or 'Shall we sit on the stoep *so long*?' (i.e. for the time being) are common among speakers of English who have been born and brought up in South Africa.

At the beginning of the century it was almost certainly assumed that the only standard of pronunciation for English in South Africa was the accepted standard of pronunciation of English in England. Indeed there are many people in South Africa who still believe that the only respectable standard. They are mainly people who were born in England or the children of such people. In other words the continual flow of newcomers from England during the last fifty years has helped to preserve the belief that the Standard English of England is the only possible standard, and that anything that is different is colonial and inferior. Many of these newcomers have been of the type that when abroad is more British than the British and has therefore done little to promote good feeling with Afrikaners. They have been people who have not hesitated to express their opinions of South African pronunciation plainly and loudly, and people who have been in positions where they could make their opinions influential: businessmen, employers, editors, teachers and parents.

There is therefore a distinction to be made to-day between those speakers of English born in Britain and those born in South Africa. Those born in South Africa often marry Afrikaners, the ultra-British never do.

To the Afrikaners the preservation of the Standard English of England as a standard for South Africa appears just another indication of the desire of English South Africans to 'put England instead of South Africa first'. Since an overseas standard is regarded as another symbol of bondage and as an unattainable ideal for Afrikaners, since a different standard is already adopted in practice by South African born speakers of English, and since even the English born find some cultured South Africans with whom they are willing to associate (correctness in speech being only what is acceptable socially), it seems as though it would be wise to acknowledge a different standard officially.

Naturally there are in South Africa as elsewhere different levels of usage. But whenever anyone talks of South African English the English born think of the extremes of uncultured usage, and throw up their hands in horror at the suggestion that any form of South African English is respectable. The importance of a form of speech depends on the importance of the speakers of it, and the reliance on England has for long kept the English born in the most influential positions; but it is a fact that a cultured form of English, yet one recognizably South African, is already accepted socially. The South African Broadcasting Corporation tends to support Standard English, but even it has appointed some announcers whose pronunciation is evidently acceptable but can still be identified as South African. It would be better for everyone if some such standard were accepted openly, in theory as well as in practice. For the insistence, even in theory, on an overseas standard is a source of a feeling of inferiority in English-speaking South Africans and of resentment in the Afrikaans-speaking. The disposition is already there in some groups to condemn an overseas standard as 'un-South-African'.

One of the real though probably unconscious reasons for the unwillingness of the English born to recognize openly any form of South African English as respectable is possibly that one or two characteristic South African pronunciations are very similar to pronunciations regarded as inferior socially in England. For example, words like *gate*, *pale*, *train*, tend to be pronounced in a way that sounds to English ears very like a Cockney pronunciation. In fact, it is almost certainly another case of Afrikaans influence and not Cockney at all.

There is no doubt that the attitude of the English born towards the English of those born in South Africa produces an apologetic and self-conscious manner in those who have to admit that they were only 'born out here'. It may be only coincidence that almost the only South African writers in English who have achieved any reputation have been people who were either born overseas, or who were born here but have lived largely overseas. On the other hand, with their tradition of servants, plenty of manual labour, and a wonderful climate, there are very few South Africans beyond the first generation who retain any cultural interests, and very many ready to swallow the digests and surrender to all passive forms of entertainment.

AUSTRALIAN ENGLISH

ERIC PARTRIDGE

Both as a whole and in several important aspects, Australian English has received more attention than any other form of Dominions English. Not only has Mr Sidney J. Baker written a very good book upon 'the Australian language', but both he and Professor A. J. Mitchell, of the University of Sydney, have dealt, separately, with that, to certain unduly sensitive souls, thorny subject, Australian pronunciation; and even Australian slang has on several occasions been recorded in dictionary-form, most recently and best by Mr Baker.

Pronunciation can be a question not only (to those who lack a sense of proportion) extremely offensive but also (to those who possess that sense) extremely tedious. First of all, it must be borne in mind that the natural conditions, the physiography of Australia have, like the very similar conditions of South Africa, tended to produce a certain type of speech-organs, to which the dulcet sounds of Southern Standard English are not merely alien but impossible; they are equally, though in a different way, impossible to those people who live in the colder moister climates of Canada and New Zealand; the compara-tively high-pitched voices of Australians (and of South Africans) resemble those of Indian people, especially the men, when they speak English—and for much the same climatic and other physiographic reasons. The nasality characterizing the speech of most Australians has arisen from the same influences: compare the nasality of much American pronunciation, a nasality more marked than that of Canadians.

Then there are influences of a different order. The earliest inhabitants of Australia were either convicts, mostly speaking either Cockney or some provincial dialect, or soldiers, mostly speakiug either Cockney or dialect, and a few officials mostly speaking standard English. The convict influence upon Austra-lian heredity has, by Australia's greatest native-born historian, Professor W. K. Hancock, been proved to be slight, and most of that slight influence to be beneficial. Probably the convicts

were, in the aggregate, 'better types' than the majority of the
soldiers. To be touchy upon the subject of convicts is as absurd
as a bustle and as antiquated as a dodo.

But that Cockney element, so often—and so rightly—
mentioned in reference to Australian speech, constituted only
one of the five principal factors in the genesis of Australian pronunciation and, as has been ignored by almost every writer, in
the genesis of Australian English as an entity. How strong the
Cockney element still was in 1916, although more in the large
cities, especially Sydney, than in the country districts, can be
perceived by a careful reading of C. J. Dennis's poem, *The
Sentimental Bloke*: nor has that influence weakened. The Cockney element has affected speech and vocabulary alike.

The second enduring influence upon Australian English has
been that of the English dialects, soon reinforced by those of
Scotland, Wales and Ireland. Every single one of the British
dialects has, in Australia, ranked always as being as good as any
other, if not rather better; moreover, every dialect has, except
by a comparatively very few purists, been regarded as almost
equal in merit to Standard English—and that holds good of
Cockney too.

Upon the triple basis of Standard English, of Cockney
(greatest of urban dialects) and of the various provincial dialects of the British Isles, there impinged two powerful factors,
the one immediately influential, the other rarely operative
before the twentieth century. The former, already touched
upon, consists in the tremendous impact effected upon the
colonists, not only by the climate and other physical features,
all so different from those they had known, but also by a
strange flora and a still stranger fauna and, again, by the
Aborigines, a native race so utterly different from any they had
seen or even read about. So many new things to name! (The
Aborigines have not very extensively influenced the vocabulary, apart from that of place-names and the names of a few
birds, beasts and trees.) This impact exemplifies a factor common to the evolution of language in every new country.

Uncommon, however, is the factor of a powerfully Nationalist movement, not politically away from Britain but away

from the English spoken in England rather than from that spoken in (say) Scotland. In literature it began with such writers as A. B. ('Banjo') Paterson and Henry Lawson, yet it did not become at all marked until immediately after the war of 1914-1918; then it suddenly became rather obstreperous. Yet this factor has proved less powerful than those of Cockney, the other dialects, and the impact of the continent itself, probably because most of the best Australian authors and journalists pay to this nationalism only a smiling lip-service.

It is true that the Australia of 1950 or 1951, as compared to that of 1900, has a more definitely Australian version of English. But that, names being changed, is equally true of Canada, South Africa and New Zealand. The effective inauguration, on New Year's Day, 1901, of the Commonwealth of Australia did much to render Australians, all Australians whatsoever, far more Australian-minded than they had been when 'all were for the State' and few for the country. Australians at last became conscious that now they possessed a dual heritage. That of the homeland and that of their home. There arose a co-ordinated or communal sense of independence: and in the main that independence has borne good fruit.

Australian writers have retained all except the subtleties of English syntax and all except a few superfine points of accidence; mostly they have learnt to fuse the specifically Australian vocabulary with the general vocabulary of the language, instead of plastering the general vocabulary with as many Australianisms (few of them known outside Australia) as they could lay avid, sometimes rather indiscriminate, hands upon. If the reputable writers employ more slang and colloquialism than do their English compeers, the proportion is still reassuringly small. The English of such post-1914 Australian writers as Leon Gellert, Jack Lindsay, Brian Penton, Godfrey Blunden, Leonard Mann, James Aldridge, differs only slightly from that of their English contemporaries. They have been influenced far more by English than by American writers, whether novelists or poets.

And thus we finally arrive at the last of the five principal factors in the development of Australian English. This factor of American influence is particularly hard to assess. Lawson's short stories, of which the best appeared during the seven years ending in 1900, had exhibited the influence of Bret Harte; yet only slightly. The six notable writers mentioned in the foregoing paragraph show likewise only a slight American influence; the most notable of these influences would seem to be that of John Steinbeck.

American humour, beginning with that of Bret Harte and Mark Twain, has been well received in Australia. In the present century, the kind preferred has been the boisterous and the slapstick; a subtle, humorous American writer (for instance, Robert Benchley or Christopher Morley) stands much less chance in Australia than does the American comic strip—but then, that's true of almost every other country. Very few Australian humorists have directly imitated the Americans.

American influence has, in the twentieth century, come mainly from the cinema and, only since about 1940 and, even so, much less, from the radio. In 1943-45 American soldiers, sailors and airmen temporarily blitzed Australian English; as in New Zealand, the craze departed with their departure. Yet that friendly invasion has left a residue of Americanisms, which have joined the already existing stock. Those American servicemen made no permanent mark upon Australian pronunciation, nor has there, at any other period, been an appreciable number of Americans resident in, or even visitors to, Australia.

Like the Cockney, the American influence has always been strongest in Sydney; next strongest in Melbourne; then in the other continental capitals. Inland, especially in the rural areas, the American influence has been slight. In these rural areas, the geographical—the general physical—influence has preponderated over any of the others; there, too, has influence of the English dialects—at least, during this century—been stronger than in the cities. In a few rural areas, one finds a fairly strong German influence; in sugar-cane districts, an Italian. Yet neither the German language nor the Italian has much influenced Australian English.

Australian English has never had to combat the deadly competition of another European language—of a language

always preponderant—as Dutch, evolved into Afrikaans, has
been in South Africa; nor to contend with two great racial influences, as Canadian English has had to do with French
(evolved into French Canadian and also into that very different
thing, Canadian French) and with American English; nor to
struggle against what is numerically an immensely superior
native language, as English has had to do in India; nor with
the somewhat slighter obstacle of a small, isolated community
which New Zealand English had diminishingly encountered.
By New Zealand, Australian English has been scarcely affected.
Because of the distance of Australia from Britain, Australian
English will probably increase its Australianism; as for Canada,
the momentum of a rapidly growing population and of a
rapidly approaching economic self-sufficiency will do much to
ensure that increase. Whereas, except in pronunciation, New
Zealand English has tended to remain as English as possible,
Australian English has tended to become Australian; yet that
tendency remains far more of a tendency than a fact.

NEW ZEALAND ENGLISH

Arnold Wall

Emeritus Professor of English in the University of New Zealand

The English language as spoken and written in New Zealand during the last fifty years shows, in speech, a slow, gradual, but indubitable divergence from the home standard; in the written language, however, this tendency is far less remarkable, though there is a general trend towards laxity in grammatical forms, a lack of observance of certain traditional habits such as, e.g., the rules of punctuation and the use of inverted commas. Those who are concerned with the results of the system of education complain that a large proportion of the younger generation seem to be unable to construct sentences coherently or to express themselves with accuracy. In other respects the written language, as it appears in the newspapers and in books, written by New Zealand authors, conforms closely to English custom and usage. American words and idioms do not appear to have infiltrated to a greater extent than in Britain, and New Zealand compares favourably in this respect with Australia, where the American influence is far more marked. The influence of the Maori language remains much as it was during the nineteenth century; few, if any, Maori words have been added during the last half-century to the small number which were established in English in earlier times. But there is a tendency, as yet regrettably slight, to adopt a more correct pronunciation of Maori words and names, a tendency which is encouraged by the example of some of the broadcasting announcers who have made a special study of the subject and pronounce the Maori names with precision and accuracy. Many of the established mutilations of Maori names, however, hold their own in popular speech, such as *Oterhu* for *Otahuhu* and *Paraparam* for *Paraparumu*. Australian slang, though always popular and perhaps increasingly so in speech, hardly affects the written language except in 'sporting parlance'.

In the field of pronunciation the picture is very different. Not only has there been a remarkable increase in such details as gabbling and nasality and in odd mispronunciations of particular words, but certain general tendencies towards change in sounds affecting large groups of words have developed rapidly during the last fifty years. Six tendencies of this kind are observed. (The pronunciation of final -*y* as *ee*, as in 'citee', 'likelee', etc.; and the fronting of long *a*, as in 'farm' and 'large' are both older than the present century, having been noted by McBurney in 1887).

(1) Reluctance to pronounce long *o*, whether close or open, especially in initial syllables; this affects a large number of words, e.g. *toll, knoll, oral, choral, floral, orient, auction*, all of which tend to be pronounced with the short sound of *o* as in 'top'.

(2) Stressing the first syllable of words which in standard English are stressed on the second, e.g. lúcerne, mágazine, mánkind, and very many others; this tendency appears also in certain phrases such as 'áll the săme', 'áfter ăll'.

(3) Substitution of the voiced sound for the voiceless, *zh* for *sh*, in such words as version, immersion, Asia, Persia, etc.; this seems to be due to American influence.

(4) Obscuring of *i* when unstressed, especially in final syllables, e.g. *Phyllus, Maurus, Allus* (for Alice), *charguz* (charges). Monosyllables having the short *i* are similarly pronounced, *ut uzz, uzzn't ut* (it is, isn't it), and such words as 'did'.

(5) Words which have a short *e* in their first syllable tend to be pronounced, not with short *i* as in the standard, but with a clear and often quite long *e*; e.g. *beefore, beelong, reeport, eeleven*, etc. This seems to be a bit of pedantry due to the influence of those teachers who apparently regard the short *i* in these words as a slipshod or vulgar pronunciation simply because it conflicts with the spelling.

(6) The names of many places tend to be pronounced 'as spelt', not with the traditional English pronunciation, e.g. *Roll-is-ton, Well-es-ley, Ha-wawden* (Hawarden), *Arúndel* (as in the U.S.A.), *Mahlborough* for Mawlborough, *Heethcoat* for Hethcut, etc. These pronunciations are of course due to the weakening of the home traditions among the members of the third and fourth generations of New Zealand speakers.

Editor's Note

But New Zealand English is particularly interesting because New Zealand is the most British of all the dominions, yet the furthest from Britain. Despite the influence of Australia and the United States of America, despite also the small population, New Zealand English has, except in several quite superficial aspects, remained, like the people, remarkably (but unobtrusively) independent. I have, therefore, invited a second consultant's opinion.

NEW ZEALAND ENGLISH

HAROLD ORSMAN

Postgraduate Research Student in the University of New Zealand

1900 is not a specially significant date in the history of colloquial New Zealand English. The main drift towards an independent idiom started much earlier. Social and political independence was almost worshipped in the colonies. The first settlers had to name the strange situations and objects of a new environment. They had a Maorified whaler/sailor argot to help them. During the 1850's—1870's emigration was the vogue.

'New-chums' constantly arriving sought to get 'colonized' as quickly as possible. To escape ridicule and criticism they adopted among other things the more violent traits of 'colonial speech' and exaggerated them to fit their preconceived ideas of 'colonialism', taken from the highly-coloured accounts of emigration-touts and tourists. The nostalgia, the efforts to create a 'Britain of the South', flaunted by the 'colonials', were too superficial and self-conscious to assert 'Home' idiom over the forming New Zealand idiom. It certainly did not stop both the recently-arrived and New Zealand born 'colonials' thinking of themselves and not of the Maoris as New Zealanders. The feeling was perhaps a mere self-justification for 'deserting Home' for better conditions overseas. The word 'home', most of its original associations lost, can now mean Europe or even America. Catholics speak of 'going Home' for the Holy Year celebrations. The conditions were excellent for generating an impulse towards unconventional speech. Miners' language of the 1860 'rushes' was colourful and cosmopolitan. Sailors added their jargon; 'agricultural labourers', a little dialect English.

This drive towards independence of speech persists into the twentieth century. (E.g., older *spell* 'rest' instead of English 'period of work' is paralleled by the modern *jack up* 'arrange, get up' for English 'hinder'.) New Zealanders have always preferred native to overseas language resources that are hard to modify to express their own interests. Comparatively little new material came out of two wars. Farming, bush and seasonal industries and 'national' sports yield vivid expressions: *be on one's muttons* 'alert', *bushwhacked* 'beaten', *hook your mutton* (freezing-works modification of 'sling your hook'), *be a starter* (horse-racing).

Maori words do not figure as much as they could. Few New Zealanders speak or use Maori, although most recognize commoner words. Some older usages are fixed—*whare* 'hut' (even in legal documents); others, once popular, are now obsolescent—*kit* (from *kete*) 'basket', *hoot* (from *utu*) 'money'. We prefer the original Maori natural and place names. *Rimu/Kahikatea* displace older southern *Red/White Pine*.

Borrowed Maori expressions are mainly localized—current in one district and not in another—and are perhaps commoner in the more largely Maori-populated North Island. The phrase, *Ko had it* 'it's had it/finished (Maori *ko* 'it'), current in the comparatively isolated North Auckland area, is the kind of purely local usage which will probably spread no further. The same happens with Pakeha expressions. In Dunedin, *crib/sulky* displace general New Zealand *bach* (weekend cottage)/*pushchair*.

Many New Zealanders mistakenly believe that most of their slang comes directly from America or indirectly through Australia—that they are imitators, not inventors. They have thoroughly assimilated what they have really borrowed from America. The 'American invasion' of 1942-1943 left little lasting impression on the language. 'Americanisms' are recognizable, but the American origin of many common expressions is not. *Canned* for *tinned* fruit would be felt an unhappy usage, but not *canned* (drunk). New Zealanders think their drinking reputation secure; their fruit-tinning, not so. They will add to a familiar vocabulary, not to an unfamiliar one. American terms are popular with special groups—e.g., jazz-collectors and broadcasting people use *disc* for the more general *record*.

Australia, bigger and older, has certainly anticipated New Zealand in the use of many terms; and many more are common to both countries. Words like *fair go/do* are not considered Australianisms as *dinkum* or even *cobber* are. It would probably be hard to prove that Australia accepted the common expressions first.

Vagueness, which results from persistent use of slang and unconventional speech, has influenced New Zealand syntax. The sentence-structure of colloquial 'New Zealandese' is drawn out and overloaded with many colourless words and phrases. *Too right, right-oh, good-oh, she's right/jake*, adverbial *pretty, bloody*, hypocoristic *bastard* have no precise meaning and weaken the sentence. *A bit* is tacked on as a diminutive—*a bit crook, a bit of a kid, hold on for a bit.* An indefinite *it* conveniently forms durative verbs—*bush it* (live a bush life), *rough it, soup it* (live on soup).

New Zealanders seem to enjoy (but not seriously condone) ungrammatical English. *Might of, they come yesterday, they was* are not used only by children. This is perhaps carrying unconventionality too far.

THE POSITION OF ENGLISH IN INDIA

SAMUEL MATHAI

Secretary of the Inter-University Board of India

By the beginning of the twentieth century English had become well established as the official and academic language of India. English education, which had begun in the early years of the nineteenth century, had received the support of Macaulay and others, and the East India Company had accepted a proposal for the establishment of Universities in India. The first Universities were established in 1857 in the three presidency towns of Calcutta, Bombay and Madras. By the end of the nineteenth century there were two more Universities—the Punjab University at Lahore and the Allahabad University at Allahabad. These Universities were of the affiliating type. A number of Colleges scattered all over the country were affiliated to these Universities, which prescribed courses of study and examined students and awarded degrees.

The growth of University education implied a spread of knowledge of English, as English was the medium of instruction and examination. The numbers of those who received any kind of education at all was very small in relation to the total population of the country as a whole. In 1901 only 0.04 per cent. of Indians could speak any English. It would be incorrect therefore to say that the knowledge of English had become widespread in India by the beginning of the century. But in a society which was mainly feudal in character and in an economy which was predominantly agricultural and dependent on peasant labour the significance of the spread of education and the knowledge of English could not be measured by numbers. There was growing up in the early years of the twentieth century, before the first World War, a small but influential middle class and lower middle class who had had some education in English and who carried on their business, be it administrative or commercial or educational, in the English language. The Indian element in the civil services, in the legal, medical and other professions, and in the teaching faculties in Schools and Colleges, was drawn from this class. English was the language of the courts and it was rapidly becoming the language of commerce and social intercourse among the educated. If husbands did not write to their wives in English, fathers wrote to their sons in English; and English provided the only common medium of communication among the many different linguistic groups in India.

In most of the Colleges and many of the English Schools—especially in the larger towns—there were usually some British or American men and women on the staff, and this helped to give to the English language learnt by many Indians a fair degree of approximation to the speech and idiom of those whose mother-tongue was English. Added to this was the fact that in those days English was taught in Schools by drilling students in English grammar. The result was that most of those who learned English learned it well, at least in the sense that they were sure of their grammar. It was also not unfashionable to play the sedulous ape to one or more great English writer: and not a few, obeying the injunction of Dr Johnson, gave their days and nights to a study of Addison or some other accepted classic in English literature.

Indians love oratory, and among English writings that specially interested students and teachers were the speeches of Burke and other great English parliamentarians. Some of the most skilled Indian users of English were the great lawyers and public speakers in the early twentieth century. In passing it may be also mentioned that the great utterances of British and American democracy had a profound influence on the movement for political emancipation in India.

But though on the whole the Indians who learned English in the first two decades of the twentieth century learned it well, there were certain limitations in their mastery of the language which in some instances produced amusing results. Although there were 'English' teachers of English in many of the Schools and Colleges of India, inevitably the Indian learned a great part of his English from books. Indian English was therefore always inclined to be bookish, and not adequately in touch with the living English of the day; and when we remember that the books which we re-read as models of good English were the works of Shakespeare and Milton and the other great English poets and dramatists and prose-writers, it is not surprising that the more eloquent utterances of Indians (whether spoken or written) were often freely garnished with phrases and turns of expression taken from the great writers. Sometimes these phrases were used without proper recognition of their archaic or obsolescent or purely poetic character.

As education spread, English was necessarily learnt by many Indians from other Indians and they had hardly any means of discovering the difference between literary English of an older day and contemporary English in its colloquial forms. The person (he was actually a lecturer in English) who on seeing the sea for the first time and noticing a ship on the horizon solemnly asked, 'Is that a ship on the bosom of the sea?' was typical of many Indians who could not always distinguish between a literary phrase and a common expression.

There were also other tendencies in Indian English arising from the influence of the syntax and idiom of the Indian mother-tongue and from a failure to distinguish among the various levels of English speech—the poetic, the colloquial, the slangy and so on. After the war of 1914-1918 there was a considerable increase in the number of Schools and Colleges and Universities, and the knowledge of English spread further among the middle and lower middle classes. Necessarily this knowledge was carried by Indian teachers of English; and in the more rural areas where English was taught there was an increasing tendency for the language to be influenced by the speech-habits of the region. Teachers themselves were likely to mix up genuine English idioms with literal translations of Indian idioms. After the war the old practice of drilling students in grammar was more or less abandoned and English was taught in Schools through a so-called direct method. Whatever the arguments in favour of the direct method, the actual results of learning a foreign tongue through teachers who themselves had learnt it at second-hand were not very happy.

Indian English has sometimes been the subject of amusement and has been made fun of under names like 'Babu English'. It is true that some Indian users of English made amusing mistakes not only of the kind referred to earlier but in unwarranted coinages and 'portmanteau' expressions. As examples of un-English expressions that may be met with in the speech and writing of even well-educated Indians we may cite 'to marry with', 'to make friendship with', 'make one's both ends meet', 'England-returned', 'A pindrop silence', 'A failed B.A.', 'A welcome address' (for an address of welcome), 'to give a speech' and so on. Expressions such as these are recognized as wrong or clumsy by the more careful writers and speakers in India, but certain neologisms of Indian origin are frequently used even by the most careful. Thus even Vice-Chancellors of Universities have been heard to speak of 'freeships' for free studentships. On the analogy of 'inter-marry', Indians who have taboos about eating with members of castes and sects other than their own speak of 'interdining' when they participate in a common meal.

Indian pronunciation of English words is considerably affected by the phonetic tendencies of the speaker's mother-tongue. Thus the East Bengalee is unable to differentiate between *heard* and *hard*, *guerdon* and *garden*, *fir* and *far*, because in his language he does not have the sound of '*e*' in h*e*r. He pronounces *young* as *yawng*, *among* as *amawng*. He tends to pronounce *virgin* as *bharjeen*. In other regions there are other peculiarities, as for instance pronouncing *school* as *ischool*, *offspring* as *offispring*; or *end* as *yend*, *only* as *wonly*; or *lawyer* as *layyar*; or *turnip* as *taynip*; or *seven* as *sayvhen*, which can be related to phonetic characteristics of different regions.

But such peculiarities in accent and pronunciation and occasional blunderings in idiom did not prevent the English used by a very large number of Indians from attaining a high degree of effectiveness and accuracy. Indeed it may be said that of all foreigners who have learnt English, Indians have had the most success. If at its lower levels Indian English degenerated into 'Babu' English, at its higher levels it flowered forth into the English of a Gokhale, a Tagore, a Gandhi, a Sarojani Naidu and a Jawaharlal Nehru.

Although great pains continued to be taken and much

enthusiasm shown by Indians in teaching and learning English in the second quarter of the century, there was a gradual change of attitude towards the language. With the growth of the National movement there was an increasing feeling that English was a foreign language forced upon the Indian people and there was a tendency not to strive too much after accuracy or literary quality in the English they used. So long as one could make oneself understood it did not seem to matter if one's English did not quite approximate to King's English. The great increase in the number of persons receiving education through English during and after the second World War added to the difficulties of achieving a really accurate knowledge of the language.

During the fifty years of the twentieth century a great many English words have passed into the vocabulary of the Indian languages. The British connection meant also contact with Western civilization; and the enlargement of the mental and spiritual horizon of the Indian people is partially reflected in the many English words that have become part of the language of the common people. These include words relating to new modes of transportation like the bicycle, the motor-car, the railway train; to electricity and electrical appliances; to school and college and University; to courts of law and various branches of administration; to the cinema and many sports and pastimes; and also to parliamentary and democratic institutions in general.

With the coming of independence in 1947 there was naturally a marked change of attitude towards the English language: and although there was a strong feeling in many quarters that India should not lose the advantage of her knowledge of English, it was thought that English should give place to an Indian language as the official language of the country. The constitution of the Republic of India (written in English) has laid down that Hindi shall be the official language, but that English shall continue as at present for fifteen years more. But in some provinces steps have already been taken to discard English, and one or two Indian Universities have begun to experiment with an Indian language as the medium of instruction and examination. English has been removed from the courses of study at the earlier stages of school education almost everywhere.

When we remember that after nearly a century of English Education only something like 3 per cent. of the population know English, it seems obvious that English cannot be the language in which the millions of India will be educated. In 1900 the urban population of India received English as the language of the future, a knowledge of which was essential for their advancement. To-day, though English is still the only language that serves as a *lingua franca*, and a knowledge of it is still necessary for participation in national and international affairs, it seems certain that the future in India does not lie with English. What will actually happen in the future it is difficult to say, but it seems clear that for many years to come it will be in India's interest to retain English at least as an important second language and thus keep open her only door to the knowledge and culture of the larger world.

CHAPTER FOUR

DIALECT: A NOTE

With a Story, in Dialect, by Neil Bell

Dialects are not in all cases mutilated or corrupted forms of their standard language, for not only does every great language owe its origin to dialects, but is merely a promoted or elevated dialect itself. ... Great languages need centuries to grow; their ... grammatical frame-work and vast vocabularies represent the contributions of untold thinkers and writers. Dialects, on the other hand, are not consciously created; their primitive origins are veiled in obscurity. ... They grow and develop naturally like trees. But a tongue that is merely spoken or not extensively written cannot well become fixed: for that a literature is necessary. ... As regards the English literary language, it would be more correct to call that a dialect than some of the 'provincial' variations, for it is constantly changing, both in spelling and pronunciation, whereas the 'dialects' in remote places preserve their forms with but little divergence from those of their ... ancestors.

HENRI F. KLEIN, in *The Encyclopaedia Americana*, 1937.

DIALECT has been defined in the chapter 'Non-Literary English' and something more will be said about the subject in 'General Trends and Particular Influences'. It should be clear that a dialect, so far from being a degraded form of speech, represents merely the survival of that variation of the original form of the language which was spoken in that region.

In *Breaking Priscian's Head* (1928), J. Y. T. Greig, having remarked that 'all the authorities are agreed that pronunciation has been standardized in America to an extent hitherto impossible in any European country', quotes an important statement from H. L. Mencken's *The American Language* (edition of 1923): 'This uniformity is especially marked in vocabulary and grammatical forms—the foundation stones of a living speech.

There may be slight differences in pronunciation and intonation—a Southern softness, a Yankee drawl, a Western burr—
but in the words they use and the way they use them all
Americans, even the least tutored, follow the same line. One
observes, of course, a polite speech and a common speech. But
the common speech is everywhere the same, and its uniform
vagaries take the place of the dialectic variations of other
lands.'

In the main, that statement is strikingly true. 'The same is
obviously not yet true of the British Isles; perhaps it never will
be.' (Probably it never will. But it would, I think, be a bad
thing for British English if ever it did become true.) 'Skeat
[*English Dialects*, 1911: and still invaluable] distinguished nine
dialects in Scotland, three in Ireland, and thirty in England and
Wales. Yet even in Great Britain, with its thirty-nine dialects,
a remarkable degree of uniformity in speech has been laid upon
the people in the last fifty years [i.e. 1878-1928], chiefly by
compulsory education. We hear complaints on every hand
that children are being taught to speak a bastard tongue, which
is neither standard English nor their own local dialect but combines the faults of both.'

What usually happens is that the children whose parents,
relatives and companions speak dialect revert to dialect immediately they leave the classroom. I cannot, therefore, agree
with Professor Greig when he adds, 'Dialects are vanishing
quicker than philologists can record them, nor does any pure
dialect exist any longer in the British Isles. Folk move about so
much that the dialects are getting all mixed up.' The number
of dialect-speakers has been steadily decreasing, it is true; but
decreasing very slowly, as countrymen go to the towns—and,
even then, only when they go to such towns and cities as do
not predominantly or notably speak a dialect; for instance, a
Warwickshire-dialect man going to live in Birmingham is unlikely to begin to speak Standard English.

Factors making for uniformity, and therefore militating
against the continuance of dialect, are education, as noted
above; increasingly rapid and easy transportation; the Press,
especially the Popular Press; the radio, since the early 1920s;

and the cinema, since the early 1930s. Yet the influence of any or all of the Press, transportation, the radio, the cinema, is smaller than many journalists, publicists, writers and scholars apparently suppose: this influence very rarely affects syntax and accidence, rarely affects pronunciation, and into a dialectal vocabulary insinuates only a few slang terms, a few catch-phrases, a few scientific and technical words, and occasionally a vogue-word such as *glamour*. Only very rarely indeed is a dialectal supplanted by a Standard English word; a dialectal phrase, almost never. If a new word or phrase is adopted, its well-established rival usually remains as a homely alternative.

That very great philologist, Edward Sapir (1884-1939) once wrote (1931) that 'it is very doubtful ... if linguistic localism can win out in the long run. ... Compulsory education, com-pulsory military service, modern means of communication, and urbanization are some of the more obvious factors in the spread of these attitudes'—i.e., those implied in Sapir's dictum that 'the modern mind is increasingly realistic and pragmatic in the world of action and conceptualistic or normative in the world of thought'.

All the various undermining forces that have been men-tioned (and several that, even by Sapir, have not) may, in the end, cause the disappearance of dialect in England, then Wales, then Scotland, and finally Ireland. But that would not happen for a very long time, even in England; nor will it ever, I think, in Scotland and Ireland, and only very improbably in Wales. For linguistic reasons—notably the enrichment, re-freshment, invigoration, individuality of British English (hence, ultimately, of all English whatsoever)—I hope that the dialects will never die out. Like Sweet, Skeat, Bradley and Pearsall Smith before him, Professor Greig (*Breaking Priscian's Head*, pp. 87-93) has some very interesting things to say about the value of the British dialects to English as a whole; but either to quote them or to express myself on this subject, would be to exceed my brief.

Since Cockney, the most important of all British dialects, has a chapter to itself, we shall here exemplify dialect with a passage from another that is realistically, conservatively, thoroughly and sturdily English—the East Anglian—well exemplified in the following passage* from one of Neil Bell's novels, *Forgive Us Our Trespasses*, 1947.

Did I ever tell yew abewt Tosh Muir? They called him Tosh becoz he'd gret buck teeth what stuck ewt in front. Betterin'[1] this net reminded me on him.

I don't think so, Father.

Tosh lived by Tibbies Green. He'd a punt *Mary* and a young wife Lily. Lil he called her. They hadn't been married long. Very fond o' one anawther they both war. And then Tosh began to change. He was still kind with Lil, for he war a softhearted man, but thar warn't no lovemakin'. Lil didn't say nawthin' neether to him nor nobody else for a long time, but at last she up an' arst him ewtright whass[2] the matter. And o' course he say nawthin', but she wouldn't hev that an' she say thar's anawther woman; an' he looks straight at her an' then he say, 'Yes, Lil, thass[3] right, thar's anawther woman.'

'Whew is she?' she say, an' Tosh say, 'I dorn't know whew she is, Lil, but she's a marmaid.'

'A *what*?' Lil say.

'A marmaid,' Tosh say; 'when I'm ewt at nights she come an' lean over the bort[4] an' make love t' me.'

'Whass she say?' Lil say.

'She dorn't say ezzactly nawthin',' Tosh say, 'but she lean thar over the bort an' look at me.'

In a way that war a load off Lil's mind. There warn't anawther woman. A marmaid! He war just duzzy,[5] that war what it war. Still, it warn't healthy. Lil went to see Ted Ashmenal, he war chemist hare then, an' he gave her sutthin', but it didn't dew Tosh any good an' he still loved his marmaid an' didn't love Lil, an' so she told some of the neighbours an' the women told their men, an' presently it war all arranged an' the next night Tosh went ewt tew or three other borts kept him in sight, an' when they war off Dunwich an' abewt three

* With the author's generous permission.

mile ewt he'd got his net down an' they overhauled him, an'
sure enough there war a marmaid lookin' over his gun'ul an'
makin' eyes at him an' makin' a sort o' crunin' noise tew.

Not a *rale* marmaid! There aren't *rale* marmaids, Father!

Well, a seal then, Bor[6]; a young female seal; an' by starlight
they dew look sutthin' like a young woman. She war off in a
flash as soon as the other borts drew alongside, an' Tosh in a
nasty temper arst them what they warnted.

'We came t'see your marmaid, Tosh,' said old Alf Craigie
(he's dead now, yew never knowed him). 'Well,' Tosh say,
shewin' all his big teeth at them, 'yew seen her, new yew kin
gew.'

'Thass not a marmaid, Tosh,' old Alf say; 'thass a seal, a
young female; I've seed hundreds.'

'Yew're a liar,' Tosh say, 'an' I dewn't warnt yew nosin'
abewt here. You slosh off[7], all on yew.'

Well, they went off an' they came an' told Lil, but it didn't
make no difference to Tosh; they could call it a seal if they
liked; he knowed it war a marmaid, an' he got more an' more
in love with her an' hardly spoke to Lil. An' so the men, old
Alf Craigie an' four others, Ted Denny war one on 'em, they
planned to capture the seal an' prove it warn't a marmaid to
Tosh, an' they put a twalve hook[8] in a harrin[9] an' caught her
with it, an' the hook must've caught in her stummack an' she
screamed just like a young woman screamin', an' Tosh came
up with them an' he started screamin' an' jumped aboard Ted
Denny an' old Alf's bort with his guttin' knife, an' Ted had to
knock him ewt with the gaff. But they'd got the young seal;
it war dead by now, an' when Tosh came rewnd they shew
him the seal, but he didn't take no notice, an' he say nawthin'
but set thar leanin' against a thwart (they'd taken his bort in
tow) an' starin' ewt over the sea. An' when they got ashore
Tosh picked up the seal an' went off with it in his arms, leavin'
his bort, an' no one sayin' or dewin' nawthin'.

Warn't he never seen again?

Yes, he war home before it war dark. He didn't say nawthin',
an' Lil she say nawthin'. An' he went ewt arly the next mornin'
an' didn't come back; run dewn in the roke[10] they reckoned;

but nawthin' came ashore. Rum cuffer,[11] aren't it? Thass what comes o' pokin' your snout into other people's business.

Most of the dialect words are self-explanatory. A few readers might, however, be glad of this key to the less obvious terms: [1] *betterin'*, mending; [2] *whass*, what's; [3] *thass*, that's; [4] *bort*, boat; [5] *duzzy*, 'dizzy'—daft; [6] *Bor*, term of address—from *neighbor*, *neighbour*; [7] *slosh off*, make off, go away; [8] *twalve hook*, a large, very strong hook, such as would be used for the catching of congers; [9] *harrin*, herring; [10] *roke*, reek—i.e., fog; [11] *rum cuffer*, strange and astonishing tale.

CHAPTER FIVE

COCKNEY

'A PEOPLE'S VOICE ...'

JULIAN FRANKLYN

'THE Greeks had a word for it', but in that respect the Greeks were in no way superior to the Cockney.

Let it be new, striking, stupid or superior; let it be what it may; and immediately the Cockney will give it a name. Always a pithy one, often a rude one, sometimes a mildly obscene one; but invariably a name that is suitable, inevitable and overwhelming: a name that will inhibit the title bestowed, after painful cogitation, by originator or by manufacturer, and will become *the* name for the thing.

His tongue kills cock-robin every time. Who christened a Ford car a 'Lizzie'? Who called a German a 'Jerry', and branded a police constable a 'copper'?

Who is this wizard of words with his irresistible impingement on standard English, where does he live, what does he do to secure that end?

He is tough, he is rough, he is raucous; he is also polite and accommodating, he is impertinent and respectful, easy-going but unimpressionable, sentimental and unemotional.

He lives in the Old Kent Road and in Camden Town, in Camberwell and in Hoxton, in Hammersmith and in Leytonstone, but none the less in Putney and in Hampstead, for he is the whole native population of the Metropolis and its environs. He does not belong to one specific class or caste—he is the Smiths, the Browns, the Joneses and the Robinsons, whether he went to Sayer Street Board School or to one of the London Grammar Schools.

No matter how carefully he may watch his tongue, how hard he may labour to eradicate his native dialect, he can never wholly succeed, and it does not even require moments of stress for him to forget himself. The sound of his voice will betray him in moments of calm. Such words as 'sale' and 'towel' will forever lay bare his secret to the sensitive ear.

Of course, the down-to-earth Cockney has no stupid linguistic pretensions. He is as proud, and rightly so, of his county peculiarity of speech as any other dialect speaker in the country. He cultivates it, for he believes that the language of London, *his* London, and *his* language, is English. The only English.

Other people talk 'like country-mugs' or 'well orf' or 'wif da goiver' or 'dead Yank', but if you 'tork proper' you talk Cockney and no nonsense.

You seek and win no medals at any amateur society for poetry-speaking; you never articulate, you seldom part your teeth. You crush your vowels either right out of the word, or into a misshape; you slur your consonants, you run words together, you abbreviate by truncation or by dropping internal syllables, you dispense with an aspirate where it belongs, and sometimes, in order to aid the smooth, almost imperceptible journey from word to word, you slip one in, as a kind of verbal hyphen or bridge. 'Igh O'bun', shouted the bus conductor. '*High Holborn!*' corrected the pedant. 'Yhus!' retorted the man behind the bell-punch, 'an' if yehu was shartin' it aht undred toimes eh daie like wot hi am, yeoud soon git thet there funny little corf o' yourn cured, gubner!'

Bus and tram conductors, contrary to popular belief, do not make their stopping-place calls, and their demands for fares, in typical Cockney. Not by any means. They have developed a sort of bus-conductorese. 'All fares, please' was cleverly rendered as 'Oile rairze filllsssst' in a sketch by J. B. Boothroyd, in *Punch*, 28 December, 1949.

A. W. Tuer, in his *Old London Street Cries* (1885), quoted by Professor Wm. Matthews in *Cockney Past and Present* (1938), claims that only one of the station names on the Inner Circle is pronounced correctly by the Cockney. The present writer differs slightly; the fact is—*none* of them are, or ever were.

Tuer gives: 'Emma Smith, South Kenzint'un, Glawster

Rowd, I street Kenzint'un, Nottin' ill Gite, Queen's Rowd Bizewater, Pride Street Peddinten, Edge-wer Rowd, Biker Street, Portlend Rowd, Gower Street (this one, Tuer assumes, is pronounced correctly), King's Krauss ("sometimes", he says, "abbreviated to 'ng's Krauss"), Ferrinden Street, Oldersgit Street, Mawgit Street, Bishergit, Ol'git, Mark Line, Monney-m'nt, Kennun Street, Menshun Ouse, Blekfriars, Tempull, Chairin Krauss, Wes'minster ("Sometimes," he states, "one hears Wesminister"), S'n Jimes-iz Pawk, Victaw-ia, Slown Square.'

Apart from the changes that have taken place in the naming of stations, the above Cockney renderings are a little misleading. 'Emma Smith' should be *Emma Smif*; 'South Kenzint'un', *Sarf Kinzey't'n*; 'Glawster Rowd', *Glawster Roaed*; 'I Street Kenzint'un,' *Oi Stree' Kinzey't'n* (but on most occasions it will be abbreviated to just *Ken*); 'Nottin' ill Gite', *Nod' Nill Giate*; 'Queen's Rowd Bizewater', *Queen's Roaed Biazewa'er*; 'Pride Street Peddinten', *Priade Stree' Ped'n'tn*; 'Edge-wer Rowd', *Essh-wer Roaed*; 'Biker Street', *Baiker Stree'*; and so on, until we reach Gower Street, which should be, most emphatically, *Gahr Stree'*. Not 'Tempull' but more like *Tempowl*; not 'Chairin Krauss' but *Cherin Craws*; not 'Ol'git' but *Aw'git*.

One does not condemn Tuer as wrong, since there are numerous sub-dialects within the main dialect. Cockneys are closely patri-local, patri-lingual, and endogamous. Not only does the intonation, the accent, and the consonantal slipshodness vary from district to district, but the physical type varies with it. South of the Thames Cockneys differ in physique, as a whole, from the North of the Thames population.

Mac Kenzie Mac Bride in *London's Dialect* (1910), says: 'The London dialect really, especially on the south side of the Thames, is a perfectly legitimate and recognizable child of the old Kentish tongue to which we owe our earliest written language. ... The dialect north of the Thames has been shown to be one of the many varieties of the Midland or Mercian dialect, flavoured by the East Anglian variety of the same speech, owing to the great influx of Essex people into London.'

Areas hemmed in by canals, railways, docks and ware-
houses, develop, again, a peculiar ethnic type, and a speciality
of tongue. These minor linguistic varieties, though marked,
are not, however, of sufficient importance in themselves to
prevent generalizations on the Cockney dialect of the whole
Metropolis from being applicable.

It is also worthy of note that individual words, in the mouth
of the same speaker, vary with the context. For example,
'water' may be, in the tones of the whining child, 'Mum—gis
a dwink er war-er'; in the urgent suggestion of the cheerful
child, 'Let's plai wif dah warder!'; and in the shout of the
frightened child, "Arry's fall'n in dah wah'r?' The favourite
word 'guvnor' may be 'gubner', 'gufner', 'gumner', or
'gunner', although in very recent times there has developed
a general tendency to abbreviate it to 'guv'. *Drury Lane* may
fall anywhere between 'Doory' Lane, and 'Jeowry' Lane.

A further complication in the rendering of the Cockney
dialect is the impossibility of spelling the words in a way that
will convey their true sounds.

No alphabet has letters that go off at half-cock or letters that
represent two different but related sounds, or even letters that
have no sound at all, but only a value. For example, though
'street' is wrong, so is 'stree'', for the apostrophe cannot give
the key to the final sound of the word, which, though far from
'eet', is by no means non-existent. 'D' does not adequately
replace 'T' in 'water', but the sound partakes of the flavour of
both.

Even if it were possible, it would still be inadvisable, for the
nearer the writer achieved complete success the less readily
readable the matter would become. In fact, it would be unintelligible to any save a Londoner, who would be able to make a
sort of mental auditory reconstruction from the visual appearance of the strange, written words. Writers of Cockney stories
and sketches, therefore, fall into two main groups. Those who
portray the life and character of the people accurately, and leave
the dialect to suggestion, and those who write what they believe
to be good dialect, but sometimes misinterpret the characters.

Because of the great subtleties in the Cockney tongue, the

native of London is able to make a much better job of imitating the speech of a visitor from the North, than any visitor from the North is of imitating the Cockney speech, though a provincial person resident in London over a number of years, and engaged in a calling which brings him in contact with the tough, inflexible, linguistically invincible Cockney type, will, often much against his inclination, develop the Cockney accent in certain words and phrases—particularly place names. His carefully enunciated 'Holl-bourne' will comparatively rapidly turn into the slick 'Oh-bun' (or 'Oh-burn').

The basis of the Cockney dialect remains stable. It has not altered for centuries. Mac Kenzie Mac Bride traces Cockney spelling as far back as A.D. 825. Be that as it may, it is at least certain that, in 1580, John Stow wrote 'bylyffe' for *bailiff*. Some sixteenth-century spellings, given by Matthews, might well be used by Cockney dialect writers to-day. *Towle* (toll); *towld* (told); *colles* (coals); *poll* (pole); and the passion for abbreviation, too, is there: *salt* (assault); *countable* (accountable); *stallyd* (installed); *paringe* (repairing), and so on; but, in other respects, Cockney changes fundamentally and rapidly.

The ready wit, and the link-up with life as it goes by in the biggest city in the world, account for the ever-changing slang in current use by the Cockney. It accounts, too, for changes in inflexion and stress, and in the currency of catchwords and phrases.

Occupation has much bearing on the mode of speech, and the changing means of daily life exercise a strong influence. In 1900, slow horse transport and few diversions drove the consciousness of the people inward, and forced them to provide the bulk of their own amusements, to which end there was a more vital social intercourse, and with it the need for witty or, at least, vivacious conversation. To-day, speed and the wireless hold the people apart.

In 1900 there were no official shortages of commodities, and the street trader, as well as the shopkeeper, was forced by keen competition to use his voice to its fullest advantage. To-day he has merely to mumble, 'Git on da queue, missis; yull git served in yeh turn.'

Fifty years ago freedom enabled the Cockney to 'irabarrer' (hire a barrow) and, after loading it up at Covent Garden Market or elsewhere, 'git eself a bob-a-teuh' as an itinerant street trader. To-day, such perambulating hucksters are swept off the scene by one-way traffic, speed, 'No parking', and a thousand other irksome regulations, quite apart from controls of labour, goods, and the private lives of the population.

The standardized accents of the B.B.C. do not materially affect the speech of the established Londoner. The occupants of the little houses in back streets, houses and streets that have often been populated by the same families for several generations, behave towards the elocution-conscious announcers' careful English in much the same manner as they reacted in childhood to the authority of provincial-born teachers in the elementary schools.

How shocked the grave broadcaster would be, if, a few minutes after he had made his final verbal flourish, he heard himself retailed over the garden-wall: 'Yhus—it jest come ofer da whylis. E sed sum'in' abaht wot we all got eh deu, is git aht o' de 'abit o' finking we knows wot we're a-torkin' abaht, 'cause we don't, an' start a-doin' wha' e sais!'

What would probably hurt the gentleman still more deeply, is the retort that might be expected from the average Cockney —'Sorse!—Shime yeh cawnt oller aht beck attem, enit?' Rhetoric, logic, and eloquency, leave the Cockney stonily unmoved—the mute appeal, as for example that of a dumb animal in distress, stirs him to the core, urges him to a frenzy of activity, will probably rouse him, good-natured, peaceful, friendly fellow that he normally is, to indulge in fisticuffs, and even to invoke the law.

In his childhood, while at school, and for those hours only, he articulated carefully, employed aspirates in the right place, watched his syntax and his grammar. It was so much more comfortable than running foul of authority, for in 1909 the London County Council issued a *Report of the Conference on the Teaching of English in London Elementary Schools*, in which the following passage occurs: 'It must not be forgotten that London has a special responsibility for the maintenance of a satisfactory standard of English as a spoken or a literary medium. Many of the so-called provincial dialects are ... survivals of older forms of the language, and are thus historically and phonetically justified. When a boy or girl in Devonshire, Lincolnshire, or Yorkshire is taught to acquire the constructions of the King's English at the expense of his native forms of speech, there is a balance of loss and gain in the process. But with the pupil in the London elementary school this is not the case. There is no London dialect of reputable antecedents and origin which is a heritage for him to surrender in school. The Cockney mode of speech, with its unpleasant twang, is a modern corruption without legitimate credentials, and is unworthy of being the speech of any person in the capital city of the Empire. There, if anywhere, the endeavour should be made to diffuse as widely as possible the standard English which, as the result of a long process of development, has become the normal national means of expression.'

Thus, by people ignorant of its antecedents, the Cockney dialect was condemned as the spawn of the slums and the product of crass vulgarity. Had the children been encouraged to express themselves naturally, they would have learnt more and developed a balanced form of speech. The result of repression and artificiality in school, led to a reaction in a contrary direction out of school. Children developed a stronger dialect than their elders, employed more slang, sang only the dialectal and sometimes disreputable ditties of the music-halls, instead of, as they might well have done, the English classic ballads they were taught in school.

The influence of the L.C.C.'s *Report* ... upon the method of teaching English may have been profound. Its influence on the dialect of London was contrary to its intention, and the result of the revised method of teaching must have been galling indeed to the 'Education Authorities'.

At the present time there seem to be no particular cranks with a mission to force 'standard English' (like a gag) into the mouths of the people. This is perhaps because it is slowly becoming clear that, although there is a standard English spelling, and there might be a standard English writing, there is not, and never can be, a standard English speech. The 'King's English' is all the English that is spoken in the King's domains. It includes Scottish English, Welsh English, Yorkshire English, Devon English and London English. These dialects can and do develop and grow. All of them, and particularly Cockney, are living organisms, and as such obey the law of life, which is fundamentally to eliminate waste and disused material, and to assimilate new. This the Cockney dialect does intensively, while it retains its own morphology. Accents and slang, imported by the gramophone record and the film from America, are assimilated selectively, not swallowed whole, and only such words and tones of voice as suit the Cockney are retained. The rest is tasted, chewed perhaps, then rejected.

A dialect that has survived a thousand years of history need not fear the attacks of pedants and purists. Occupations may change, ways of life may be altered, transport, housing, trading and modes of amusement all be revised, but the basic speech of the people of London will survive, and the Cockney of A.D. 2000, and even of A.D. 2050, will be supporting the statement made by 'Billicks' (Mr A. St John Adcock's character, Bill Hicks, horse-bus driver) in an altercation he had with a policeman of Scottish origin, as so many were at the commencement of this century.

Said Billicks, 'Fact is, there's no sich thing as a Cockney dialeck. The Cockney's is the real, original, correct English, an' all the rest is dialecks. This is the capital, remember, and nat'rally the man that's born in it knows the language of the country better than the josser thet comes in from outside to see what he can pick up.'

21st Birthday
(dahn da Warwoff Roaed)*
By JULIAN FRANKLYN

Young Alf, the protagonist, had imbibed enough beer even before dinner. That was Uncle Charlie's fault. The square-built

* Down the Walworth Road, one of the centres of the Cockney kingdom: Southwark, London, S.E.17. *Roaed* is pronounced, briskly, as two syllables: *rō-ĕd*.

greengrocer with the gruff voice, who thought in terms of gallons, and was always the life and soul of any party he attended, and where he invariably appointed himself master of ceremonies, had arrived early.

Quart bottles in crates were loaded on to his cart. He announced his presence by shouting 'Hi! Pig's ear[1] up!' in at the open door, and as his widowed sister-in-law emerged from the back-kitchen, wiping her hands on her apron, he greeted her with, 'Ullo, Marfa. Got some Guinness fer yeuh an' de uffer[2] laidies,[3] an' all da rest's brahrn[4]—jes' plain wallop[5]—no shorders.'[6]

'Come in 'ere, Uncle Charlie!' Alf called from the front parlour, which to-day was to be put into full service.

Uncle Charlie entered: hauled from each of the outside pockets of his check jacket a large bottle of beer and they commenced right away.

When the first bottle was empty they went outside to unload the crates from the cart. Joe, a lad of twelve, Uncle Charlie's youngest, was in charge, acting very superior to a group of boys and girls who surrounded the interesting equipage. He was in intense, almost violent, conversation with another boy of about his own age—'... wot? wiv Arsnul two none, an' Chowsea aht o' da cahnt[7] awready an' Totnum[8] dahn[9] da pan[9]—wot cheu torkin abaht!'

'Nah, Joie!' The sharp gruff voice of his father cut in upon the conversation—'Drop chewin' da fat, an' 'elp yeh cousin Alf an' me wif dese 'ere bo'hls![10] Yus! Come orn!'

They piled beer crates in the corner of the parlour. They lined the wall with them almost to the ceiling in the narrow passage, leaving barely room to pass through. When all was done Uncle Charlie poured out a Guinness for Martha and took it through to the kitchen. She protested, but who could resist Charlie (even if one really wanted to!)? 'Gooo on!' he urged. 'Knock it beck![11] Git it dahn—wot d'yeh fink dey goes teh all da trouble o' makin' it fer!'

'Well—they do sai it's ony dirdy waw'er[12]—doan they?' Martha answered, reducing the contents of the glass by half at a gulp, after which she wiped her mouth on the back of her hand, then smacked her lips appreciatively.

'Nah, Joie!' cried the energetic greengrocer emerging on to the street, 'git orf 'ome wif da cart, an' tell yeh muffer not teh be laite rahnd 'ere fer dinner or yeh auntie Marfa won't arf clean[13] 'er!'

Joe must have been a faithful and impressive messenger, for he, in clean Eton collar, best Norfolk jacket, and with face and ears scrubbed to a shining pink, arrived with his mother in ample time.

Auntie Rosie with Bill, her bald-headed, grey-faced, weak-stomached husband, a house-painter by trade, was there already. Uncle Charlie stood with his broad aggressive back turned to Rosie's husband, thereby demonstrating his dislike of men who couldn't or wouldn't drink beer when it was there for the drinking.

Alf, his sleek black hair taking advantage of the situation, and hanging a greased rat-tail or two over his face, was a trifle more bright-eyed and had a little more of pallor than usual.

'E'yar,[14] Sal!' cried Uncle Charlie as his wife entered. 'I got one poured aht fer yeh!'

'Yers—an' I cen deu wif it, teuh!' Sal took a long pull at the liquor. 'Well, Alfie,' she said on regaining her breath, 'it's your pah'y,[15] ain't it! I bo'ght[16] yeh a little present, I 'ave—it's from me an' yer uncle.' She produced out of her voluminous hand-bag a rectangular something wrapped in slightly crumpled, rather grimy tissue paper.

'Oo—fenk yeh,' simpered Alf, taking the parcel and remov-ing the wrapping. It was a shining, in fact glinting, cigarette case.

'Eepee[17] Eness[17] is wot they calls it—ingeein-turned, so the man tol' me—d'fink ye'll loike it?'

'S'grend.'[18]

'Nah doan' yeh be shoy if yeh don't,' Uncle Charlie cried reassuringly, ''cause we can chainge it, yeh know!'

'Yus, I loike it—straite[19] up[19] I do—it's grend—jes' wha' I wan'—fenks, Uncle; yeuh too, ahn'ie.[20] Look, mum!' he con-tinued, addressing his mother, who entered in the first stage of serving the dinner.

She deposited her various burdens on the table, unnecessarily wiped her hands on her apron and took hold of the present for closer inspection. 'Yeh shouldn't eh[21] done,[21] Charlie!' she protested by way of appreciation.

When Aunt Rosie's turn to inspect it closely came, she extracted a packet of cigarettes from her bag and filled the case. 'There!' she said modestly.

'Yeh shouldn't eh done, Rosie,' said Alf's mother again.

'Ow—*fenks*,' Alf said weakly. One did not expect anything from Aunt Rosie. Uncle Bill was generally out of work over his weak stomach.

'Fegs!' Uncle Charlie shouted, not to be outdone. 'Plen'y[22] fegs!'[22] He dragged crumpled part-used packets from every recess of his clothing and tossed them on to the table.

'Oi, nark[23] it! Cawnt yeh see I'm a-gittin[24] da table on!'[24] cried Martha, but Charlie was impervious. He was refilling everybody's glass. Sal came to the rescue. With a drink in one hand she employed the other to remove the cigarette packets to the mantelpiece and the little shelves of the overmantel.

'*Ain't* thet a lufly vawze?'[25] she said rapturously to Auntie Rosie, who was helping in a reticent half-hearted sort of way. The specimen of ceramics that so thrilled Auntie Sal was large and shapeless. Its bulging sides were painted a bright yellow, and further adorned with the reddest of red roses garnished with the greenest of green leaves.

'Yers,' drawled Rosie in awed admiration and with bated breath. 'It's vallable, y'know!'

Any further conversation between the connoisseurs was checked by the onrushing clatter of feet and the shrilling of loud voices in the passage. The children had come home from Sunday School.

'Coo! look a' all the bo'hls!' shrieked young Clara, age ten.

'Garn!' roared her twelve-year old brother Tom, aggressively and in contempt, 'thet ain't nuffink! If yeuh was teh go dahn Boney Street—' But what glory might meet her gaze there was never revealed.

'Goo on! go an' wash yeh 'ans an' faice an' come teh yeh dinners!' cried their mother in an aggrieved falsetto. 'Wheres yeh bin? Din I sai come straite 'ome, an' look at da toime nah! Where yeh bin?'

'Ain't bin nowhere!' retorted Tom indignantly.

'Don't answer me beck or I'll clip yeh rahnt de ear 'ole! Goo on an' wash dem 'ans an' come in teh yeh dinners. Wot d'yeh taike me fer?'

The ablutions were achieved. The parlour seating accommodation was eked out by a board resting between two chairs, making a kind of form on which the children, Clara, Tom, and their cousin Joe, perched themselves. Martha, assisted somewhat by Rose, served the dinner. It was ample, and reasonably well cooked, but quite cold, largely on account of the unaccustomed journey from kitchen to parlour, which transport was not too well organized.

The matter of temperature, however, was one that passed unnoticed. Uncle Charlie kept the ball rolling, the bottle flowing, the party going, and the entertainment hot.

Bacchus calls for song. Uncle Charlie, conducting with a table-knife for baton, lead the discordant chorus. 'It tis moi birfday—fill 'em up, fill 'em up, fill 'em up!' was first favourite with him, but 'I'm twen'y one teh-daie!'[26] had to be made use of at reasonable intervals, and 'A boicycle built fer teu' interposed itself without effort.

Uncle Bill, who, on account of his inability to eat, drink, or smoke, always felt that at a party life was harder than any other place on earth, was, as early as seven o'clock, agitating in a stage-aside to go home. He did it with his eyes swivelled into the extreme corners, his teeth clenched, and with only one side of his mouth engaged upon the task of articulation.

Uncle Charlie, the essence of discretion even without a load of beer aboard, decided to help.

'Gah blimey, yeh misery-gutted lahse,[27] cawnt yeh lit no one else enjoy theselves noither?'

'I wasn't addressin' *yehu*, Mr Noakes,' Uncle Bill protested feebly.

'Oh! wasn't yeh! Gor[28] blimey,[28] s'good job yeuh tol' me so, or else I wouldn't a-knowed, I wouldn't. 'Ere! Woi de 'ell doan' yeh go an' dhrand yehself an' leave yeh missus alone teh enjoy 'erself fer onct? Some people wan' a bit o' barney[29] nah'n'den.'

'Yehu moind yeh own affairs.' Uncle Bill tried to assert himself once again.

'Shurrup,[30] Charlie, yeh drunken ole coot. Let Bill alone,' chided Sal. "Ere, wot[31] ser marrer[31] wif yeh? Slippin', ain't cher? Moi glars 'as bin enty dis tin minnets!'

'Fill 'em up, fill 'em up, it tis moi birfday ...' Young Alf commenced to sing, and the infection, spreading rapidly, overcame the effect of the congenital depression of Uncle Bill and the diplomatic interference of Uncle Charlie.

It was past eight when the children came in from the street. They clamoured for food. Their mother drained her glass, and with a 'Scuse me, woncha' went to the kitchen where she provided them with huge hunks of bread and jam. They rushed out again, biting into the slices as they went. Their mother's gentle tones followed them down the dusk-filled gaslit street.

'Nah, doan' yeuh go slingin' it rahnd all[32] ofer de awktion[32] an' comin' in fer more—yeh won't git none—yeuh eat it. See?'

Now was the hour when it was respectable for unbidden neighbours to look in.

Mr Thompson from over the way pushed his whiskery face round the door. 'Jes' wan' teh sai "many 'appy returns" an' all thet ol' kibosh,[33] yeh know.'

'Jolly goo' luck. Come ri' in!' Uncle Charlie blared a bleary welcome, filling a glass and handing it to the newcomer, who took it, nodded, held it up, stepped fully into the crowded room, and drained the dark frothy liquid at a gulp. Uncle Charlie approved and instantly made good.

Taking this one slower, Mr Thompson toasted Alf: 'Well—'ere's teuh yeh, mate—on'y 'appens onct in a loiftoime, yeh know.'

Mrs Simmonds, who explained she 'was on'y parsin'', had knocked timidly at the open front door, and taking courage had readily responded to Uncle Charlie's shout of 'Nah, walk right in—doan' 'eng[34] abaht rahnd da doorstep!'

Her eyes gleamed at the Guinness. 'Goo' luck, Alfie!' she

croaked over the top of it and took a long sip. 'Why! I remimbers yeh wen yeh was so 'igh. I remimbers onct wen
yeuh come rahn to moi plaice to play wi moi 'Arry an' yeh
goes an' falls dahn all ahr apples³⁵ an' pears³⁵ ...'

'Yah!' Uncle Charlie interrupted in a boisterous blast of
mirth, 'I reckelleck onct wen 'e come dahn teh moi shop an'...'

The reminiscences, to Alf's occasional embarrassment, continued; the room filled to bursting point with neighbours as
the more retiring, emboldened by the apparent success of the
forerunners, followed suit. Mrs Simmonds was gradually
pushed from her perch beside the doorpost to the centre of the
arena.

Dick Hawkins came in and brought his concertina; there
were two mouth-organs at work already.

Midnight chimed, and Martha, who was now so far gone
with mingled fatigue and beer as to have forgotten to pack the
children off to bed, was nodding in the corner of the room.

Alf, who had by now really come to the conclusion that
something somewhere ought to have gone click and converted
him into a man of consequence who could shoulder responsibility, took a cigarette from his glittering case and lighting it
pushed his way (a little unsteadily) to where his mother dozed.

He shook her by the shoulder. 'Nah c'm on, ol' gal!' he
commanded.

The charm worked better than might have been expected.
From heavy somnolence she jumped briskly to her feet. The
concertina, scenting trouble, stopped dead in the middle of a
bar.

'Oi! Look 'ere! Doan yeuh gimme none o' your sauce, me
boy, or I'll slosh³⁶ yeh right acrors da clock,³⁷ an' no mistake,
soon³⁸ 'slook atcher³⁸—twen'y-one or no twen'y-one.'

'"Ooray!' yelled Uncle Charlie. Then words and music
appropriately burst out together.
'Go it, Muffer Brahrn ...'

The numbered words call for some comment.

¹ Rhyming slang for *beer*.
² other. Compare *Marfa* for *Martha*, and *Muffer* for *Mother*.

³ Instead of the usual *i* (*lidies*), Julian Franklyn employs the phonetically preferable *ai*; such a word as *straight* enforces a deviation. Other examples: *sai*, for *say*; *laite*; *chainge*; *faice*; *straite*, for *straight*; *taike*; *daie*; *plaice*.

⁴ brown (ale).

⁵ beer.

⁶ *shorters*, i.e. colloquial *shorts*, spirits. This *d* represents a consonant that is a shade closer to *d* than to *t*. Compare *dirdy* for *dirty*.

⁷ count, i.e. reckoning.

⁸ Tottenham (Hotspurs) Association football team; other London teams mentioned are Arsenal and Chelsea.

⁹⁻⁹ 'down the pan'—done-for; out of it; compare slangy *down the drain*.

¹⁰ or *bo'ls*, i.e. bottles. The word exemplifies the glottal stop so characteristic of Cockney; *cf.* note 12.

¹¹ back.

¹² water.

¹³ reprimand.

¹⁴ Here you are!

¹⁵ party. (Glottal stop: *cf.* note 10.)

¹⁶ brought.

¹⁷⁻¹⁷ E.P.N.S., i.e. *electro-plate* on *nickel silver*.

¹⁸ It's grand.

¹⁹ I.e. honestly.

²⁰ auntie. (Glottal stop.)

²¹⁻²¹ have done (it).

²²⁻²² plenty of fags. (Cigarettes.) For the *e* instead of *a*, *cf.* No. 11.

²³ stop.

²⁴⁻²⁴ laying the table.

²⁵ vase.

²⁶ to-day.

²⁷ louse.

²⁸⁻²⁸ *Gor* (often *Cor*) *blimey*, literally 'God blind me!'—the most popular of Cockney oaths.

²⁹ (noisy) fun or amusement.

³⁰ Shut up!

³¹⁻³¹ What's the matter.

³²⁻³² *all over the auction* (room): all over the place.

³³ *bosh*, nonsense. (Not the usual sense of *kibosh*.)

³⁴ hang.

³⁵⁻³⁵ rhyming slang for *stairs*.
    ³⁶ strike.
    ³⁷ face. (Short for *old Dutch clock*.)
³⁸⁻³⁸ as soon as look at you.

Note that *wot* is not unnecessary for *what*; for *wot* indicates the slovenly, unaspirated pronunciation of *what*.

CHAPTER SIX

THE TEACHING OF ENGLISH

FRANK JONES

Formerly Second Master at King Edward's School, Aston,
Birmingham, and author of *A New English Course*, *A New English
Composition*, *How We Speak*, etc.

IN 1900 English was the worst-taught subject in most schools.
In 1950 it is much the same. In all other subjects, notably in
art, physical drill, science, mathematics, modern languages
and even Latin, great and obvious advances have been made.
The advance in English teaching is undoubtedly much less.

At the beginning of the century the boy of 15 or 16 was supposed to have a sound knowledge of English Grammar, most
of which, based as it was on Latin Grammar and using its
terminology, was of little practical use. Much time was spent
in 'parsing', i.e. in telling the part of speech and every other
category of accidence of each word in a sentence. Thus 'Save'
in 'God Save the King' would be parsed: 'Verb, weak, transi-
tive, active voice, Subjunctive mood, third person, singular
number, its subject being the noun God'. This was doubtless a
salutary exercise but scarcely likely to improve one's power of
writing English, though done once or twice a week throughout one's school life.

'Literature' was generally represented by a play of Shakespeare or possibly by two. Modern prose or verse was considered too trivial for consideration. About the beginning of the
century doubts began to be born about the usefulness of formal
grammar teaching. But instead of winnowing the wheat from
the chaff and retaining that irreducible minimum of English
grammar obviously necessary for the learning of a foreign
language and the correction of vulgar errors in the mother
tongue our reformers, to change the metaphor, emptied the
baby out with the bath water with the cry, 'No Grammar!'

and for twenty years the only thing we could be certain about with regard to the boy from the more progressive Grammar School was that he knew no grammar. And strange to say, his powers of Composition showed no signs of improvement! The establishment of an English Language paper in the School Certificate Examination restored, let us hope, a more sensible study of that essential subject.

The Essay made its appearance at examination time but, if my memory serves me well, the schools that demanded a weekly essay from the boys were few. I suspect that in those days, before the time of 'free' periods for marking, the schoolmaster made fewer encroachments on his leisure for that hateful though necessary work.

Then, as now, the incompetence of the examiner and the necessity of satisfying his demands were the chief obstacles to any improvement in teaching methods. It may be that English is an unexaminable subject (though I don't believe it is); but certainly in those days fifty years ago the examiner called the tune and woe betide the teacher who dared to play another. And the same is true to-day.

A typical Shakespeare examination paper of those days would show the baleful influence of examination on the teaching. The very last requisite was a knowledge of the play itself or any appreciation of its merits. Question 1 would probably deal with the origins and date of the play, points doubtless of interest to scholars but scarcely likely to arouse the enthusiasm of a boy of 15. Question 2 almost invariably dealt with 'contexts', the only question requiring any knowledge of the play itself. The speaker and occasion had to be given. Context questions where the passage concerned is well chosen are probably the best questions that can be devised to test a close reading and understanding of the play. But many of the passages were not well chosen and might have been put into the mouth of any character in any play, with the result that Shakespeare himself might have experienced difficulty in allotting them. At any rate, I, both as candidate and later teacher, often did! Question 3 generally required the boy 'to describe the character of ——'. Doubtless the examiner meant the 'of' to be appositional but as a boy I thought that what was required was to give the person a character, as if he were a domestic servant.

The 'character' question was the crammer's joy. My own headmaster, a prince in the art of cramming (and strange to say one of the greatest schoolmasters I ever knew), always ensured that this question should bring us full marks. For our note-books told us, e.g. that Henry V was (a) patriotic, (b) brave, (c) religious, (d) sympathetic, (e) humorous, (f) a skilled soldier, (g) kingly, and when it came to the examination every single boy in the form with absolute unanimity was ready to vouch that Henry possessed these qualities in the same order and to substantiate the claim by the identical quotations from the play.

Question 4 would deal with difficult words and archaic expressions duly recorded on the back of maps or even on a roll of wallpaper, quite divorced from their context. To this day I remember:

'Dearest chuck'—a term of endearment.

Question 5 was distinctly more tricky and its anticipation called for the highest experience and skill on the part of the teacher. It might deal with Shakespeare's use of metaphors ('give two examples') and similes (ditto) or Shakespeare's love of nature ('give five examples') or 'the value to the play of the clown'. But the real crammer was never defeated. Occasionally the examiner would kick against the uniformity in the answers. I remember one occasion when she (for it was a woman) fell foul of me. A week before the examination a diploma student at the University arrived at the school without notice and begged me to give a lesson to a Certificate Form. I protested that all teaching was at an end and that the form were revising their notes. But the lady pleaded so hard that at last I consented and gave a lesson on Macaulay's prose style. With his essays before us we printed up examples of all his tricks. A few days later in the examination there was a question, 'Discuss Macaulay's prose style, quoting extracts to illustrate your answer'. Naturally, the form jumped at it to a man. The examiner's criticism was: 'The answers to the question were entirely worthless. Instead of giving their own views they repeated those of their master and in many cases the quotations were identical.' At the time I was old enough to be the good lady's father, if not her grandfather, and could afford to smile at such criticism, but I could not help thinking how much damage such condemnation might have done to a younger man.

Modern methods of the teaching of Shakespeare afford one of the most pleasing improvements in English teaching. The average English master of to-day recognizes that Henry V is not a dry-as-dust library book to be inflicted on a boy because it is a classic, but a play. The boy therefore studies it as a play, quite possibly acting it with book in hand on a platform in Big School. With the play, thus taught, it is astounding how many of the difficulties experienced in the older method of teaching automatically disappear. The master may from time to time give brief *sotto voce* explanations but they interfere very little with the dramatic representation of the play and if skilfully made cause little distraction from it. This is not to say that the microscopic examination of every line in the play given at a different type of lesson altogether has not its virtues. Shakespeare deserves some study and without it his full beauty cannot be appreciated. But 'the play's the thing' and they should be reserved until the play as a whole has made its impact.

It would be well if English teachers would follow the example of the Romans. The Roman schoolmaster set himself the task of training his pupil to speak clearly, concisely, logically and persuasively in the courts. No one can claim that the British schoolboy to-day in any type of school can do this. The very last thing the average sixth-form master thinks of is to teach his pupil to write English. Some of them cannot write themselves and more seem to despise this most important branch of English teaching. No boy would dream of devoting the time and thought to a short English composition that he would to a Latin prose. He will spend hours on writing a sonnet or a triolet, but the writing of a piece of 'simple' prose is beneath his dignity.

One important part of the Roman teacher's curriculum was the training in clear, articulate, correct and pleasing speech. So far as I know the highest English honours may be gained at every British university without the Candidate ever opening his mouth. It is not surprising, therefore, that the teacher of English thinks pronunciation no concern of his. Any interference with a pupil's natural speech is always calculated to raise a storm of protest from lovers of 'dialect'. Be it noted that this desire to preserve the local 'lingo' is always for other people's children, and those who advocate it are themselves prepared to pay exorbitant fees for inefficient private schools rather than subject their own offspring to the contamination of a Council School. The elimination of the grosser forms of 'town' accent is one of the most important branches of English teaching. *It can be done.*

English teaching will always be governed by the examiner. He may seem to do his job (i.e., of passing and failing candidates) reasonably well. A change in the nature of the questions asked might make little difference in the order of merit, though it would undoubtedly make some. But far more important than this essential part of his work is the examiner's effect on teaching. A really good English paper at the Certificate examination would change English teaching in every English school overnight. Could not English teachers get together and devise one? the fee paid at present to the examiner for setting a paper is £5 or less. The right paper would be cheap at £100,000!

Postscript (by E.P.):

Mr Frank Jones is one of the leading writers upon English from the angle of teacher and taught. He would agree with me when I add that, in the present century, the most influential writer upon the teaching of English is George Sampson (died February 1, 1950)—the author of *English for the English, Cambridge Lessons in English, Seven Essays,* etc. A third notable writer upon this subject is Mr L. A. G. Strong, with his *English for Pleasure* and *An Informal English Grammar.*

CHAPTER SEVEN

GENERAL TRENDS AND
PARTICULAR INFLUENCES

ALTHOUGH the title of this chapter is far from being
synonymous with 'The Ethical, Intellectual and Cultural History of the Twentieth Century', yet language
(since, obviously, it is inseparable from speech and from the
written or printed word) responds intimately and profoundly
to many factors outside itself, such as the 'climate of opinion'—
to quote, once more, a phrase so much used by the intellectuals of 1940 onwards—prevalent economic conditions—the
impact of three wars—the influence of cinema and radio—the
fungoid growth of bureaucracy—and many other so-called
'externals'. These factors and others 'to be hereinafter considered' combine to form the very soil by which language is
nourished; their effects are sometimes hard to distinguish and
always difficult, if not impossible, to assess; but, by any writer
worth the name, they must—even if that writer be not (as I am
not) a professional historian—at least be attempted, not ignored in a silence hardly less undignified than ill-advised, and
hardly less stupid than deceptive.

General Trends

One of the gravest and most portentous trends of the
twentieth century is the decline of formal religion. (To differentiate denominationally, the decline is at its gravest in the
Church of England; in the Catholic Church, at its least grave.)

This decline seems to have begun in the 1860s and 1870s,
with the popularization of the theory of evolution; during the
1890s, it became evident to all; throughout the present century,
the rot has continued to spread. In February 1950, *The Month*

prefaced its series, 'A Decade in Retrospect: 1939-1949', with an 'Introductory Note' by the editor, whose opening paragraph runs thus: 'If the past ten years have to be characterized briefly, they might be called "A Decade of Disinheritance". Throughout what once used to be called without irony "the civilized world" these years have spread an empire of perplexed and anxious instability which must be preparing the way for a less ambiguous condition of one kind or another.'

In such an atmosphere—an atmosphere that had pervaded the civilization of the British Isles from soon after Hitler's accession to power early in 1933—religion and the spiritual life in general were bound to suffer; and in much the same atmosphere are they still suffering. Only the spiritually elect seem able to withstand such intangible influences. In the April 1950 number of *The Month*, F. A. Voigt—that eloquent and most courageous crusader, and, by the way, an Anglican—has, in respect of the decade ending in 1949, written a remarkable article, wherein he says, 'What I do see—"subjectively" or "objectively" (or both)—is the preponderance of evil and the ascendancy of Antichrist.

'The ultimate character of every age is determined not by its art or science, not by its philosophy, not by its social or political order, not by its "civilization". All these, and the character of the age itself, are determined by religion. Beliefs are decisive. Beliefs made the Ten Years what they were. Catastrophic beliefs engendered catastrophe.

'What are those beliefs in the present, the eleventh year, 1950?

'These are the articles of the contemporary creed:

'Religion without God; Christianity without Christ; Christ without Antichrist; Heaven without Hell; works without faith; a God of love but not of wrath; a Church that can bless but cannot curse.'

This fiery, yet sympathetic critic of our age goes on to amplify those 'articles'. In the ethical, as distinct from the purely religious field, he finds that:

'We believe in order without hierarchy, in progress without direction, in freedom as an end and not a means, in justice as a means and not an end. We believe that justice can be qualified, that there is political justice, social justice, economic justice, or historical justice, or any justice other than justice.' Phrased differently, this is tantamount to saying that we are ready enough to take, but remarkably reluctant to pay: that we want everything both ways, and resent any inability to achieve this egomaniac purpose: and that we most certainly do expect to 'have our cake and eat it'.

'All articles of our creed,' Mr Voigt continues, 'can be summed up in one phrase: "the Christian ethic".

'The "Christian ethic" is the Antichrist of the Western world. It is the most insidious and formidable corruption that ever affected that world. ...

'The "Christian ethic" is preached from innumerable Anglican pulpits. It pervades art, letters and science. It is proclaimed daily by the Press and is propagated by wireless. It is the "philosophy" of the Pacifists.'

But, himself no misanthrope, this critic asks, 'In what is our hope? In the famine and the thirst! ['*Not a famine of bread, nor a thirst for water, but of hearing the words of the Lord*': as he makes very clear.] The danger ... is that the hunger and the thirst will be stilled with the frothy pabulum of the "Christian ethic", and that the people will be full and yet not fed. But there are signs ... that there is distrust of the prophets that prophesy falsely.'

For *The Month* of May, 1950, that equally fiery character, Roy Campbell, toreador, soldier, distinctive poet, penned—for the occasionally provocative but always instructive and often quite invaluable series 'A Decade in Retrospect'—an article that, even now, brings anguish and anger, malaise and murderousness, to all the effete intellectuals that lack his vigorous manhood, his insouciant courage and gay fortitude, and his widely recognized literary power and virtuosity.

'It is,' he writes, 'the intellectuals of this world, and Britain in particular, who have by far the least faith: and once faith is removed, credulity is its inevitable substitute. Man is a believing animal. If he is not allowed to believe *sense*—he believes any *rubbish*, especially if it pays as well as Bolshevism does to-day. It is true that Faith can move mountains, but it moves them slowly and painfully, inch by inch, though generally in a profitable direction.

'The terrible thing about credulity is that it can move, not only mountains, but whole continents, at a prodigious speed, and infallibly in the *wrong* direction, to wholesale disaster. ...

'That is why, during the last forty or fifty years, coincident with the decline in Faith, "progress" has assumed the momentum of an almost vertical Gadarene stampede: the most rapid and disastrous "progress" ever witnessed; and all for want of those two sensible stand-bys (a brake and a steering-wheel) *Tradition* and *Reaction*. A body without reactions is a corpse. So is a Society without Tradition.'

From the once 'revolutionary' Roy Campbell, who is still (and why not? he was born in 1901) far from being a reactionary, those are extremely significant and thought-provoking words. He implies that the train of humanity—especially that part of it which inhabits Britain—has gone off the rails and that the passengers imagine they are still destined to reach the stars alive whereas they are, in fact, headed for a crash, unless the brake of Tradition be applied before the train overturns.

After quoting two laymen, one of them a self-proclaimed Anglican, I shall, in fairness, quote a Canon of the Catholic Church. He prefers to remain anonymous, but I am free to say that he holds a very good degree and has at least thirty years' experience in 'the cure of souls' and almost as much in the teaching of the young. He traces the 'decline of religion' to 'confused teaching' and to the 'lack of good example on the part of so-called religious people'. 'Saints', he believes, 'are badly wanted.' To this decline in religion he attributes the 'decline in family life, for instance in England once renowned for it because of its Christian tradition (which has, in the twentieth century, greatly weakened) and because of its respect for Christian ideals'. He mentions the effect of multiple divorce 'upon the children of such broken marriages' and deplores the 'mania for taking people away from their homes—women in industry, organized activities and recreations *away* from home, schooling at a distance from home influence.'

Very closely linked with—in some respects, inseparable from

—the decline in formal religion is the ever-increasing lack of moral discipline, and of the general principles of ordinary decency, throughout the twentieth century. There has, since the late 1890s, been an increasing tendency, among those who merely think as distinguished from those who have 'a mind that feels, a heart that thinks', to forget that 'cultivation of the mind without a corresponding cultivation of character constitutes, not an asset, but a danger, to society. From neglect of discipline in the home there follows, inevitably, a weakening—indeed, a neglect—of discipline in many schools. Humanitarianism and education of the mind are not enough; H. G. Wells and his fellow progressives have been completely refuted by events. You won't cure the world until you have better people in it.' The Canon thereupon suggests that those better people can be ensured only by the precept and the practice of religion. He further suggests that all these post-war conferences fail or, at the least, tend to fail because 'there is no unity of principle—no established agreement on fundamental ideals'. Sir Hartley Shawcross has said that Parliament is 'so much the only source of Law in Britain that if it were to decide that all blue-eyed babies should be destroyed at birth, *that* would become the Law of England'. In 1917 Lord Sumner declared, in the House of Lords, that the dictum *Christianity is part of the Law of England* is 'really not law: it is rhetoric'. (See *Under God and the Law*, edited by Richard O'Sullivan, K.C., 1949.)

To the orderly religious or philosophic mind there seems, at times, to be not merely a lack of moral discipline, but also sheer chaos. 'It is, therefore, not surprising that in the painting, sculpture, architecture, and in poetry and the novel, of these times we should have confusion, ugliness, lack of form (there's no unity of principle in the artists themselves), preoccupation with sex (no self-control is recognized), despair and pessimism (even in the Catholic authors, Greene, Waugh, Mauriac)'—to quote the Canon.

The war of 1939-1945 brought to a head certain tendencies latent in the thirty or forty years preceding it, and F. A. Voigt, summarizing the general spiritual character of 1939-1949 and speaking of the power of evil, has said that 'The menace to civilization is incidental and, ultimately, perhaps of small account. The menace is to man. The Ten Years were not years of clear purpose, they were years of the utmost perplexity and confusion. Men were able to make war, but they were unable to make peace. It is easy to make war, because war can be organized. Peace cannot be organized, because it is organic. Man was never so helpless as he was in those Ten Years, not even in "primitive" times. ... The open confusion of those years was preceded by confusion of the mind. Outward confusions begin in the mind and Babylon is but the work of the Babylonian heart.

'Alas, the Ten Years are not the end of confusion ... "Collective man" is formless. Absolute freedom is the end of freedom, for the free will is left with nothing more to will.'

There has, in the fact (as opposed to the Utopian theory), been throughout the twentieth century more talk of liberty than at any time since the French Revolution: yet, after 1914, less civil liberty than at any time since the Middle Ages: and, after 1941, less personal liberty than at any time since the days of formal slavery. Nowadays, we call slavery by the resounding but pretentious and dishonest name 'State control'. A friend, who happens to be a man of some note—one of several to whom I applied for their frank comments upon some of the subjects forming the matter of this chapter—has sent me the following 'merest jottings' upon the 'grave decline of liberty', a decline that I date from the compulsions imposed upon the nation in the war of 1939-1945 but that he dates from the rise of Mussolini in 1922 and attributes to Fascism, Nazism and the later forms of Communism. He points to the 'ironing-out of all differences between peoples and between individuals on the plea of equality—in many instances an equality of misery'; thinks that the fostering of class-hatred (by those very persons who formerly preached that there is no such thing as class— that Britons have a classless society) constitutes an indirect yet powerful cause of the decline in liberty; and remarks upon the pernicious results of the theory that there should be no opposition to the will of the State—i.e. to what, in more honest times, we called 'the will of tyrants'—even in literature and the arts, where, in all the totalitarian states, 'genius is in danger of being quashed because it will not fit in a mould'. More, 'religion is denounced because it recognizes the overlordship of God—an overlordship which is above man-made laws'. It is obvious that, if the tyrants in totalitarian states are either logical or practical, religion *must* be denounced: it would never do for them to admit that there exists a power greater than theirs, whether that power flows from God in the absolute or Catholic sense—formerly, of course, also the Protestant sense—or even from a God in the restricted modern sense current among the majority of non-Catholics. Persecution of religion is always the result of fear, whether that fear cloaks itself as hatred or as political expediency.

What was formerly—and, by the minority, is still—hoped for, if not always expected, from religion is now expected, not merely hoped for, from the State. Hence the pathetic, the literally (not just the slangily) fantastic degree of credulous (or is it rather the desperate?) trust reposed in the benefits derivable from the Social Services: for communion with God we, the larger (not necessarily the greater) part of the Western World, have substituted communion with one another: for Heaven, the Utopia of false teeth and free medical attention: for Hell, the atom bomb: for God and His power, the State and its juggernaut. Such is the opinion of many thinking men from among not Catholics only, not other practising Christians only, not the entire body of Christendom only. Many unreligious men, most of them anything but irreligious, firmly think and strongly feel that these substitutions, equivalent to attempts to blueprint human happiness and the world's spiritual and moral, no less than its material welfare, are, after all, substitutions tragically artificial and attempts woefully inadequate.

'Not surprisingly after two world wars', the benefits of material security have been over-estimated. Along with all the preoccupation with social services, there has gone, as an almost, perhaps absolutely, necessary concomitant, a manifest and alarmingly rapid decline of initiative and of enterprise; a decline hastened by the prevailing egalitarianism and certainly not checked by the 'rationalization of industry' and the nationalization of certain industries and services. The outlet for creative talent, like that for craftmanship, has almost everywhere been dammed. To most workmen, work no longer affords happiness: hence their 'desire to get away from it as soon as possible with as much money as they can collect to spend on things in which they really are interested—their hobbies and their pleasures': far too often, their 'work is now so dull and monotonous that it gives them no true pleasure and no sense of achievement'. Much slacking and much 'go-slow' arise from that monotony, but also from 'that fear of unemployment which constitutes a reasonable excuse for many who remember the inter-war years'.

Loss of initiative and the decline in the spirit of enterprise are having an even graver result: the loss of the desire for independent thinking, whether by others or by oneself: hence, the loss of the power to think. That increasing inability to think independently—for acting like a flock of sheep and toeing the party-line (whatever the party) cannot be called thinking, it's merely the illusion of thinking—this inability, which has increased so rapidly during the years 1941-1951, has begun to exercise a most deleterious influence upon the life of the nation as a whole. Even writers and artists and composers have been deluded into imagining they are following a star, whereas they have merely been following a will-o'-the-wisp into a morass of ineptitude and stultification. But there are not very many writers; and of these (comparatively) few, the majority are now sceptical, and some downright rude. Most of them have recanted, bravely and handsomely, as in that damning indictment of Communism, *The God That Failed*, published in 1949, edited by Arthur Koestler, and written by six distinguished Europeans—insular as well as continental.

An inevitable result of the decline in moral discipline and of the confusion and uncertainty in all moral and spiritual matters has been an increasing freedom of speech; a freedom that, in certain cliques and circles and even classes, has reached the stage of licence, with the counter-result that, if one wishes, there, to achieve a spectacular effectiveness, one has to resort to a rather prim, entirely 'proper', understatement, couched in terms of the severest simplicity. To use a sexual or a functional image where an ordinary word or phrase would serve as well or, rather, would serve better; to employ verbal violence where violence is entirely unnecessary; to use any coarse word or phrase where a good ordinary word or phrase is available; to exaggerate not only picturesquely but also salaciously, and thus to diminish the picturesqueness: to do any or all of these things, which suspiciously resemble the self-assertiveness of the inferior, the noisiness of the half-wit, the boasting of the coward, is to debase both oneself and the language one uses. Oneself may be a moron, of little importance. The language, however, is very important. In the desert one does not befoul the well that others will have occasion to use.

This freedom of speech is creeping even into written English; very extensively and very decidedly—despite the restrictions imposed by law and by common decency. In dialogue one expects a certain degree of realism, although, there too, certain conventions need to be observed. But an exaggerated realism has often found its way into narrative and description. A 'tough' character acts 'tough' and talks 'tough': but the writer doesn't have to keep him company and 'go all tough' in the passages *about* this 'toughie'.

Between moral discipline and mental discipline the division is theoretical: neither can exist without the other. Yet one may regard mental discipline as an aspect of moral discipline; one may, therefore, speak of mental laziness. Such laziness tends to be produced by the cinema and even more by the 'popular' (or National) Press, especially in its cartoons and comic strips, and most of all by the 'picture papers', designed for those who cannot read—except in the purely physical sense. The 'popular' Press rarely presents the grounds and the steps of any argument more difficult than could be understood by a fairly intelligent child of ten; it 'pots' every scientific discovery that has a 'story' and all wisdom that isn't profoundly wise. Almost every leading article is drastically, not to say insultingly, simplified and the cause or message thereby misrepresented. To avoid wearying the readers' brains, every leader (or editorial) and every other article are short.

Having for years looked up and not been fed, readers, developing a contracted stomach, no longer wish to be fed; a little soothing-syrup or an ice-cream or a cocktail, and all is for the best in the best of lousy worlds. Certain newspapers would panic if they learned that their readers had begun to Think. Yet the editors and journalists concerned are hardly likely to learn any such thing, for there is only a very slight risk that their readers, or most of them, will examine any other newspaper, especially if it has no, or few, or unsensational pictures, or do anything so epoch-making as to read a thoughtful book.

With the improvements that have taken place in facilities for education and with the raising of the school-leaving age, there has—the externalists and the mistakers-of-means-for-ends have hastened to tell us—been an increase in literacy. Unfortunately, there has been no corresponding increase in education. It almost looks as if the cynic were, in the first two of his propositions, right when he exclaimed, 'The more literacy, the less education; the more subjects, the less learning; the more learning, the less thinking; the less thinking, the more action'. Even the cynic admits that to have something to think *with* is a great help, and that a potentially, or a nominally, good brain cannot get far without accurate information and without the vocabulary required for the acquisition of that information and for summing it up and imparting it. This very general desire to give everybody a fairer chance of winning the prizes of life—and, with that end in view, to provide better schools and numerous scholarships—this, in its way, is excellent.

But the utopians hope for too much. There are painfully obvious differences in mental equipment and in moral stamina; many children and young people are quite incapable of profiting by the opportunities provided with the moneys extracted from their parents. (I've met parents so stupid that they believe 'the guvment' pays for their children's education.) There is this extraordinary tendency to believe the contrary: to suppose that every child will benefit: to imagine that it would do a working-class child good to go to Eton or Winchester, exactly as if education depended upon being housed in this rather than in that aggregation of bricks and accumulation of mortar; that one set of apparatus rather than another will make a Watts out of Willie; that this equipment, here, and not that equipment, there, will produce a Lister out of Les. If a child has character, all except the gravest material obstacles tend to become of small account. Far more important than buildings and equipment are the teachers: teachers that are intelligent and cultured, capable and good, exercise a lasting influence on those whose minds they impress at a receptive age: so, unfortunately, do the doctrinaires, the slackers, the self-seekers and the careerists.

Those who doubt the validity of 'more literacy, yet less education' may care to ponder a comparatively unimportant but illuminating fact. Because of the influence of three wars, of numerous scientific inventions and discoveries, of rapid growth in industrialism, of borrowings from other languages, and for various other reasons, the English vocabulary has enormously increased among all classes of people and in every trade and profession: but has that enlarged vocabulary improved the education of the millions of persons concerned? (Not unless a smattery knowledge is equated to education. Knowledge is only a part of education—the smaller part.)

There we verge upon a matter of the greatest and gravest importance: the teaching of English. This matter particularly concerns the schools, for by the time the young people are launched upon the troublous seas of contemporary life, nearly all of them have so much to do to keep the ship afloat that they feel (quite mistakenly feel) no, or little, compulsion to rectify the errors or, far more often, the defects of those whose profession and duty it had been to start them off on the right foot and with sound equipment; and by the time the more fortunate or more ambitious enter a university, the harm has been done and is only occasionally undone. 'As the twig is bent ...': it should be clear that upon the way English is taught depends the way the pupils, later the citizens, will speak and write. 'But perhaps as much depends on the home as on the school!' Very well; that merely throws us one generation back—how were the *parents* taught?

Not until George Sampson published his *English for the*

English had this subject, the teaching of English as distinct from the assimilation, by the young, of English, been adequately recognized. Until his death early in 1950, Sampson maintained the fight; there is, for instance, a long and pertinent article in his *Seven Essays*, 1947. Mr L. A. G. Strong has done much for the cause. So also has Mr Frank Jones, who contributes to this volume an article upon the teaching of English. (I too have tried—so far, with little success—in *English: A Course for Human Beings*.)

Certain schools teach English very well; a few, quite admirably; many, fairly well. But the majority teach it inadequately; of these, some teach it perfunctorily. Yet, compared with the year 1900 (to take a convenient date), 1950 shows up very favourably, despite the fact that the teaching of English has not kept pace with the teaching of geography or mathematics or physics or, indeed, several other subjects. Dr G. Pratt Insh, historian and educationist, writes thus upon the change: 'Behind both journalism and broadcasting lies the problem of the schools. Until recently they had the great majority of the children only up to fourteen years, and you cannot do very profound language study at that ripe age. But the schools did a great deal—they threw out (despite the lamentations of the classical master and the modern languages master) the old formal, dogmatic, sawdusty conning of the grammar book; inspired by George Sampson, Sir Henry Newbolt [†1938: general editor, 1925 onwards, of the "Teaching of English" Series, later edited by Dr Richard Wilson] and Sir P. J. Hartog, they encouraged the children to write prose and verse and to appreciate the simpler English classics. Many who began to write school essays under their influence brought into journalism and literature a fresh, personal approach, in work very different from the products of the study of the eighteenth-century men of letters' (private communication, 24 June 1950).

But in the schools, where the pupils are, mostly, rather too young to resist the tendency or even to recognize the danger, and out in the world among the seniors, who might be expected to do both, there has—according to a number of acute observers—been an increase of fluffy thinking and (this being one of the results of such inchoate thought) of incoherent speech and writing.

In reference to the late George Orwell's charge that much of the writing in the 1930's and 1940's suffers from two widespread faults, 'staleness of imagery' and 'lack of precision', J. Y. T. Greig (*Keep up the Fight for English*, 1946) remarks that these faults are 'plain signs of incoherent thinking. That is what our scattered and incoherent education is doing for us: it is turning out fluffy and incoherent thinkers, an endless succession of them, like motor-cars coming off the assembly-line. We might have expected the strong emphasis on science to produce an effect quite opposite. It has not; and mainly, I believe, because, in spite of all the big talk about it, we have not been training young men and women in science; we have been training them in sciences, which is quite a different matter. It is notorious that outside his specialized science, the typical scientist of to-day is as fluffy a thinker and as gullible a person as you could wish to find in a day's march. He may be a good chemist, geologist, or bacteriologist, but he is all too often a pretty poor citizen in a democratic country—thinking even more incoherently and emotively on questions of general interest than the man whose education stopped at the early age of fifteen or sixteen.'

As Professor Greig goes on to say, 'The truth may be unpleasant, but do not let us shy away from it for that reason. A generation which when it has reached maturity after passing through primary schools, secondary schools, and universities, persistently writes such down-at-heels English as we find in the specimens [cited by George Orwell in the already mentioned article on "Politics and the English Language" in *Horizon*, and in several from Professor Greig's own reading], is one whose education went wrong. Those of us who are trying to teach a generation that has not yet reached the maturity of Professor Laski [who, it must be admitted, wrote very bad English] ... are painfully conscious that the education we are giving it is no better, and perhaps worse—more frothy, more discrete, more incoherent. We cannot flatter ourselves that the output of woolly and incoherent thinkers is declining.'

That is a very serious charge. But it is not the only serious charge brought against twentieth-century English, whether the literature or—or to separate the inseparable—the language. There has, many say, been a decline in both; most of the doctors, however, hold out some hope—several of them hold out considerable hope—that the patients are already convalescent and may well be healthier and stronger than they had been for a very long time. That recovery, although indicated, has not yet been firmly established. To the harm done; to the writing and speaking of English, by speakers and writers upon political theory—mostly dogmatism parading as enlightenment—and upon psychology and, especially, psychiatry; we must add the much greater harm that could be done to English by the members of literary and artistic coteries. We must also admit that, so far, the harm has not been irremediable.

In John Hayward's shrewd pamphlet, *Prose Literature since 1939*, published in 1947 but, at almost every point, as pertinent to-day as it was then, we read that although the creed of 'giving people what they want' runs counter to a proper respect for literary values, yet, 'if literature is to continue to be a civilizing influence in society, it must do more than preserve a tradition; it must develop its capacities with the needs of the times' and learn how to control, or at the least to make itself respected by, the expanding market that those needs have evolved. If literature fails in this task, 'it will be reduced to the status of an art pursued for art's sake by isolated groups of writers, segregated from the world in their ivory towers and "private worlds" '. The amazing thing is that these seclusionists tend to think of themselves as cosmopolitans—nay, as Olympians set far above the dust and the dirt and the strife—whereas they are manifestly parochialists.

Such a 'decline into parochialism', although an ever-recurrent threat, has not yet become a serious danger to literature; the 'little reviews' that have flourished, on and off, ever since the war of 1914-1918, have so small a public, always 'high-brow' rather than possessed of first-rate minds, that they never inaugurate a trend; they merely express it in an exaggerated form, or when, usually in revolt or merely to attract attention, they attempt to set up a trend of their own, they again exaggerate and thus defeat their own ends, as *Horizon* did. Yet *Horizon*, edited by Cyril Connolly, and *New Writing*, edited by John Lehmann, performed, during the war of 1939-1945 and for several years after it, a splendid service to English literature, 'by maintaining intellectual relations with the Continent', for 'without these slender links with Continental thought a vital and vitalising source of strength might well have been lost to English literature for many years to come. For all the apparent insularity of the British people, their literature is indiscerptibly rooted in the European tradition. ... Those who have lately [1945-47] condemned ... an excess of Francophily in certain quarters would be better occupied in diagnosing its causes, which lie deep in the common origins of Western Civilization' (John Hayward).

The same critic has strongly upheld his salutary opinion that writers should not 'take sides' in the social revolution; that they can best serve the cause of mankind and civilization, of spirituality and morality, and of literature itself by recording, untendenciously, and by expressing, without bias and as well as they can, 'the drama of the human condition'. 'There was' (John Hayward maintains) 'enough of this kind of polemical writing in Britain during the 1930's to show that it is not on public platforms, any more than in ivory towers, that literature prospers.' He then rises to an eloquence far too rare in British criticism. 'The integrity of the individual writer', he says, 'can best be defended from all the forces currently arrayed against it, by an attitude of absolute intransigence towards the philistine and all his works. Not only in the immediate post-war era now over but during the years of man's painful spiritual recovery which lie ahead, such an attitude must be preserved if, out of disintegration, a scheme of values is to arise and out of disillusionment a dynamic faith in the power of the printed word to express the finest operations of human thought and sensibility.'

Still on the subject of trends in literature, I must briefly mention one that concerns language no less than literature; a trend manifest in that indissoluble link, style. By taking as their example Kipling's early, more journalistic prose and verse, instead of his mature, literary (yet no less vivid), thought-out, balanced, no longer fashionably bitter work, many writers of the 1890s and of the first quarter of the twentieth century allied themselves, most of them unthinkingly or imperceptively, with the better of the slick writers enlisted by the *Daily Mail* and thereby hastened the popularity of a 'modern' writing that possessed rather more numerous and perhaps more funda-mental faults than virtues, defects than merits. Dr G. Pratt Insh has pointed out that, 'working independently of the *Daily Mail* school of writers (for instance, G. W. Steevens), Kipling —the Kipling of *Plain Tales from the Hills*—had, in *The* Allahabad *Pioneer*, evolved a technique similar to that which was to be practised by "the Northcliffe School"; a technique intended for the delectation of readers in clubs and messes and for the itinerant and jaded palates of Indian railway bookstalls' (communication of 28 June 1950).

If there were influence, it issued from Kipling (*Plain Tales*, 1888; *Soldiers Three*, 1888, No. 1 of 'H. H. Wheeler & Co.'s Indian Railway Library'; and in verse: *Departmental Ditties*, 1886, and *Barrack-Room Ballads*, 1892) and flowed into the mind of Alfred Harmsworth, hence into the *Daily Mail* (May 1896). I cannot quite share Dr Insh's view that Kipling and the Northcliffe school exemplify just such another inde-pendent origin and activity as those exemplified in 'the inde-pendent approach to the theory of natural selection by Darwin in England and by Russell Wallace in the Moluccas': this sort of approach to writing may have been 'in the air', as such things often seem to be: but, no believer in parthenogenesis, I think that it was Kipling who put it there. Whoever the originator of this type of writing, the type had, by 1920 or so, passed from the fumbling grasp of authors too feeble to handle it into the deft, firm grasp of journalists, who had always—though sub-consciously—been aware that it was literature's, or Kipling's, gift to journalism.

Thus we arrive at the decline in 'English itself'; in the lan-guage, considered—so far as it can be considered—apart from literature and journalism. That very capable novelist and short-

story writer, Neil Bell, who, in his quiet way, is something of
a scholar, has, in response to my suggestion that a practising
writer's, a creative writer's, opinion upon the language he must
perforce use would be more valuable than that of any theorist,
sent me a letter (20 June 1950) in which he says this. 'To read
anything written in English between (say) 1880 and 1950 is to
feel that one is reading a "dead language": a language that has
at least come to the end of one of its lives or periods. All writers
in English are at present using a language that is worn out—
all the blood sucked out of it.

'But the language began to die, or, at any rate, to ail, long
before 1880. I should say that the first symptoms of this mortal
sickness began to be apparent round about the turn of the
previous century. It was a dying language when the middle-
aged Lamb, Hazlitt and Wordsworth and the young Tennyson and young Dickens were using it, and by the time Trollope
and Meredith came along, it was past saving and could only
linger on, mortally ill, until Kipling, Wells, G. B. Shaw,
Bennett, Galsworthy and down to our own time.

'One doesn't need to worry about what is happening to a
corpse, although, of course, one can hold a post-mortem upon
it.'

Yet even he, a vital writer, has to admit that written English
is, as he phrases it, 'incubating a new birth' and has, indeed,
been doing so ever since 1918 or thereabouts; he thinks that this
new birth or re-birth will take place during the decade 1950-59
and that the resultant literature, with its vehicle, language, may
prove to be no less vigorous and no less vivid than those of the
Elizabethan period. He further points to D. H. Lawrence,
James Joyce, T. S. Eliot as three of the most important heralds
of this period of renewed vigour, and, of the younger men,
names Dylan Thomas as a potential. Moreover, it is in barest
justice to Neil Bell that I add that, after stating his fresh and
independent views, he says, in the concluding paragraph of his
letter, 'All this being perhaps a mere bee in my bonnet, it is of
no use to you, unless you wish to invite derision and brick-
bats'. Only those who think that twentieth-century English
has not exhibited a dangerous valetudinarianism will throw

brick-bats and only the hasty and the crusty will deride an opinion expressed by an acute observer and unconventional thinker. Before cremation, one thrusts a needle into a corpse—to see whether it is not perhaps alive, after all. To reassure the pompous, I add that this is precisely what Neil Bell has done.

Taste and Fashion

This sectional sub-title is far too pretentious, for the section merely constitutes a breathing-space between the general trends and the particular influences: and some of the themes that are but glanced at, not treated, might—in one or two instances, at the cost of some violence—have been included among the trends or among the influences. But let us not make critical mountains out of the molehills of unavoidable arbitrariness.

Precisely as *Punch* has never been what once it was, so taste has never been what, in some golden age, it was—or is said to have been. Is there, however, any justification for a charge that, since the war of 1939-1945, has often been laid?

To the June, 1950, issue of *The Month*, M. André Simon contributes an excellent article on the decade 1939-1949. What he says about taste can fairly be applied to the entire period 1900-1950 or, at the least, to the years since *ca.* 1915. 'I cannot help being afraid,' he writes, 'that mass production will become universal on account of the stress of present economic conditions and that the standards of good taste will fall inevitably. The fact that the original handiwork of a gifted artist or skilled artisan must necessarily be dearer than mass-produced goods or shoddy imitations may be more of a limiting factor than when the cost of living was so much lower than it is now, but the loss of leisure and opportunities is an even greater handicap for the boys and girls who left school and college during the past two decades than the lack of spare cash. There is no great harm done when we ... go without that which is best; what is disastrous is not to *know* the bad from the good, and the greatest tragedy of all is not to *care*. There cannot be any hope where there is no desire to train one's taste, to recognize, to appreciate, to enjoy the slight yet all-important differences between fair and fine, good and great. Taste cannot be bought over the counter. ... What does matter is that the masses of the people are losing their power of appreciation as well as the power to think for themselves.'

Towards the end of his entertaining, instructive and uncomfortably shrewd article, André Simon remarks on the fact that recently a minister of the Crown 'declared that Taste was merely one of the obsolete privileges of the idle rich'. The day after this fatuous statement was made, a Socialist friend of mine exclaimed, 'The man's a moron'; I could not help thinking that he was fulsomely overrating the man's mental equipment. But to return to M. Simon. 'What a libel on the poor! Taste, talent and genius, feeling and understanding are the common heritage of rich and poor alike, and since there always has been a great many more poor than rich in the world, it is by no means surprising that in all lands and times many more poets, artists and men of genius were born poor than rich. Taste cannot be bought, but it can be killed by the planners planning mediocrity for all.'

Concomitant with a decline in taste—or perhaps only so radical a change that we are shocked into so describing it—has gone a decline, or at the lowest a disquieting change, in culture. Culture (by the way, a continuing process, not a 'Thank heaven, we've got it' state) is apparently more widely diffused now than it was in 1900, but it is also shallower in the lustrum 1946-1950 than it was in (say) the lustrum 1910-1914. In fairness to ourselves, however, it should be said that the wars of 1914-1918 and 1939-1945, to which must be added the economic depression of late 1929-1933, overlapped by the uneasiness slowly, sinisterly creeping over the body politic of Europe from the very day, January the 30th, 1933, Hitler became Chancellor—that those wars and that distress and that mounting tension have so unsettled Britain and France and Belgium, and Germany too, that culture perhaps inevitably declined from the (in the main) serene profundity of the lustrum ending at Sarajevo on June the 28th, 1914. That sort of thing is disturbing.

But in 1914 the writers of belles-lettres, especially of essays, were reluctantly beginning to admit what their publishers had, perhaps a year earlier, begun to suspect: public taste was moving away from belles-lettres in general and from the essay in particular. By 1919 or 1920, the recession had become a retreat; by 1931 or 1932, that retreat was a rout. In a letter written shortly before his death in 1938, E. V. Lucas asked me whether I had noticed 'the very odd fact that an essayist can have a considerable reputation on the strength of an average sale, per book, of two or three thousand copies'. He deplored the decline of the essay and spoke of belles-lettres being 'as extinct as the dodo'. That, as he himself admitted, was an exaggeration. Nevertheless, if in the years 1948-50 a volume of essays sold 3000 copies, the publishers (and the booksellers) thought it 'quite successful'.

The great age of the English essay—at least, after the Lamb, Hazlitt, Leigh Hunt period—was *ca.* 1890-1912. Leading into and continuing in that period were such essayists as Robert Louis Stevenson, Oscar Wilde, Andrew Lang, Augustine Birrell, Vernon Lee; leading out of it was such an essayist as E. V. Lucas; among the post-1920 essayists in the true line, there have been W. R. Inge, Robert Lynd, C. E. Montague, George Gordon, Rose Macaulay, Virginia Woolf, and Ivor Brown, to name seven representative exponents. Within the great period, 1890-1912, fall many of the best-known essays of such writers (in addition to those already named) as Havelock Ellis, Edmund Gosse, Max Beerbohm, A. C. Benson, G. K. Chesterton, Hilaire Belloc.

Space lacks for a linguistic analysis of the works by these and other essayists: yet, since those who have read them do not need the analysis and to those who have not read them the analysis would mean nothing, the lack hardly matters. The following imperfect yet not, I believe, misleading list of some of the most important volumes of essays published since about 1890, will convey to the knowledgeable some idea of the changes that have affected this delightful form—and perhaps even of several of the forces that lay behind those changes.

1890 *The New Spirit*, Havelock Ellis.

1891 *Gossip in a Library*, Edmund Gosse.
      Views and Reviews, W. E. Henley.
      Diary of a Pilgrimage, and Six Essays, Jerome K Jerome.
      Essays in Little, Andrew Lang.

1892 *Science in Arcady*, Grant Allen.
      Res Judicatae, Augustine Birrell.
      Studies at Leisure, W. L. Courtney.
      Miscellaneous Essays, George Saintsbury.

1892-96 *Eighteenth Century Vignettes*, Austin Dobson.

1893 *Questions at Issue*, Edmund Gosse.
      Pagan Papers, Kenneth Grahame.
      An Agnostic's Apology, Leslie Stephen.

1894 *Essays about Men, Women and Books*, A Birrell.
      Intentions, Oscar Wilde.

ca. 1894-1904 essays and studies by Lafcadio Hearn.

1895 *Essays*, A. C. Benson.
      Essays and Studies, J. Churton Collins.
      Adventures in Criticism, A. Quiller-Couch.
      Corrected Impressions, G. Saintsbury.

1896 *The Works of Max Beerbohm* (seven essays).
      Scholar Gipsies, John Buchan.
      Critical Kit-Kats, Edmund Gosse.
      Father Archangel, R. B. Cunninghame Graham.
      The Colour of Life, Alice Meynell.

1897 *Limbo*, Vernon Lee.
      [*The Treasure of the Humble*, Maeterlinck.]

1898 *Affirmations*, Havelock Ellis.
      The Second Thoughts of an Idle Fellow, Jerome K. Jerome.
      London Impressions, Alice Meynell.

1899 *More*, Max Beerbohm.
 A Paladin of Philanthropy, Austin Dobson.
 The Decay of Sensibility, Stephen Gwynn.
 The Spirit of Place, Alice Meynell.
 Frames of Mind, A. B. Walkley.

1901 *The Defendant*, G. K. Chesterton.
 Essays of an Ex-Librarian, Richard Garnett.
 The Plea of Pan, H. W. Nevinson.

1902 *Twelve Types*, G. K. Chesterton.
 Letters from John Chinaman, Lowes Dickinson.
 [*The Buried Temple*, Maeterlinck.]
 The Household of Faith, G. W. E. Russell.
 Horae Solitariae, Edward Thomas.

1903 *Ideas of Good and Evil*, W. B. Yeats.

1904 *Essays on Life, Art and Science*, Samuel Butler.
 Hortus Vitae, Vernon Lee.

1905 *In the Name of the Bodleian*, A. Birrell.
 Heretics, G. K. Chesterton.
 Idle Ideas, Jerome K. Jerome.
 Adventures among Books, Andrew Lang.
 The Enchanted Woods, Vernon Lee.
 Essays on the Art of Writing and *Essays of Travel*, R. L.
 Stevenson.

1906 *Hills and the Sea*, Hilaire Belloc.
 From a College Window, A. C. Benson.
 Progress, R. B. Cunninghame Graham.
 Fireside and Sunshine, E. V. Lucas.
 Some Irish Essays, G. W. Russell ('A.E.').

1907 *Character and Comedy*, E. V. Lucas.
 Discoveries, W. B. Yeats.

1908 *On Nothing*, Hilaire Belloc.
 Some Eighteenth Century Byways, John Buchan.
 All Things Considered, G. K. Chesterton.
 From a Hertfordshire Cottage, W. Beach Thomas.

1909 *The Hand of God*, Grant Allen.
    Yet Again, Max Beerbohm.
    On Everything, Hilaire Belloc.
    Tremendous Trifles, G. K. Chesterton.
    Laurus Nobilis, Vernon Lee.
    One Day and Another, E. V. Lucas.
    Ceres' Runaway and Other Essays, Alice Meynell.
    Essays in Freedom, H. W. Nevinson.
    Memory Harbour, Filson Young.

1910 *On Something*, Hilaire Belloc.
    The Silent Isle, A. C. Benson.
    Alarms and Discursions, G. K. Chesterton.
    Old Kensington Palace, Austin Dobson.
    Essays, Edward Dowden.
    Attitudes and Avowals, Richard Le Gallienne.
    Philosophical Essays (in 1818, renamed *Mysticism and Logic*),
      Bertrand Russell.

1911 *First and Last*, Hilaire Belloc.
    Romance and Reality, Holbrook Jackson.
    Old Lamps for New, E. V. Lucas.

1912 *This, That and the Other*, Hilaire Belloc.
    Essays, Augustine Birrell.
    A Miscellany of Men, G. K. Chesterton.
    Simplicity and Tolstoy, G. K. Chesterton.
    Posthumous Essays, J. Churton Collins.
    The Inn of Tranquillity, John Galsworthy.
    The Day Before Yesterday, Richard Middleton.
    Selected Essays, G. W. E. Russell.
    Walking Essays, A. Hugh Sidgwick.
    Letters from Solitude, Filson Young.

1912-1913 *Collected Essays*, Edmund Gosse.

1912-1946 essays upon words, Ernest Weekley—especially:
    The Romance of Words, 1912.
    The Romance of Names, 1914.
    Adjectives, 1930.
    Words Ancient and Modern, 1946.

1913 *Modern Grub Street*, A. St John Adcock.
Loiterer's Harvest, E. V. Lucas.
Essays in Rebellion, H. W. Nevinson.
Clio and Other Essays, G. M. Trevelyan.
Collected Literary Essays, A. W. Verrall.

1914 *Southward Ho!*, Holbrook Jackson.
The Tower of Mirrors, Vernon Lee.
Essays, Alice Meynell.

1914-1923 *Impressions and Comments*, 3 series, Havelock Ellis.

1915 *Escape and Other Essays*, A. C. Benson.
The Vanishing Road, R. Le Gallienne.
The Book of This and That, Robert Lynd.
Imaginations and Reveries, 'A.E.' (G. W. Russell).
New Leaves, Filson Young.

1916 *Essays in War-Time*, Havelock Ellis.
A Sheaf, John Galsworthy.
Pebbles on the Shore, A. G. Gardiner.
Essays and Literary Studies, Stephen Leacock.
Cloud and Silver, E. V. Lucas.
Suspended Judgments, J. C. Powys.
Slings and Arrows, Edwin Pugh.
Men of Letters, Dixon Scott.

1917 *Shrewsbury Fables*, C. A. Alington.
Books and Persons, Arnold Bennett.
A Number of Things, Dixon Scott.

1918 *Essays and Addresses*, Viscount Bryce.
Leaves in the Wind, A. G. Gardiner.
For Second Reading, Stephen Gwynn.
'Twixt Eagle and Dove, E. V. Lucas.
Old Junk, H. M. Tomlinson.

1919 *Enjoying Life*, W. N. Barbellion.
Unhappy Far-off Things, Lord Dunsany.
Another Sheaf, John Galsworthy.
Some Diversions, Edmund Gosse.

1919 contd. *Outspoken Essays*, W. R. Inge.
The Phantom Journal, E. V. Lucas.
Not That It Matters, A. A. Milne.
The Cutting of an Agate, W. B. Yeats.

1919-1927 essays (art—literature—life), Arthur Clutton-Brock.

1920 *And Even Now*, Max Beerbohm.
The Uses of Diversity, G. K. Chesterton.
Sir Roger de Coverley, James Frazer.
Windfalls, A. G. Gardiner.
If I May, A. A. Milne.
The Evolution of an Intellectual, R. Middleton Murry.
About Many Things, Grace Rhys.
Little Essays, George Santayana.
Life and Letters, J. C. Squire.

[1920-1950 volumes of essays by Christopher Morley, e.g.:
Pipefuls, 1920.
Off the Deep End, 1928.
Streamlines, 1936.
The Ironing Board, 1950.]

1921 *Later Essays*, Austin Dobson.
Wiltshire Essays, Maurice Hewlett.
Light Articles Only, A. P. Herbert.
The Second Person Singular, Alice Meynell.
Essays and Addresses, Gilbert Murray.
The Pleasures of Ignorance, Robert Lynd.
Pastiche and Prejudice, A. B. Walkley.

1922 *Little Essays of Love and Virtue*, Havelock Ellis.
Friday Nights, Edward Garnett.
Extemporary Essays, M. Hewlett.
Occasions, Holbrook Jackson.
Outspoken Essays, 2nd Series, W. R. Inge.
Giving and Receiving, E. V. Lucas.
Solomon in All His Glory, Robert Lynd.
Disenchantment, C. E. Montague.
Countries of the Mind, R. Middleton Murry.
Soliloquies in England, G. Santayana.
Books and Characters, Lytton Strachey.
Cloud Castle, Edward Thomas.

1922 many true essays in his books on cricket, Neville Cardus.

1923 *On*, Hilaire Belloc.
    On the Margin, Aldous Huxley.
    Essays of a Biologist, Julian Huxley.
    The Blue Lion, Robert Lynd.
    Pencillings, R. Middleton Murry.
    I for One, J. B. Priestley.
    Some Authors, Walter Alexander Raleigh.
    The Café Royal, Arthur Symons.
    Dramatis Personae, Arthur Symons.
    More Prejudice, A. B. Walkley.
    Essays, W. B. Yeats.

1923-1924 *Collected Essays*, G. Saintsbury.

1924 *Day In and Day Out*, A. D. Barron.
    More Obiter Dicta, Augustine Birrell.
    English Portraits and Essays, John Freeman.
    Many Furrows, A. G. Gardiner.
    Last Essays, M. Hewlett.
    Encounters and Diversions, E. V. Lucas.
    The Right Place, C. E. Montague.
    Discoveries, R. Middleton Murry.
    Thirteen Worthies, Llewellyn Powys.
    Grub Street Nights, J. C. Squire.
    Unscientific Essays, F. Wood Jones.

1925 *The Muse in Council*, John Drinkwater.
    Along the Road, Aldous Huxley.
    Collected Essays, W. P. Ker.
    Reflections on the Death of a Porcupine, D. H. Lawrence.
    The Golden Keys, Vernon Lee.
    The Money Box, Robert Lynd.
    A Casual Commentary, Rose Macaulay.
    Still More Prejudice, A. B. Walkley.
    The Common Reader, Virginia Woolf.

1926 *Last Essays*, Joseph Conrad.
    A Book for Bookmen, John Drinkwater.

1926 contd. *The Return to the Cabbage*, Gerald Gould.
  Falloden Papers, Viscount Grey.
  Essays in Popular Science, Julian Huxley.
  Lay Thoughts of a Dean, W. R. Inge.
  Gorgeous Times, E. V. Knox.
  The Orange Tree, Robert Lynd.
  Catchwords and Claptrap, Rose Macaulay.

1927 *The Gorgon's Head*, James Frazer.
  Castles in Spain, John Galsworthy.
  Companionable Books, George Gordon.
  Leaves and Fruit, Edmund Gosse.
  Proper Studies, Aldous Huxley.
  The Goldfish, Robert Lynd.
  A Fronded Isle, E. V. Lucas.
  Open House, J. B. Priestley.
  Life at the Mermaid, J. C. Squire.

1928 *The Savour of Life*, Arnold Bennett.
  Generally Speaking, G. K. Chesterton.
  Essays in Satire, Ronald Knox.
  Out of the Blue, E. V. Lucas.
  The Green Man, Robert Lynd.
  Things to Come, R. Middleton Murry.
  Apes and Angels, J. B. Priestley.
  Sceptical Essays, Bertrand Russell.

1929 *A Miscellany*, A. C. Bradley.
  Now on View, Ivor Brown.
  The Thing, G. K. Chesterton.
  Some Comparative Values, H. W. Fowler.
  Do As You Will, Aldous Huxley.
  This Other Eden, E. V. Knox.
  On Getting There, Ronald Knox.
  By Way of Introduction, A. A. Milne.
  The Heritage of Man, H. J. Massingham.
  The Opalescent Parrot, Alfred Noyes.
  Casual Observations, Lord Ponsonby.
  The Balconinny, J. B. Priestley.
  The Sense of Glory, Herbert Read.
  The Aims of Education, and Other Essays, A. N. Whitehead.

1930 *Fanfare*, John Brophy.
Brown Studies, Ivor Brown.
Come to Think of It, G. K. Chesterton.
Second Shots, Bernard Darwin.
Things That Annoy Me, E. V. Knox.
Traveller's Luck, E. V. Lucas.
It's a Fine World, Robert Lynd.
A Book of Grace, Grace Rhys.
Essays and Addresses, (Sir) John Ross.

1931 *All is Grist*, G. K. Chesterton.
More Essays of Love and Virtue, Havelock Ellis.
Garnered Sheaves, James Frazer.
All about Women, Gerald Gould.
Music at Night, Aldous Huxley.
Rain, Rain, Go to Spain, Robert Lynd.
Portraits, Desmond MacCarthy.
Portraits in Miniature, Lytton Strachey.
Out of Soundings, H. M. Tomlinson.

1932 *Lost Lectures*, Maurice Baring.
The Face of England, Edmund Blunden.
Sidelights, G. K. Chesterton.
The Inequality of Man, J. B. S. Haldane.
Lemon Verbena, E. V. Lucas.
Winters of Content, Osbert Sitwell.
The Common Reader, 2nd Series, Virginia Woolf.

1933 '*All I Survey*', G. K. Chesterton.
Refuge from Nightmare, Gerald Gould.
Prefaces and Essays, G. Saintsbury.
Adventures of Ideas, A. N. Whitehead.

1934 *The Mind's Eye*, Edmund Blunden.
I Commit to the Flames, Ivor Brown.
Avowals and Denials, G. K. Chesterton.
Unscientific Excursions, F. Wood Jones.
Both Sides of the Road, Robert Lynd.
Earth Memories, Llewellyn Powys.

1935 *Artifex*, Richard Aldington.
    Collected Essays, F. H. Bradley.
    Men and Deeds, John Buchan.
    Round about England, S. P. B. Mais.
    Personal Pleasures, Rose Macaulay.
    Dorset Essays, Llewellyn Powys.
    In Praise of Idleness, Bertrand Russell.
    Reflections and Memories, J. C. Squire.
    Dramatis Personae, W. B. Yeats.

1936 *As I Was Saying*, G. K. Chesterton.
    Rubs of the Green, Bernard Darwin.
    From Rousseau to Proust, Havelock Ellis.
    Mirages, R. B. Cunninghame Graham.
    The Olive Tree, Aldous Huxley.
    Only the Other Day, E. V. Lucas.
    I Tremble to Think, Robert Lynd.
    Between the Wars, H. W. Nevinson.

1937 *Traveller's Rest*, Philip Gosse.
    Sip! Swallow!, A. P. Herbert.
    All of a Piece, E. V. Lucas.
    In Defence of Pink, Robert Lynd.
    Rats in the Sacristy, Llewellyn Powys.
    Somerset Essays, Llewellyn Powys.
    Essays ... 1931 to 1936, W. B. Yeats.

1938 *Fond Opinions*, Stephen Gwynn.
    Our Present Discontents, W. R. Inge.
    The Printing of Books, Holbrook Jackson.

1939 *Searchlights and Nightingales*, Robert Lynd.

1940 *Pleasures and Speculations*, W. De La Mare.
    Too Much College, Stephen Leacock.
    Drama, Desmond MacCarthy.
    Chiltern Country, H. J. Massingham.
    Stoic, Christian and Humanist, Gilbert Murray.
    Inside the Whale, George Orwell.
    Postscripts, J. B. Priestley.
    New Lamps and Ancient Lights, J. A. Spender.

1941 *The Silence of the Sea*, Hilaire Belloc.
Points of View, T. S. Eliot.
Life's Little Oddities, Robert Lynd.

1942 *In the Heart of the Country*, H. E. Bates.
Preludes and Studies, Alan Dent.
Field Fellowship, H. J. Massingham.
In My Good Books, V. S. Pritchett.
Life and the Poet, Stephen Spender.
The Death of the Moth, Virginia Woolf.

1942-1950 the *Word* series (six titles), Ivor Brown.

1943 *Country Life*, H. E. Bates.
The Politics of the Unpolitical, Herbert Read.

1944 *Reflections in a Mirror*, Charles Morgan.

1945 *The Condemned Playground*, Cyril Connolly.
Things One Hears, Robert Lynd.
World Still There, John Pudney.
A Coat of Many Colours, Herbert Read.

1946 *Mainly on the Air*, Max Beerbohm.
A Glimpse from a Watch Tower, Lord Dunsany.
The Discipline of Letters, and Other Essays, George Gordon.
The Reading of Books, Holbrook Jackson.
Reflections in a Mirror, 2nd Series, Charles Morgan.
Critical Essays, George Orwell.

1947 *More Companionable Books*, George Gordon.
Obstinate Cymric, J. C. Powys.
Swiss Essays, Llewellyn Powys.
Seven Essays, George Sampson.
The Moment, Virginia Woolf.

1948 *Every Idle Dream*, Bernard Darwin.
The End of an Age, W. R. Inge.
Looking Before and After, R. Middleton Murry.
Daylight and Champaign, G. M. Young.

1949 *Essays upon Literature and Society*, Edwin Muir.
     Delight, J. B. Priestley.
     Inclinations, Edward Sackville-West.
     An Autobiography, and Other Essays, G. M. Trevelyan.

1950 *Genius Loci*, H. W. Garrod.
     Shooting an Elephant, George Orwell.
     Unpopular Essays, Bernard Russell.
     A Last Vintage, G. Saintsbury.
     The Captain's Death Bed, Virginia Woolf.
     Last Essays, G. M. Young.

A close scrutiny of that merely representative list will, to those who have read at least one relevant volume of every author mentioned, indicate several noteworthy facts, the first being that no other branch of belles-lettres is so revelatory of the spirit of an age as is the essay. Apart from autobiography, which nearly always comes so long after the years concerned that it cannot hold a contemporaneous mirror to the age, the essay is the most intimate form of literature. In some ways, the essay is an even more intimate form than autobiography, for in the latter the author, although dealing with incidents, feelings, thoughts more personal and more private, is, at the same time, presenting them in a special light—usually a light favourable to himself. The autobiographer assumes a person-ality that is genuine but far from complete: to the world he shows a portrait touched up by the artist that is himself: to the National Gallery he loans a picture: and, to employ a metaphor that has become fashionable in erudite circles, he appears to his readers in a persona and thus shows not a face but a mask, as though he were an actor in a drama presented to an audience in ancient Athens. To change the metaphor: from behind that mask, as it were from behind a smoke-screen, he enfilades the reading public with subtle propaganda, the relentless propa-ganda of insatiable self. The essayist, on the other hand, is able, in talking of other persons and of things, to talk unreservedly of himself; usually by indirection, often by allusion.

The essay reflects, if not from day to day—although, in the

'fourth leaders' of *The Times*, it virtually does even that*—
then, at least, from week to week†, the vagaries and variations
of fashion and taste, the changes and developments in the
ethical, intellectual, aesthetic, as well as in the sociological life
of a people.

Soon after its acclimatization in Britain, this Gallic form
became thoroughly British or, at the lowest valuation, as truly
British as it had been French: indeed, in the eighteenth-
twentieth centuries, the essay has flourished more richly and
more personally in Britain than ever it has done in France.
What the letter is to private life, the essay is to public life; this
personalism has been a characteristic of the essay ever since
Steele (more than Addison) in his insouciant yet penetrating
Irish way decided that the Montaigne type of essay was far too
formal for those arch-individualists, his fellow Britons.

Any changes in so individualistic, so British a form as the
essay are important; so also, on another plane, is the movement
away from the essay and from belles-lettres as a whole. The
latter trend was caused, in part, by the popularity of such
popular magazines as *The Strand* and *The Grand*, *Pearson's* and
The Windsor; in part by the excitations offered by the Harmsworth Press; in part by the seductions, both of the motor-car
and other rapid transport and of the cinema—a seductiveness
merely aggravated, when most of the harm had already been
done, by the charms of the radio; in larger part, by that international unease which, culminating tragically in 1914, had been
transformed into an unrest becoming increasingly less vague
from within a few months of the death, on 6 May 1910, of
'Edward the Peacemaker'—'the Uncle of Europe'—King
Edward the Seventh.

The list of publications clearly shows that, although the
number of volumes of essays did not begin to decrease until
ca. 1940, the proportion of essay-volumes dealing with science,
morals, religion, philosophy, politics and sociology has, ever
since *ca.* 1918, been on the increase: the volumes of general
essays—in many ways, the general essay constitutes the essen-

* Compare J. M. W. Mackail's *Modern Essays, Reprinted from Leading Articles in
'The Times'*, 1915, and Oswald Barron's title, *Day in and Day Out*, 1924.
† For instance, the essays by 'Stet' (T. Earle Welby) and 'Y.Y.' (Robert Lynd).

tial form of the genre—have been numerically on the decrease, especially since 1940, presumably because the public taste for them has waned.

In *ca.* 1913, sales began to diminish; by 1931, they had very considerably diminished. In the public libraries, readers have, since 1918, borrowed volumes of essays less than they did before 1914. During the war of 1939-1945, and for a year or so after it, essays regained something of their popularity, but only because there was a dearth of new reading matter; by 1950, essays were almost as little read as they had been in 1939. That 'almost' may be indicative of some slight revival of a taste for something more fortifying, more durable, but also more aesthetic than the frothy utopias of the planners, the ephemeralities of the political theorists forced to shift from one hastily improvised position to another as world-event after world-event proves them catastrophically wrong.

The changes within the essay are peculiarly important, not merely for the essay itself but also for belles-lettres in general, hence for the entire body of literature. These changes do, in the fact, constitute changes of fashion; changes of taste; changes of the national mind: changes of the spirit, both national and international. What the essayists think to-day, the world will think to-morrow. Space lacks for a thoroughgoing examination; the few points mentioned in the ensuing paragraphs would seem to form some of the more obvious changes that have gradually taken place within the essay during the twentieth century. To gain a clear picture, one has to think somewhat exaggeratively in terms of a comparison of the types of essay prevalent in (say) 1900 and those apparently prevalent in (say) 1950. To every generalization, I can think of a not unimportant modification; for almost every forward step, there is a half-step backwards: for instance, essays published since the war of 1939-1945 have, in the main, lacked the light, deft touch of the Lucas-Lynd 'school'. (It is worth remembering that E. V. Lucas anticipated the 'tremendous trifle' essays of G. K. Chesterton, who, soon after 1909, passed to tremendous imponderables; Robert Lynd wrote in the Lucas tradition.) Perhaps the most obvious development in the essay is the very considerable widening of the scope, whether in form or in subject-matter. The latter extension has inevitably enlarged the vocabulary felt to be permissible in this form of writing, a result that will be considered later.

Despite that widening of scope, essays have tended to become much shorter. Without going so far back as Lamb and Hazlitt, one has only to think of Swinburne, Pater, John Addington Symonds, in whose day such essays as the shorter ones of Chesterton, Belloc, Lucas and Lynd were unknown. Since *ca.* 1912, the longer form has been employed only for the serious, formal essay upon religion, morals, philosophy, literary criticism and aesthetics.

The aesthetic essay so common in Pater, John Addington Symonds, Vernon Lee, A. C. Benson, Arthur Symons, has become a rarity. Essays on art in general and on aesthetics in particular tend nowadays to be written for the artistic public only; in the period 1870-1910, they were written for the general intelligent or perhaps the cultured-educated; in the 1920s Clutton-Brock formed something of an exception.

Connected with the lessening frequency and acceptability of the aesthetic essay is the decline in the literary essay, now almost entirely confined to the literary periodicals; at the present day, volumes of literary essays are, with a few exceptions, read only by those who are either professionally or scholastically concerned with the study of literature. But more important is this: that, except in specialist periodicals or specialist volumes, the treatment of all subjects has become less and less literary; of all subjects whatsoever, whether it be Proust or patience or picnics, Kafka or kangaroos, Dickens or door-knobs, Vermeer or vermilion boxes, yogi or Yokohama, salons or salt-cellars. The treatment is also less aesthetic.

And vastly less soulful and pompous, less solemn and portentous. Compare the essays of A. C. Benson, at his essayist's best during the first decade, with those of E. V. Lucas, Robert Lynd, Rose Macaulay, Ivor Brown. Admittedly, Benson tended to over-moralize his subjects and was therefore something of an anachronism even in his own day: unlike Chesterton and Belloc, Lucas and Lynd, Benson failed to profit by the

Arielistic example of Max Beerbohm. Compare Benson with C. E. Montague, another serious essayist, and you immediately notice the lightness of touch displayed by the latter when he was dealing with matters far more urgent and spirit-daunting than any that Benson handled.

This lightening of the heavy touch until the heaviness has almost disappeared does not result from the lightening of the subjects themselves, as not only Montague but Chesterton before him and the brothers Huxley after him have shown. Nor is it merely a matter of 'playing everything down' by refusing to take it seriously (an attitude far more tedious than seriousness) or, in particular, by treating it whimsically: many subjects have been made lighter by a lighter treatment, it is true, but lightness has often been achieved by another means, a process effected by aeration and illumination: whereas certain subjects have become fresher by being less stuffily treated, others have become lighter by becoming *lighter*.

Whimsicality has perhaps been overdone since, and as a result of, those volumes of Max Beerbohm's essays which appeared in 1896 and 1899. Although Lamb much, Steele a little, had employed whimsicality in their essays, yet Max Beerbohm it was who introduced whimsicality, as the primary emotional ingredient, into the recipe of the essay; Chesterton seized upon it and transformed it by a pyrotechnic virtuosity and alchemy of his own; Belloc gave it a piquant twist; Lucas used it sparingly; Lynd somewhat overused it.

Partly resulting from the lightening of the subjects and partly from the lessening of the length, general essays have tended to become more topical (not necessarily ephemeral) and more sketchy. Like the short story, the essay has tended to borrow more and more from the sketch, both in manner and in matter. Yet it has remained, in intention and in effect, the essay: it has, in widening its range and in becoming more tolerant, lost nothing of its character, none of its virtue.

In short, the general essay has become more personal, both in the choice of subjects and in the treatment of whatever the subject chosen. The vocations and invocations of even the humblest, the little everyday events, the trivial domestic objects and occurrences, the features of town and of country life, 'the common lot' seen from a personal angle: such subjects as these, comparatively rare even in Lamb and Leigh Hunt, have become 'common form'. Domestic familiarities owe their very noticeable popularity in the twentieth century essay to E. V. Lucas more than to any other writer. Did he not, so early as 1900, bring out his *Domesticities*, engagingly sub-titled 'A Little Book of Household Impressions'? Perhaps not strictly essays, they were yet annunciatory of the many charming domestic examples within the considerable corpus of his work in this genre. Reading the less formal of the twentieth century essayists—of the notable formalists, only Charles Morgan and Osbert Sitwell remain active—we share their confidences and are modestly, yet not too shyly, asked to applaud their confidence.

One apparently minor point may in reality be rather import-ant. There has, since the First World War, been an increase in the number of essays dealing with the country and the country-man. This movement was led by that true Englishman, Maurice Hewlett, and he has been ably succeeded by such writers as Edmund Blunden, H. J. Massingham, and J. C. and Llewellyn Powys; an earlier practitioner was Edward Thomas. All these writers owe something to W. H. Hudson and, also to Richard Jefferies—but in matter, not in form.

From this far too short and much too unsystematic appraise-ment of the modern essay, there should, by implication, have emerged an idea, vaguely edged yet clearly and firmly cored, of the language in which they have been—must, indeed, have been—written. Into the vocabulary of the essayists has crept almost every word and phrase that, discoverable in such a dictionary as 'The Concise Oxford' or 'Chambers's 20th Century' or 'The American College Dictionary', is neither technical (or scientific) nor slangy (or dialectal). Or if it hasn't, it well could have, done so. On the whole, the style has become less formal, less—in the intention, at least—imposing, less impressive and less literary. It has also become less architectural, less marmoreal. Sentence-structure has become simpler. Although the resources at the disposal of the essayists have been enriched, yet—apart from extent of vocabulary—their language is less rich; it is less ornate, less elaborate, with fewer patches that are purple. Perhaps the hypothetical Everyman reads essays as rarely now as ever he did: yet if he should wish to read them, he could do so much more easily and much more pleasurably than in the days before Max Beerbohm airily persiflaged the essay out of its too frequent solemnity and its insistent gravity, and rendered it light and amusing, yet without the sometimes excessively paradoxical effect and the artificial atmosphere that characterize the kind of essay affected by Oscar Wilde. In the essay, that former stronghold of literary English, the gap between literary English and the vernacular has considerably decreased.

The main trends in dramatic literature, in all non-dramatic poetry and in the novel have already been sufficiently treated in the opening chapter, 'Literary English'. There remain only two or three 'sectional' trends—literary fashions—to be mentioned in respect of the novel.

Joyce's *Ulysses*, 1922, originated the stream-of-consciousness* novels and stories of such writers as Dorothy Richardson and Virginia Woolf. Without being superseded, it has, in so far as it is (as it was originally) a fashion, been followed by the psychiatric novel, little practised in England before the American psychologist and writer, C. Daly King (author of *The Psychology of Consciousness*, 1932) published his three *Obelists* 'thrillers' in 1932-35 and several others during the next five years. Charles Daly King was succeeded in Britain by Nigel Balchin, notably in *Mine Own Executioner*, 1945, and in the U.S.A. by John Franklin Bardin, beginning with *The Deadly Percheron*, 1946. The methods of Freud have been experimented with: accelerated for speed-lovers, modified for the squeamish, and simplified for those readers who prefer the reach-me-downs of the circulating-library shelves. The result is—the better the psychiatry, the worse the novel, and, conversely, the better the novel, the worse the psychiatry. The

* Mr J. Isaacs, one of the very few genuine polymaths left in Britain after the death of Edward Bensly in 1939, tells me that the phrase has been adopted from William James's *The Principles of Psychology*.

genre of the psychiatric novel has yet to evolve a satisfactory *modus operandi*.

As a fashion, the war-novel is both earlier and later than the stream-of-consciousness novel. The Boer War produced very few novels; the War of 1914-1918, many. Yet only a few novels dealing with 1914-1918 appeared until A. H. Wheen's capable translation of Erich Remarque's *All Quiet on the Western Front* came out in March, 1927, to release a spate of war novels; by early October the spate had become a trickle; the last good war novel appeared in January 1930—Frederic Manning's *Her Privates We*, an abridgement (and expurgation) of *The Middle Parts of Fortune*, published in a limited edition late in 1929. These war novels—like the war memoirs, of a popularity less transient than that of the novels—brought into rather common use a few important 'Anglo-Saxon' words hitherto confined to low society and familiarized the general public with numerous military terms. The struggle of 1939-1945 has been slow to produce war novels, for the same reason as that of 1914-1918 had been: people no longer wish to read about war. So far, only one truly notable English novel has appeared—Alexander Baron's *From the City, From the Plough*, 1948. On the other hand, there have appeared several very good memoirs, of which the best is the fascinatingly readable, entirely credible *Private Army*, 1950, by the incredible Vladimir Peniakoff, more widely known as 'Popski'. These books, fact or fiction, are, like the earlier war books, enriching the vocabulary of the public and renewing the manliness of writers.

During a period of thirty years, 1888-1917, Arthur Conan Doyle 'started something' that neither he nor others have been able to finish; not that the public wish them to finish anything so easy to digest. *His Last Bow*, appearing in 1917 and following the *Return*, 1913, concluded the titular *Sherlock Holmes* stories that had begun, in 1893, with the *Adventures* (these, as crime stories, being themselves preceded by *A Study in Scarlet*, 1888, and *The Sign of Four*, 1890). Despite a number of imitations, Doyle encountered no rival until, in 1913, E. C. Bentley—inventor of the clerihew—delighted the connoisseurs of 'crime' with *Trent's Last Case*, which for intricacy of plot and lucidity of style, has not since been surpassed. Doyle's and Bentley's ablest successor has been Dorothy Sayers, who held the criminal field from 1926 until 1937, when she retired into more serious work. Her ablest successor is 'Michael Innes', who continues the dynasty of writers specializing in the literary detective novel. Yet the literary detective novel, represented in America by 'S. S. van Dine' (†1939) and 'Ellery Queen', may be losing its fight to the tougher, more direct, more vernacular, yet brilliantly written stories of Raymond Chandler—to name the best of the novelists in this group—a writer rapidly becoming as highly regarded in Britain as in the U.S.A. The greatest contribution made, to language, by the detective-fiction writers, British and American, comes, not from the 'literary' but from the 'tough', for the latter (especially Chandler) employ such an economy of word and phrase, of syntax and composition, as points the way—or, at least, one of the chief ways—that writing is likely to follow during the next generation or so. Moreover, the best of those 'tough' writers employ many admirable words, and words soon to be adjudged admirable; one of their contributions to English consists in their selection and apposite employment of some terse and graphic words and phrases from the language of the underworld and from that of its fringes.

To pass from the English of the detective-story writers to that of literary criticism is to pass from the dock and the docks to the drawing-room and the 'den': from the language of violent action to that of exposition, analysis, appraisal: from the material to the intellectual and the spiritual. It is all very well to gibe at literary critics as 'auteurs manqués', few critics being that. The best critics of literature, as of art and music, are recorders and preservers, guides and fosterers of much of the intellectual and spiritual, hence also of the moral, life not only of a nation and of its individual members but also of that of the entire civilized world. Some of them exercise a direct, some an indirect influence upon their fellow-men. The language of the more dilettante, as of the more aesthetic, literary and artistic and musical critics, may be precious; that of all the best of these critics is at least precise; and that of a few critics is perceptive, sensitive and subtle. Their language, at its richest, embraces the terminology of religion and ethics, psychology and psychiatry, history and sociology, as well as of literature and all the arts: and when these critics are writing for the general public, an activity in which several of them display an uncanny skill, they are contributing to the life of English as a whole.

Such men as Gosse, Clutton-Brock, Chesterton, Lucas, Desmond MacCarthy, Charles Morgan, Michael Sadleir, Edwin Muir, Peter Quennell, John Betjeman, Ivor Brown, Daniel George, and one or two others have, by their reviews and articles and essays, laid English under a debt much heavier than I can here either assess or even indicate at all adequately. Art and music receive far less attention than literature. Nevertheless, the intelligent weeklies are doing more now than they were at the beginning of the century to keep their small but influential publics informed, and so are such dailies as *The Times*, the *Manchester Guardian*, *The Daily Telegraph*. More remarkable is the fact that several newspapers belonging to the 'popular Press' are, every week, publishing upon music and painting and, occasionally, sculpture, such articles as—their publics considered—are remarkably informative, intelligent and perceptive: the coating of anecdote and wisecrack often renders acceptable an astonishingly wholesome pill of sound historical and aesthetic information and salutary criticism. The agile writers of these 'popular' articles may ostensibly deride an art term or some technicality of music: and in so doing they 'put it across'.

Particular Influences

'... I like my illusions. The universe is pretty terrifying; and so's the world—getting more so every year. People talk about the law of the jungle, but the jungle is a haven of peace and mercy compared with Europe this last fifteen years. It seems to me that the only things that now make life and one's common humanity bearable are just those little graces, the spiritual adventures—call 'em what you like—which altogether weigh practically nothing in any material scale. Why shouldn't one believe in God and Santa Claus and the Moonlight Sonata if one chooses to? Perhaps it's sad to be the victim of sentimentality, but is it sadder than to be the victim of one's own disillusion?'

She said: 'We in Europe are the victims of the time. Isn't that it? Everyone learns from experience, and we have learned that the only way to survive is to see clearly, to believe in nothing but what we personally know, to accept nobody on trust, to work for ourselves alone and to take pleasure where we find it.'—

WINSTON GRAHAM, *Night Without Stars*, 1950.

There, as conversation in a novel and not as part of a philosophical dialogue; there, in the words of a competent, popular and unfailingly readable novelist; there, where 'I' has lost faith and recovered it and where 'She' is a young European woman of a faith lost but not yet quite recovered: there, we have a dual picture of 1935-1950, a period opening in a Europe overshadowed by vague fears of war and intersected by the War of 1939-1945 and closing in a Europe still disrupted by the effects of that war and obscurely threatened with another.

Our period begins soon after the commencement of the Boer War, which (1899-1902) was, by later standards, a small war and one that, on a global view, caused only minor economic distress and had few profound, no cataclysmic, results. The Boer War popularized a number of Dutch and aboriginal terms, some of them already familiar to soldiers and officials from the earlier troubles in South Africa. To specify those terms here is unnecessary, for they* have been recorded and commented upon in almost every history of English written since 1902.

More extensive, intense, protracted and numerically significant has been the influence of the War of 1914-1918. So was the war. Whereas the Boer War influence upon slang and colloquialism had been very slight, the influence of 1914-1918 was very considerable—yet hardly our concern, except perhaps for

---

* See especially the invaluable lists, of foreign words adopted by English, at the end of W. W. Skeat's *An Etymological Dictionary of English*, 4th edition, and Mary Serjeantson, *A History of Foreign Words in English*, 1935. Perhaps see also 'War as a Word-Maker' in my *Words at War: Words at Peace*, 1948.

'to *go west*', to die, to be destroyed or ruined, hence to get lost. A large number of Army, Navy and Air Force technicalities came into general use. German and French, whether by adoption or by adaptation or even by translation, bestowed upon English such terms as *according to plan* (*plangemäss*)—*the contemptible little army* (the German *verächtlich*)—*ersatz*, substitute—*frightfulness* (*Schrecklichkeit*)—*sunk without trace* (i.e. *spurlos*)—and *Kultur*, which soon acquired an extremely ironic connotation; and *camouflage*, *dégommé*, *embusqué*, *espionage* (French *espionnage*), *estaminet*, and several extremely expressive slang words and phrases.

Still more extensive, intense, protracted and numerically significant was the war of 1939-1945, of which one of the most distressing consequences has been the increase of violence in war's aftermath contrasted with war's germination, a consequence no less manifest in communities as a whole, even in nations, than in individuals, especially when violence is employed as a rapid and drastic solvent of problems that, by peaceful methods, would take weeks, months, perhaps years to solve. Before 1914 and, quite appreciably, even until 1939, Classical scholars would proudly and hopefully quote 'Let justice be done though the heavens fall' or its Latin original, *Fiat justitia et ruant coeli* (apparently a sixteenth century fusion of the Vulgate *Ruat coelum, fiat voluntas tua*, 'Even if the sky fall, Thy will be done', and St Augustine's (?) *Fiat ius et pereat mundus*, 'Let Justice be done, even though the world perish'); but since 1939—as much after 1945 as during the war—malefactors have done their utmost to bring down the very heavens to achieve their ends, which certainly are not those of justice either abstract or legal. The violence of commando tactics and the ruthlessness of all warfare, the wholesale destruction of property (including one's allies') and the trampling of rights, the flouting of privileges: these and similar routines of war have worked violence upon society's concepts of right and wrong, of decency and quietude, with the result that, in the absence of a sense of values, human life is, by some, little more respected than property either public or private. Brutalized by lawlessness, squalor, noise, an astonishing number of persons, female equally with male, have carried over into civilian life the stigmata of their moral disintegration: violence, dishonesty (especially if 'safe' or apparently so), slack or vicious habits, an almost complete lack of consideration for others, ill-based cynicism, deficient moral stamina, and other marks of the beast.

The general impact of the War of 1939-1945 upon literature, hence upon language, has been clearly and convincingly defined and described by John Hayward in *Prose Literature* (other than fiction) *since* 1939, a British Council pamphlet issued in 1947. In the excellent introductory chapter, he notes that for almost six years, during which 'Britain was involved in the greatest crisis of her history', 'the energies, mental and spiritual no less than physical, of the whole nation were conscripted for one end; and the activities and interests of every man and woman were directed, if not actually prescribed, by the overriding needs of the State'.

'Under conditions of total war,' John Hayward goes on to say, 'literary activity, like any other, is compelled more or less to serve the interests of the community. It is not only that restrictions are applied in the interests of national security; that both the expression of ideas and the statement of facts are liable to be censored or discouraged; that the raw material of books and the means for their production and distribution are inevitably limited by their diversion to more urgent purposes; and that large numbers of those engaged in the creation of books— writers, publishers, compositors, binders, and booksellers—are called away to serve with the armed forces or in the enormously expanded departments of the central government.'

Literature is affected in still other ways, for, as the same historian has so ably summarized the position, 'the entire aspect of the human situation is altered by the violent distortions of society in war time. The disruption of domestic life; the hardship caused by evacuation, requisitioning of houses, and the absence of the breadwinner; the reorganization of industry and commerce for war production and transport; the problems of displaced labour and long hours; the boredom of monotonous diet and inadequate recreation; the depression of the blackout, the strain of air-raids, actual or anticipated—are all instruments of this change. The climate of thought and sensibility must be profoundly affected by such disturbances in the conventional and accepted order of things.'

Yet several results of those regrettable circumstances were favourable to literature—and to spirituality. The public began to read. Members of all sections of the public; not merely, as before 1940, a few of the educated, the cultured, the incorrigibly curious.

Curiosity, the greatest of intellectual virtues, now spread even to those who, previously, had wished to know only the winner of the 3.30 or what was on at the cinema. The craving of the public for books, to quote John Hayward once more, 'was doubtless stimulated by the close confinement in which most people were forced to live; by lack of other forms of entertainment; and by the prolonged satisfaction a book can give compared with the brief enjoyment of a film or radio programme. But this craving, though largely adventitious, was still the expression of a real need for spiritual refreshment, mental exercise, and emotional relief. The publishers did their best to satisfy it.' A few of those who 'took up' reading during the war have remained readers, to their own gratification and advantage: they have gained a spiritual resource: something that, more than anything else and more than any generation before it, this generation gravely lacks and greatly needs.

Another result of the war of 1939-1945 is one that we have already noticed for the war of 1914-1918. 'War is a powerful excitant, perhaps the most rapidly effectual excitant, of language. It quickens and enlivens, enriches and invigorates language as much in the twentieth century as exploration and travel used to do in the sixteenth to seventeenth centuries. In the war of 1939-1945, as in that of 1914-1918, the fighting Services have experienced a far more extensive enrichment of their vocabularies, whether technical or unconventional, than the civilian or social services have experienced; many Service terms, however, soon find their way into the civilian vocabulary.' The very conditions of Service life (its manner, equipment, companionship, strange lands and customs) lead inevitably to 'a rejuvenation of language—to vividness—to picturesqueness—to vigour; language becomes youthful, energetic, adventurous.'*

Among the words and phrases either occasioned or, at the least, popularized by the War of 1939-1945 are *phoney, G.I.* and *jeep; to take evasive action* and *to have had it; quisling* and *blitzkrieg* and *blitz; evacuee; flak* and *gremlin; gen, browned off, stooge; maquis* and *scorched earth; blue-print* and *streamlined.*

The emotion usually associated with war is fear. War, however, has been described as consisting of long periods of intense boredom punctuated by short periods of intense excitement. Boredom and excitement, quite ordinary responses to life, cause no emotional, no mental disturbances. Fear causes both. The neurosis of fear, on a large scale, began in the war of 1914-1918 among the combatants; during 1934-39, among civilians; 1939-1945, among both of these classes. Such a neurosis tended to set up a psychosis. These two terms became familiar to laymen in the 1920s, when there also arose, among educated laymen, such others as *to condition* and *conditioned reflexes; the ego* and *the id; complex* and *inferiority complex,* misused far more often than not; *repression* and *inhibition; sublimation* and *compensation. Trauma* belongs to the popularization, since *ca.* 1935, of psychiatry, to which we owe also the slangy *thing* ('to have a thing about such-and-such')—an obsession.†

Since the end of the war, the fear neurosis has persisted. In 1950, indeed, people have had 'the jitters' as badly as during the twelve months preceding 3 September, 1939. Fear of impending raids has become fear of what would be a particularly unpleasant war; an acute fear of loneliness, often felt by an individual during an air-raid, has become a vague, general fear of loneliness, a fear no less strong for being vague; and where there is no such fear, an anxiety neurosis has tended to arise in respect of one's livelihood. Men remember what happened in the 1920s, when, instead of 'a land fit for heroes to live in,' many returned men found they could barely live and

* See the essay 'Thanks to the War (1939-1945)'—whence also the terms specified in the next paragraph—in *Words at War: Words at Peace.*

† For these terms, see especially 'Words in Vogue' in the same collection of essays upon language.

the middle-aged found themselves being passed-over for ignorant louts and husky morons. They still do.

Psychiatry and psychology remain so very experimental that they can hardly be called sciences. The sciences proper, science as a body of organized knowledge, science and technics: these have, ever since the 1850s, exercised an increasing influence upon life, especially from 1914 onwards. The Canon already quoted has summarized that influence. 'Great strides in the development of physical science,' he remarks, 'have been helped by two world wars; also in surgery and medicine (e.g. the discovery of penicillin). There is less tendency than in the nineteenth century to think that this means "over-all" progress or that it lessens the need for religion or in any way discredits it. There is, indeed, beginning to be perceived the danger that man's moral progress and sense of responsibility are not keeping pace with scientific progress. Machine mastering man?'

After a cleric's a layman's opinion. John Hayward (*Prose Literature since* 1939) introduces the chapter entitled 'Religion, Philosophy, Science, Scholarship' with these pondered and temperate words. 'In a world controlled, to all immediate intents and purposes, by the power for good and evil that applied science has placed in men's hands, spiritual values have progressively declined. It is a commonplace of the pulpit and platform that scientific invention, in a few decades, has surpassed the halting moral progress mankind has made in twenty centuries. More and more importance is now attached to means; less and less significance to ends. The first use in 1945 of atomic energy*—to wipe out an entire community of men, women, and children—was an ominous and alarming symptom of this dangerous, perhaps fatal, disease of the human spirit. Widespread contempt of the moral law has led, in Great Britain at least, to a corresponding decay of religious belief and religious practice. The Church of England, though "by law established"—a phrase which must have bewildered many foreigners—has no authority, spiritual or temporal, such as the

---

* See especially the dignified, restrained and infinitely moving little book by the American author, John Hersey: *Hiroshima*, 1946.

Church of Rome has, to compel its members to worship; in recent years, consequently, its influence has greatly deteriorated. To judge only by its absence from church, the younger generation would appear to be almost wholly without religion. Such evidence is not, of course, conclusive; and it would be ingenuous to assume, even on the corroborative evidence of youth's worldliness, that it altogether lacks faith of some sort in its spiritual destiny. That a desire for it exists in some souls is evident from the recent increase in the numbers of those who have found anchorage in the Roman Church, and of those who, seeking spiritual discipline, have obtained it in the Anglo-Catholic movement.' (John Hayward has, on this subject, much more to say: and all of it worthy of attention.)

To embark upon a bare list—let alone a *catalogue raisonné*—of the words that science has, since 1900, grafted upon the English language, would be to undertake a voyage far too long and much too fascinating to be envisaged here, for apart from the language of pure sciences there are the special vocabularies of such subjects as agronomy, 'the wireless' or radio, the cinema, aeronautics and aircraft, medicine. There are even general concepts and aspects—*the cosmos* and *the cosmic process; space-time; quantum; nuclear fission* and *atomic energy; the machine age* and *the scientific attitude*.

But there is another aspect of the influence exercised by science; an aspect noted by the anonymous writer of the article 'The Immediate View' in *A Survey of Contemporary British Writing*—a special issue of *The Times Literary Supplement* of 25 August 1950. In prose, he says, 'the time is one of ability and judgment ... [The] kind of prose which has such fertility now is not poetical. We have no Elia, we have no Sir Thomas Browne, and we have difficulty in getting through the luxuriant prefaces of Shelley. The prose of English literature half-way through this century is not Stevenson's either. It is nearer to T. H. Huxley's, and for a very good reason; its matter is in the same area as his. The point is not just that we are all scientists now, although it is from the scientists that so many of our finest books have been coming in recent years—fine in their plan, in their substance, in their development and in their continuous clarity. Apart from these,' he adds, 'the historian ..., the economist, the craftsman, the writer on games —these and many others are able to uphold the reputation of our central prose.'

That criticism shows acute insight into one of the main tendencies of the twentieth century; at least from 1920, when the first of Eddington's more popular works appeared. During the 1920s, 1930s and early 1940s, Eddington and Jeans, with several very capable 'disciples', achieved a number of best-sellers. Yet not one of these scientists has written so well as Charles Morgan or Osbert Sitwell or Ivor Brown, all of whom possess a prose style that does, at times, bear comparison with the very 'unscientific' style of Lamb and Sir Thomas Browne. Not one of these scientists has written so well as any of the four greatest British philosophers of the period under review: Samuel Alexander, A. N. Whitehead, R. G. Collingwood, Bertrand Russell. To imply that the scientists and the economists, or even the historians (with several notable exceptions, e.g. Trevelyan and Powicke) are in—nay, that they constitute —the predominant line of contemporary British prose is to beg the question to a quite remarkable degree: it ignores the novelists and short-story writers, the biographers and auto-biographers, and the essayists.

But the very begging of the question is important, for it implies that the critic thinks that the best writing is that done by men certainly not in the front rank of writers and that the best writing is of the efficient, lucid, agreeable kind characteristic of T. H. Huxley. If the men he praises wrote so well as T. H. Huxley, he would have a case; yet even if he had that non-existent case, he still could say no more than: *For this sort of thing*, this sort of writing is admirable.

There are several other sorts of thing: and men better qualified to speak of the intangibles, the imponderables and the ultimates than are the scientists and the economists certainly do not think this somewhat standardized, merely efficient writing to be the best. Efficiency and lucidity are two great virtues in writing; they are far from being the only virtues. The critic means well but he doesn't mean very far. Let us hope that, some

day, he will realize that the number of persons neither bludg-
eoned nor bluffed by science is quite large and that it includes
most of the best minds and most of the best men. The influence
of science upon writing could admittedly be dangerous, but
it has not yet gone very deep nor very wide. Men of good will
are determined that it shall not.

Cinema and radio have exercised a tremendous influence,
comparable—from early in the 1920s—with that of the Press.
In *Poetry since* 1939, Stephen Spender has given it as a considered opinion that, by 1946, English had become 'a language
misused, trafficked, stretched thin, turned abstract, officialized
and castrated by all the uses of Empire, business, newspapers
and broadcasting. The most genuine impulse behind every
literary movement in recent years has been to invent a concrete and human use of this language which in millions of
minds all over the world is now no longer a living tongue but
a kind of vast calculating machine.' During the five years that
have elapsed since that was written, English has slowly been
improving its status and getting rid of at least some of its effete
and neuter colourlessness and spinelessness.

Speaking of the generation that is still at school or college,
hence by implication of those whose educational development
has been arrested either by the war of 1939-1945 or by its
almost equally pernicious aftermath, J. Y. T. Greig, writing in
the same year as Stephen Spender, has (*Keep up the Fight for
English*, 1946) given it as his no less carefully considered opinion that, 'To-day, the youngster is surrounded all day long by
confidence tricksters—the advertisers in newspapers, in illustrated magazines, in filmlets, on the hoardings, on the air; the
journalists of the daily, weekly, and monthly Press; Hollywood; and wireless broadcasting from round the corner and
from every other corner of the world. Nothing like it has ever
happened before; nothing, at any rate, on the same vast scale.
What is common to all these agencies is the emphasis on the
stereotype, since only the stereotype can be mass-produced,
and only the stereotype can be trusted to appeal to so large a

number of people that it will pay the producer. Of all the enemies of thinking, the stereotype is the worst. It is a substitute for thinking; it appeals all the time to the inherent laziness of the human mind; it is soothing; it is a mild narcotic.'

In reference to such examples of officialese as I quoted in the chapter 'Non-Literary English', Professor Greig continues thus: 'All those passages ... are packed with stereotypes ... with linguistic stereotypes, with clichés, because the minds behind them have fallen ... into the way of the stereotype, the rigid mould, which is the way of intellectual death.' Moreover, 'the number of young men and women whom the conditions of our life are forcing into the way of the stereotype is increasing every year. This is one of the most deplorable, because the most destructive, results of the Machine Age. Nor is it only a stereotyping of thought that we suffer from; along with this goes a stereotyping of feeling, of emotion, which in the long run may turn out to have consequences even more disastrous. The Machine Age ... not only actively discourages the young from thinking their own thoughts by presenting them with second-hand, third-hand, tenth-hand thoughts in the most convenient tabloid form, but also actively discourages them from responding to life with the fresh, the first-hand, the unique and discriminated emotion, by constantly presenting them with the stereotyped emotional response in film after film, magazine after magazine, best-seller after best-seller.' Two pages later (p. 25), this vigorous upholder of thinking, independence, clear comprehension sums up. 'The worst enemy of clear and precise thinking is muzzy and stereotyped feeling, which is exactly what the Machine Age, through its syndicated newspaper articles, syndicated films, syndicated magazine-stories, and syndicated radio-programmes, is spreading all over us, like the oily scum from a factory polluting a stream.'

From a rather different angle, John Hayward makes a perhaps even more direct attack upon the Press, the cinema, the radio. In retort upon the rather common opinion that 'it is better to catch the ear of the philistines than of nobody at all', he remarks that 'to argue thus is virtually to admit that a writer's business is simply to supply the public demand for "reading matter". It is an argument which has received indirect but powerful encouragement from the press, radio, and the cinema. Their influence has been harmful to literature in many ways, not least in its tendency to drive literature into the refuge of a minority.'

Two pages later in his eloquent 'Conclusion', John Hayward rallies all writers possessing character and ability to the standard-royal of independence and integrity. 'If literature,' he urges, 'is to extend its civilizing mission among the literate masses; if it is not to become the arcane cult of a mandarin class; it must impose its values, and insist on their supreme importance, no matter what the odds are against their easy acceptance. These odds may now seem heavy indeed, for the counter-attraction of working for the press, the cinema, the radio, and the purveyors of commercialized "reading matter", offers itself to any writer who is willing to prostitute himself to the public. Newspaper barons and film magnates have shown that it is not difficult to bend authors to their own desires; and the radio, if it does not actually dictate, exercises a subtle control over the ideas of its script-writers. These insidious corrupters of an artist's integrity are destructive of literary values. Resistance to them must come from within.'

The influence of the Press has been sufficiently indicated. At this point there remain but two remarks to make (several others falling more naturally into the paragraphs concerned with standardization): first, the captions of films read at the cinema, the conversations and soliloquies and speeches there heard from 1930 onwards, have constituted all the 'reading matter'—the sole intellectual, moral and spiritual pabulum and viaticum—both of myriads of young people after leaving school and of millions of their seniors, except for an occasional timid glance at something other than sport or salacity in a newspaper that, even if read from front to back page, would merely stultify or confuse them; and second, as Dr G. Pratt Insh has been at some pains to confirm, 'the microphone favours a style of simple assertion, where, in the phrase of Anatole France, the redundant wood has been planed away' and where subtlety and elaboration, whether of matter or of manner, i.e. whether of thought or of style, have been discarded.

Perhaps a third remark, applicable both to cinema and to radio, should be made, although it is impossible to assess the consequences: cinema and radio have exercised a considerable influence—so far, an inchoate influence—upon the speech of all classes and, by their special requirements, upon the style of novelists writing with two eyes upon the film and of dramatists writing with one eye upon the film and the other upon broadcasting. By 1960 it may be possible, though still difficult, to render a fairly adequate account of the influence exercised, the potential power inherent in, 'the talkie' and the radio; here and now, however, we can and should record the negative yet informative fact that 'the book of the film' has exercised as little influence in the twentieth century as did, in the nineteenth, 'the book of the (particular) opera' and that the film script-writers' scripts, seen by very few persons indeed, have, like the 'little book' or libretto, 'the book of the words', exercised precisely no influence at all upon either literature or language.

Largely owing to the influence of American soldiers, sailors and airmen stationed or on leave in Great Britain and Ireland during 1917-1918 and 1942-1945 and to that of the cinema (the majority of films come from Hollywood), and, in much slighter degree, to that of American magazines and books and, even less, to that of the radio, British English has, during the twentieth century, become increasingly Americanized. Yet the Americanization has, in the main, affected only cant, slang, colloquialisms and catch-phrases; indeed, the Americanization of Standard English, whether spoken or written, has been astonishingly slight. All things considered, American English has been far less influential in the British Isles than in Australia, where even American spellings are infiltrating. Although no one has thought of mentioning the fact, the American influence on Standard English during the twentieth century has, both quantitatively and qualitatively, been smaller than the British on Standard American English—an influence that is, however, confined almost entirely to the field of literature.

To mention a very few of the features characterizing this

influence, as astonishing to Britons as to Americans, we should ponder and attempt to assess the impact of G. B. Shaw's, Noel Coward's and T. S. Eliot's plays upon the American stage, both immediately as presented there and, more slowly, upon certain 'high-brow' American playwrights; the extent to which the novels of Kipling (his short stories too), Conrad, Galsworthy, H. G. Wells, James Joyce (much of *Ulysses* was published in America before it appeared in Europe), Virginia Woolf, Aldous Huxley and several others (including, on a lower plane, Edgar Wallace) have been read and, by certain authors, imitated—this extent exceeds, proportionally, the influence of American fiction upon the British Isles, or rather, it did until about 1946 or 1947, for, during the last three or four years of the decade, the balance has, just perceptibly, swung the other way; in non-dramatic verse during the twentieth century, no entirely American poet has impinged upon British poetry as much—little although it be—as Walter De la Mare, T. S. Eliot, and the Auden-Spender-Day Lewis-Macniece group of the 1930s; whereas the influence of American upon British essayists has been null, that of British upon American essayists has been not quite null, for Max Beerbohm, G. K. Chesterton and Hilaire Belloc have had their practical admirers in America, this constituting, however, an influence that, since *ca.* 1939, has been gradually diminishing until, in 1951, it no longer exists; and, to take two branches of knowledge, no American historian has, in Britain, exercised the posthumous influence of Acton (†1902) or the genial influence, since *ca.* 1930, of G. M. Trevelyan, in America, and likewise no American philosopher has a transatlantic reputation comparable to that of either Whitehead or Russell. Britain, one suspects, is not quite the spent force she has, in unthinking belief, so often been adjudged; nevertheless, one must emphasize the fact that this influence-in-reverse has, except in the essay, affected literature far more than it has affected language.

We now arrive at a set of influences rather different from those we have been considering; in respect of literature and language, they are perhaps less obvious and certainly more difficult to determine than the influences exercised by the three wars, science, the Press, cinema, radio, America: and this difficulty arises mainly from the fact that these yet to be treated influences are so appallingly material and, in a sense, materialistic that one often finds it hard to say what, precisely, the results are and, still more, how they have come about. These material factors may be summarized as transportation; urbanization and conurbation; regimentation and standardization: all of them becoming noticeable by (say) 1914 and all having, by 1949 or 1950, achieved—at least, for the time being—a maximum of intensity. They are factors that, in themselves, are easy to describe; essays are written about them by pupils aged 15-18. *How they have affected language* is a question vastly harder to indicate and perhaps impossible to settle.

Transportation is inseparable from speed. Speed has become an end in itself. Not one man in a million had thought of the following aspect before Monsignor Ronald Knox remarked that the only true test of the desirability of aeroplanes is, How much nearer do they bring man to God? Reducing that 'Chestertonian' question to a level more comprehensible to the laity, we might ask, What spiritual and moral benefit have aeroplanes conferred upon mankind? The number of lives they have saved is perhaps one-tenth of those they have destroyed. 'This marvellous, comparatively recent facility of communication and intercourse has made the world, so to say, a much smaller place and therefore a much more dangerous place if international relations are not good' (the anonymous Canon). Increased speed has partly sprung from and partly subserved the passion for hustle and bustle, the imaginary necessity to reach nowhere in particular in the shortest possible time or to arrive at somewhere particular, for no imperative reason, even faster than that. The tempo of living has accelerated; feverish haste to do things essentially trivial has become ever more noticeable since the Economic Depression of 1929-1932; it began soon after the war of 1914-1918, if not, indeed, as early as 1910 or 1911.

The spirit restless, restless the style; the mind in an overpowering haste; the wording and phrasing, the syntax and composition deficient in precision, in calm and balance, in sanity; beauty too often forced to disappear, trampled beneath the feet of the robots, the careerists, the materialists; gracious leasureliness become rare, and with it that poise of spirit which was so much more prevalent before than after ca. 1911.

Except in the strong-minded, the style, whether of prose or of verse, tends to be febrile—when it is not stale and nerveless. Books begun at white heat backslide into the hot-and-cold of the fever of living. The effect upon language is so subjective and pervasive that it is almost impossible for the historian to achieve objectivity and particularity: he feels rather than sees the results of this senseless hustle, this obsession by speed, this mad tempo that overshoots its goals.

That hustle, that passion for speed at any price, that haste to reach the end of a journey only vaguely foreseen, with an arrival longed-for rather than expected—those symptoms characterize life in large cities far more than life in the country or in small towns. Unfortunately that drift to the cities which began during the Industrial Revolution has continued and shows little sign of ending; nor has the fault been entirely that of the drifters. More young fellows and girls have gone to the cities because of the folly and ingratitude of governments than because of any imagined or supposititious attractiveness inherent in cities, although clearly a number (mostly girls) have yielded to the lure of the lights, the charms of the cinema, the dreams of the dance-hall.

In Cobbett's day, there existed 'the Great Wen', but it was the only wen in the whole of the British Isles; now there are at least six others: Glasgow, Birmingham, Manchester, Liverpool, Leeds, Sheffield. Such urbanization grows worse as a snowball grows larger, for to it is inevitably added the disease of con- urbation—the connecting and then the coalescing of the Five Towns or the six or the seven. Communities with corporate lives of their own, idioms of their own, dialects of their own are, like particles compelled by centripetal action, gradually absorbed into the great city they had, unfortunately for them- selves, happened to neighbour. Civic individualities, possessing a vigorous, well-defined personality, become a neuter, emasculated by collectivism. The certitudes philosophically evolving from the uncertainties of farming and market-gardening or orcharding turn into the cynical or the moronic hesitations and doubts of the rootless 'city slicker': and that unhappy change is reflected in the very language they imitate and then tentatively adopt, a language more 'educated' but far less meritorious than the provincialism they ashamedly abandon. They exchange the tang and the pithiness and vivid simplicity of their rural or predominantly rural speech for the slang and catch-phrases and catachreses of their new environment; all they retain of their place of origin is accent, and even that is mongrelled by contact with meritless composites.

Such influences are manifestly linked with regimentation and standardization, which themselves are very closely related the one to the other. Regimentation began during the War of 1914-1918 and increased with a gradualness that seemed to stamp it with inevitability; the war had been in progress for more than a year before conscription was introduced, nor did 'Dora' (the Defence of the Realm Act) seem anything more terrible than a war-time expediency. Only when it was retained long after the need for it, did Britons finally wake up and realize that their once vaunted liberty had gone: that what remained to them was a liberty so restricted that it survived as a name, not as a fact. A few lucid minds were perturbed by the rapid consequences, in Germany, of Hitler's accession to power, not only because (more than a few said this) they feared a Germany reborn but because they were witnessing the whittling-away of liberty along lines foreshadowed by Dora; to these few minds, in the middle thirties, a nation regimented appeared to constitute a menace, first to others and finally to itself—whether that nation were Germany or Britain—and that it was gaining a soulless advantage to the detriment, perhaps irreparable, of liberty, individuality, personality.

During the War of 1939-1945, regimentation increased. Most of it was, if the nation wished to survive, unavoidable; it was essential, imperative—so long as the war lasted. But no longer necessary once the war ended in August, 1945. Now in 1951 regimentation is almost as thorough-going as in 1948, and in 1948 it stretched wider and went deeper than in the earlier half of 1945. That literature, hence language, should, to a considerable extent, be regimented during the war years, John Hayward has, in a passage already quoted, shown to be inevitable: the tremendous compulsion was tolerated because of the tremendous need. That need has gone.

Under a deceptively quiet exterior of usualness, numerous intelligences are seething in revolt against regimentation. That revolution, which has commenced (a fact known only by the perceptive), will be one of the mind and the spirit: its manifestations will take place, its battles be fought, in the fields of popular religion, everyday ethics, and unpopular philosophy, and in those of music, art, literature. The ferment has been at work for so long as a decade or two; the retention of wartime restrictions, or of restrictions appallingly similar, has hastened the fermentation; unless there be another World War (and those who panic at the idea are dangerously helping to bring it about) or a comparable catastrophe, British and American literature—hence, yet at the same time partly because of important internal changes, the English language —will perhaps burgeon in a gigantic efflorescence, no less vigorous, though probably shorter-lived, than the Elizabethan, as we have seen prophesied earlier in this chapter. (For an aspect of the efflorescence in language, see the next section: 'The Vernacular'.)

Clearly, regimentation forms one aspect—one of the more ominous aspects—of standardization. The Press, the radio, even the cinema, Public School and elementary school, propaganda public and private, these are factors in the standardization of any and every people in this our wonderful century. As M. André Simon has noted ('The Decade in Retrospect' in *The Month*, June, 1950): 'The technique of mass persuasion has been brought to such a pitch of efficiency that knowingly or unconsciously the younger generations have their own minds made up for them by the Press, Publicity, and Propaganda experts. ... Men of my generation [M. Simon was born in 1877] still refuse to surrender their right to have a critical opinion of their own' (so, by the way, do those of my generation, we who were born in the 1890s); 'we were brought up upon a deeply rooted tradition of independence and individualism, and we cannot help viewing with the utmost distaste the trend towards the so-called "democratic" uniformity which has been such an outstanding feature of the past decade.' It is worth nothing that M. André Simon sets off 'democratic' in quotation marks; he does not despise democracy; I suspect that he despises those who don a cloak of ostentatiously democratic home-spun, but wear a haircloth neither devised nor woven at home.

To deal adequately with the effects of standardization upon language would require, not a paragraph or two but a rather lengthy monograph. Some of those effects have been glimpsed in such sections of 'Non-Literary English' as those treating of the Press and Officialese; several others have been glanced-at in the opening section ('General Trends') of this final chapter; another aspect of standardization has been treated (very briefly) in 'A Note on Dialect'; yet another can be narrowed down to Pronunciation. Something has already been said, either explicitly or implicitly, about this thorny and tricky subject. Little more needs to be said in so general and conspective a view of English as forms—or should form—the subject of this book; at least, in the British part of it.

All the forces of standardization, which is mainly deliberate or, at the least, conscious, and all the forces of conformity and convention, of which more perhaps are unconsidered than considered, make for uniformity of pronunciation. These forces have been more numerous in the twentieth century than at any other period in history. The 'talkie' (since *ca.* 1930) and the radio (since *ca.* 1920) are new; propaganda has, since 1914, been more intense than ever before; the Press has, since the late 1890s, been the pleasure of the polyarchy whereas, until then, it had been the prerogative of the oligarchy and the privilege of the well and comparatively well educated. Within a period of forty years, three wars—at their height in 1901, 1916, 1940— were mingling townsmen and countrymen, artisans and artists (painter, sculptor, musical composer and musical executant, novelist and poet), clerks and technicians, factory hands and shop-hands, farmers and engineers, professors and preachers,

Public School and Secondary School and Elementary School masters, scientists and shoemakers, underworld and over-world, mingling them and shaking them up, all together and altogether, and mixing, admixing them into a strange and fateful hotch-potch that turned out to be distasteful to a few yet edible by all and acceptable by many. Partly through Parliamentary law and partly for vocational convenience, vehicled in the various almost statutory examinations, and partly from humanitarian motives, expressed in communal non-scholastic activities, education has succeeded in binding to a Procrustean bed many an unwilling patient, many a rebellious victim. To or towards uniformity in pronunciation have snobbery and convention intimidated the weak and the meek and those whom destiny or evolution or chance has cast into the form of sheep instead of shepherds: and for many persons this uniformity has merely proved a 'comfortable' thing to observe. The insidious, virtually inescapable influence of en-vironment, lapping one about as the sea does or investing one's sleeping, no less than one's waking life almost as inevitably, almost as decisively, almost as uncannily as does the air about us: all these factors make for uniformity of pronunciation.

Yet look at the reverse of this deceptively engraved, mis-leadingly worded coin of the realm of speech and you will find that, despite all the prohibitions of the law-givers, all the regulations of the planners, all the *don'ts* of the teachers, all the horrified exclamations of the conventional (themselves often the most horrible sinners); that despite all the economic and material and physical, as well as all the educational and cultural, forces consciously directed to or unconsciously working to-wards uniformity; that despite these forces and these factors, pronunciation, although appreciably more uniform in 1951 than in 1900, is, regarded dispassionately, far more varied, divergent, irregular than regular, convergent, uniform.

To pretend anything else is to pretend a sham; to believe anything else is to show oneself singularly credulous. Examine the staffs of the universities of England and you will discover that, whereas, at Oxford and Cambridge, a slight majority of professors, readers, lecturers speak Public School Standard, and the remainder some form of Modified Standard, at the other universities the majority speak a Modified Standard (Midland or Northern or Scottish or Irish) and only a very small minority —usually Oxford and Cambridge graduates—speak Public School Standard. Then go into the Faculties of Medicine or Science or Engineering and you will notice that the majority of the staff, in no matter what English University, speak a Modified Standard. Since that is the state of things in even the most august, the most efficient, universities (and, with obvious modifications, the same holds good of the universities of Wales and Scotland, as of Eire and Northern Ireland), what do you suppose is the state of things in any university in any of the Dominions? And what do you expect to find outside these closed corporations the universities? When you have succeeded in picturing these states and conditions, turn your minds to the —at first thought—very odd fact that educated Americans *have* a far more uniform pronunciation than educated Britons *happen to have*. Reluctant to encroach upon the ground my American collaborator will be covering, I need only remark that uniformity of vocabulary is obviously more important than uniformity of pronunciation.

Standardization; an almost neurotic urgency and an almost psychopathic impatience; the inroads of propaganda; the exotic influence of the cinema, the soothing speech of the radio, the frightening power of the popular Press; the preponderance of science; the esoteric allurement of psychiatry; the fear neuroses and the economic, intellectual and moral disturbances of the two great wars: not a pretty picture. Yet a one-sided picture.

'Is the desire for hiking, mountain climbing, cycling, country excursions a welcome sign that people want to get back to a saner form of life?' asks a correspondent I've already quoted three or four times. Certainly there is, proportionally, far more exercise taken, and exercise taken by many more individuals, than there was in 1900; certainly the sun is now welcomed, not avoided, and fresh air sought after, not evaded; certainly there is less pub-crawling, less fugging in billiard-saloons, less smut on street-corners, less boredom among young ladies in drawing-rooms, less city-keeping by factory girls; and sport has spread to every class of our so-called classless society and to everyone who can bat an eyelid or bowl or roll a ball or manipulate something or other. Thus there is less of sniggering salacity and more of honest lust, more sexual freedom and less sexual immorality. And all these changes have had their consequences in literature, in journalism, and therefore in language.

What, however, of the future? I am no prophet. But I should like to quote a relevant passage from an alert poet and vigorous prose-writer, who—with no pretentions to prophetic ability— has at the end of his contribution (May, 1950) to the 'A Decade in Restrospect' symposium conducted by *The Month*, written thus: 'People will have to begin minding their own business and reforming themselves before they try to reform others. Minding one's own business is an all-time job too! So it may be that, through non-interference, things will be allowed to look up, and life to circulate normally. At no other time, nevertheless, was it more thrilling and enjoyable to be alive than it is to-day, when the life of the whole planet is triggered by a hair, and the roar of chaos is challenging from us all every atom of our faith, hope, charity and courage ... Above all we need that stand-by of all good soldiers, laughing gaiety which shows up best against the blackest background; to live without that is an insult to Creation and makes nonsense of living at all.'

Roy Campbell's gay courage, spiritual integrity and intellectual worth and independence remind us of the existence of intangibles, and hearten us by the persistency of imponderables, two sets of powers and potentialities indefeasible by all the Kaisers and Hitlers, by all the tyrants and dictators, by all the bureaucrats and morons, by all the philistines and barbarians. Among all such men and women as are neither nit-wits nor sheep, there has, very clearly since 1890 or 1900 (and perceptibly since 1860 or 1870), been an ever increasing individual as opposed to collective feeling and sentiment—personal as opposed to mob-moved, and widely spiritual as opposed to narrowly moral—of authentic, deep-based independence; and to some extent they have achieved the independence.

This independence has begun to set up a conflict, and will maintain the conflict, between individual, i.e. personal, liberty whether physical, mental or moral, and bureaucratic bullying, a bullying carefully collective and soullessly impersonal, revering itself and delusively thinking it should be revered. That conflict will inevitably lead to crime and near-crime among the lawless and to an exacerbated individualism, an exaggerated solipsism, among those with capable minds of their own and the courage to use them. True; but better that than the death of the spirit, the decay of the mind, the abdication of liberty. It is to such men and women that we owe civilization: without them there would have been none.

Linked with independence and individualism is that experimentalism in creative work without which all intellectual and ultimately all spiritual life would stagnate; an experimentalism that has underlain every period of scientific and political and other activity; an experimentalism that, ever since 1900, has existed almost continuously and, usually, fruitfully; an experimentalism seen at its strongest and clearest in the work of James Joyce and Virginia Woolf in prose, in T. S. Eliot and 'the group of the 1930s' in verse, and in G. B. Shaw, T. S. Eliot and Christopher Fry in the drama. To Eliot's dramatic work, the United States of America shows a fairly close parallel in the plays of Thornton Wilder; on the other hand, Britain affords no close parallel, either as literature or as language, to the plays of Eugene O'Neill.

The British writers mentioned above have experimented more with method than with language, yet several of them have conducted some fascinating, though not always fruitful, experiments with language; and all of them have added much to the enlargement of our conception of style. (The interdependence of language and style—the impossibility of separating them, style being one's choice and handling of language —need not be emphasized here.)

The Vernacular

The usual twentieth-century definition of the predominant twentieth-century sense of *vernacular* is: 'written in the native as opposed to the literary, language' or, as noun, 'the native, as opposed to the literary, language'. The meaning intended is fairly clear, but the scope is obscure, for manifestly the native language, e.g. Modern English words deriving from Old English, may be as literary as the highly Latinized language of erudition. Can one think of anything more 'literary', more dignified, more apposite than 'Be still and know that I am God'? Yet every word (*Psalms*, 46, 10) is 'native', none is 'literary', none erudite.

That introductory paragraph serves merely to clear the ground. There has grown up another sense of the noun *the vernacular:* and this is a sense approximating to the primary literal etymological meaning of the originating adjective, *vernacular*, derived from Latin *vernaculus*, 'born in one's house; hence, domestic; hence, native', from *verna*, 'a slave born in one's house'. (*Verna* itself is of obscure origin.) But you will consult in vain the standard dictionaries for *the vernacular* as it is used to-day by those thoughtful, well-educated persons who do not regard language as a set of conformations to philological 'laws' and who bear in mind, instead of paying lip-service to, the fact that language has been made by ordinary men and women, not by a learnèd committee, and that it is made for mankind, not mankind for language.

Precisely because this sense of *the vernacular* has not yet been embalmed in a dictionary, one can define it only hesitantly and tentatively. One could short-circuit the difficulty by defining *the vernacular* as 'informal spoken English' and, by so doing, go fairly close to the mark. There is, however, 'more to it than that'. What sort of informal spoken English? That of the literate? That of the illiterate? That of the vast number of persons neither quite the one nor quite the other?

A rough-and-ready answer is that the spoken vernacular consists of the words, phrases, idioms, the accidence and the syntax, the pronunciation and intonation that are common, or acceptable, to all three, but with the pronunciation and intonation of the very literate (that is, the literary and the literary-minded) and the cultured ruled out—on the grounds, either that they sound affected or that they would be condemned as 'talking "posh"'. There is also a written vernacular; to this we shall return. A more satisfactory definition will slowly crystallize and finally emerge as this much too brief discussion continues. So far, the subject has not been discussed. In the recent, fully authoritative British history of the English language —Professor S. Potter's (1950)—it is not even mentioned; in *The Story of Languages* (1949) Professor Mario Pei hovered tantalizingly on the fringes of this unmapped territory.

Yet so long ago as 1928 a scholar indicated some of the changes he thought would eventually take place; changes that would form part of the development that is being, and that, before long, will perhaps be much more rapidly, effected by the vernacular, both in the United States of America and, with more opposition, in the British Isles. In *Breaking Priscian's Head, or English as She Will Be Spoke and Wrote*, Professor J. Y. T. Greig does not discuss the vernacular, nor has he envisaged—at that date, he could hardly have envisaged—the problem in the same manner as I am now doing. That he does not use the term 'the vernacular' in no way lessens the significance and importance of that movement towards the vernacular which is imperceptibly, yet (I believe) irresistibly, taking place, has long been taking place and has always been taking place, whether in American English or in British English or in Old English or in Latin or in Greek.

After remarking that 'the reform of English spelling must wait for the reform of English pronunciation. To reform it now, while the dictionary-makers are still countenancing Public School Standard, would be a calamity' (they continue to countenance and vigorously inculcate that Standard), Professor Greig launches a direct attack. 'As to English accidence,' he writes, 'reform is bound to come slowly at best, but anything we can do to hasten it will be a public benefaction. For though English has got rid of most of the inflections that burdened its youth a few still remain, and of these the majority could be discarded without loss.'

Unlike many revolutionaries, Professor Greig (a revolutionary in the sense that Shakespeare was one) is practical; he is also courageous, for he has said in particular what he means in general. 'Inflections in a language simply aren't needed', he declares; a declaration footnoted thus, 'How difficult it is to drive this idea into the heads of scholars, especially of classical scholars!' Continuing, he says, 'One or two [inflections] may be a convenience, a means of avoiding clumsy periphrases; but only when the language has failed to throw up the suitable auxiliaries'. He then advances a number of practical suggestions: if at first they make you squirm, think, think again.

'The habit of English-speakers being to use the preterite much oftener than, for instance, the French do, it is perhaps desirable to keep -ed or -t as the sign of the preterite in English verbs; but if we could get into the habit of using the perfect (e.g. *I have looked*) on all occasions where we now use the preterite (*I looked*), even this inflection could be dropped; *I have look* and *I have go* are inherently just as good, because just as unambiguous, as *I have looked* and *I have gone*. It is perhaps desirable, too, to have some simple means of denoting plural number in nouns, and -s is as good a way of doing it as any. The sign *'s* is a neat device to mark possessives. *Whose* is a handy variant of *who*, though *of who* would be better'—but why not *who's*? 'Certain irregular ... preterites have diverged slightly in meaning from their present tenses, as *would* from *will*, *might* from *may*, and *could* from *can*, and had better be retained as separate words. But all these are of the nature of luxuries. We *could* do without them, and in a language like Chinese one has to. ... The same ease and simplicity could be attained in English if only we would relegate our few remaining grammatical fossils to the proper place for fossils, our museums.'

Professor Greig reminds us that 'we have all spent a deal of time and mental energy on getting the distinction between *I* and *me*, *who* and *whom*, *know* and *knew* and *known*, firmly into our heads, and it's little wonder the phrases *between you and I*, *I seen him* [or *I seed him*], *says I sharplike*, and *he knowed what us wants* tend to make us squirm'. Note, however, that *between you and I* is rapidly becoming common, that *It's me*, when self-contained, is now a widely accepted form, and that *Who is it for?* or *Who do you mean?* or *Who do you take me to be?* are now more usual than *Whom* ...

'Many of us,' fears the same authority, 'desire the retention of grammatical difficulties chiefly from snobbery: the ability "to speak good grammar" raises us above the vulgar herd. Others happily forget how long it took them to master even the simple accidence of English, and so cannot see why the common people should have difficulty in it. Well, the common people have. And so in our childhood had we, who are now alleged to be educated and therefore common people no more. And the mischief is that half our difficulties, and theirs, are needless. If every remaining inflection disappeared from English to-morrow, we should have learned in a few months how to avoid every possible ambiguity due to the loss.'

Referring to the *between you and I, Who do you mean?* constructions, Professor Greig has recalled the fact that 'nominatives have always shown a tendency to devour their objectives [—although the objective *you* has devoured the nominative *ye*], and ... they ought in future to be encouraged in this gruesome but desirable work. Further, irregular plurals like *oxen* and *sheep*, and Latin plurals like *curricula* should be regularized at once (*oxes, sheeps, curriculums*). As to verbs, the *-s* of the third person singular indicative [e.g. *he hits*] should be gradually dropped as unnecessary, much as we have already dropped its Southern-English predecessor *-th;* the present participle and verb-noun in *-ing* might usefully be kept for a time, since many English idioms depend on it, but it ought to be sacrificed in the end; and so-called vocalic verbs (e.g. *bind,* making *bound, bound,* and *begin,* making *began, begun*) should be gradually transformed, as every child now does until he is mistaught better, into consonantal verbs making *-ed, -ed* (or *-t, -t*) in the preterite and past participle—that is to say, for as long as we resolve to keep preterites and past participles at all.'

Such changes are in the right line of natural development in language: they also form part of the onward sweep of the vernacular. These simplifications have always been, either wholly or mainly, caused by the influence of the vernacular; manifestly they constitute something of what we call the vernacular. This phenomenon obtains, certainly in English, almost certainly in most other civilized languages. In 1928,

Professor Greig warned us that the 'improvements' he proposed would probably come very slowly. 'The old pedantic grammarians ... have done their work too well, for they have induced in nine out of ten educated Englishmen to-day a greater fear of committing a solecism in grammar than of committing one of the seven deadly sins. The result is that grammarians of the modern school—like Professor Otto Jespersen ... —are forced to waste nearly half their days in clearing away the rubbish deposited by their predecessors in the minds of our contemporary schoolmasters, and in persuading the rest of us of the simple truth that grammar has no intrinsic value, but acquires such minor value as it does have, only in so far as it makes, by the shortest and quickest route, for ease, clarity, and flexibility in human speech.'

Nor has Professor Greig been alone among British grammarians in vigorously attacking the imposition, upon English, of rules drawn from Latin. Such scholars as Sweet and Dr Onions and, above all, Jespersen have shown how natural are certain tendencies deplored by the very strict grammarians. Even the author of *Modern English Usage* once admitted that 'what grammarians say should be has perhaps less influence on what shall be than even the most modest of them realize'. Since that admission is true of many good writers and eloquent speakers, how much more widely true it is of the rest of us— especially in Speech, where, except on formal occasions, we are less concerned to preserve the proprieties of language.

The strength and the driving force, the pervasive generality, and the tacit acceptance, by men outwardly 'respectable', of the vernacular can perhaps be seen best in Cockney. Linguistically a dialect, Cockney is also a vernacular; it arose in London; it has, over many centuries, developed in London. Despite all the standardizing influences of trade and commerce, of government and tradition, of literature and the arts, of science and technics, of the visits and sojournings of foreigners and Colonials, and despite the weighty pressure exercised upon it by the vast mass of London—despite all these and other influences, Cockney has preserved a healthy, independent life. Cockney possesses tremendous vitality, almost infinite resourcefulness, swashbuckling picturesqueness, and a kindly clear-eyed realism. It may be said to form a heightened vernacular, a vernacular *in excelsis*. I do not for a moment suggest that the vernacular predominant in (say) A.D. 2050 will, in the main, resemble Cockney, whether in vocabulary, phrasing, style, or, much less, in pronunciation, this last approximation being improbable and perhaps not altogether desirable, and the former characteristics impossible—for, in these respects, the vernacular simply could not keep up with Cockney. I do suggest that the forces and qualities of Cockney are, in lesser degree, present in the vernacular as a whole; that they will preserve it; that they will perhaps bring to it a slow, gradual, for the most part imperceptible and unconscious ascendancy over literary English; and that, with probably some benefit deriving from it, they will perhaps absorb literary English and even incorporate all Standard English, whether British Standard or American Standard.

The tendency of the vernacular to overcome the literary is as old as the existence of a literary standard. That, in almost every language, literary speech and writing had evolved from the vernacular is a truism, so blindly, unthinkingly accepted that very few scholars, or others, have mentioned the fact. That the literary could, entirely or mainly, be re-absorbed into the vernacular is an eventuality hitherto unstated, except, by implication, in terms of the daunting possibility of a victory by barbarism over civilization.

Jespersen, Greig and one or two others have recommended, in particular, the discarding of inflections and, in general, the simplification of English; but nobody, so far as I'm aware, has advanced the view that English will gain, for itself and all those Britons and Americans and others who use it, a remarkable victory if the vernacular absorbs all other forms, the more so, assuredly, if it takes a few hints from those other forms—as it probably will, the spirit of the vernacular being in no way doctrinaire or arrogant or narrow-minded or little-souled. All-embracing in its tendencies, the vernacular will, in effect, embrace everything, from the 'highest' to the 'lowest' and from the 'least' to the 'greatest'. No one will need to appeal against the vernacular, for the vernacular will be the speech of all: not a speech superimposed by law-givers thinking only of their own needs; not a speech superimposed at all; but a free growth. And the written vernacular will be identical with the spoken, speech and writing being merely two aspects of one thing.

In point of fact, changes of accidence and syntax may be neither so drastic nor so wide-ranging as Professor Greig has envisaged; nor does the vernacular much depend upon such changes. Yet there will almost certainly be a thoroughgoing regularization and simplification. The gap between the spoken and the written language will gradually close. Idiom and vernacular, already so intimately related, will merge, in the sense that idiom will form a part of the vernacular. But idiom is also an integral part of all English, whether vernacular or literary; idiom forms one of the channels by which English has been irrigated and kept fresh; so that, to an increasing yet still very far from predominant degree, the vernacular itself forms one of those channels of beneficial—indeed, necessary—irrigation. 'The enemy' is already within the gate, and well beyond; the revolt has only to grow, as grow it will; and finally the revolutionary rule will be the accepted form of government; 'vernacular English' will become 'English'.

Even more widely and profoundly than in ancient Rome will the vernacular predominate. In the Rome of the late Republican and early Imperial era, perhaps 5 per cent. of the population could write Classical Latin and perhaps 10 per cent. speak it, the rest speaking Vulgar (or Low) Latin and, if they could write at all, writing it; Vulgar Latin was spoken by the slaves, whose vernacular partly determined the nature of Vulgar Latin and, in turn, was gradually so influenced by it, that the vernacular, in its literal sense, became identical with Vulgar Latin. It was the speakers of Vulgar Latin—soldiers, hangers-on, sailors, merchants and tradesmen—who startlingly predominated, numerically, in any army serving beyond Italy: it was they who, in Spain and Portugal, France and Rumania, founded, upon a basis of Vulgar, not of Classical Latin, the languages that, diverging ever more and more from the parent stock, we know as Spanish, Portuguese, French, Rumanian. The Medieval Church preserved and later the Renascence introduced many words from Classical Latin, both for the Romance languages and for those Teutonic (including Scandinavian) languages which came under the influence, ecclesiastical or linguistic, of Rome; yet the Vulgar Latin stock was never submerged, the old Roman vernacular persisted.

There is, however, no need to invoke either the historical or the moral example of Vulgar Latin to account for the persistence of the English vernacular. When the vast majority of any nation speaks the 'vulgar', not the literary tongue—and most nations do—that vulgar tongue (the vernacular) will not, for it cannot, be ousted by the literary. The literary may gain the mastery in the field of writing; the Standard may gain the mastery in that of speech; but not for always; sometimes, by the reckoning of history, not for long. Take Italy itself! In the Middle Ages, monks and a few others preserved literary Latin, yet even literary Latin had been and was still being so transformed that few persons would, even in those days, have called it Classical. Elsewhere, Vulgar Latin and Classical Latin were merging: changing into Italian.

In the Old English period, what proportion of the population of England spoke anything other than the vernacular— or wrote anything at all? We don't know more than this, that the proportion must have been very small. The Normans drove English underground: yet English finally overcame Norman-French, by which, English having always been an acquisitive and chameleon language, it had, all along, profited considerably. The Renascence soon discredited the vernacular: yet the vernacular was, from the beginning, able to insinuate many a 'good old Saxon word' into the mass of ink-horn terms, and was to continue to do so.

Often contemned, usually frowned upon, the vernacular has irresistibly marched towards its unconscious goal; precisely because of that unconsciousness, the goal is the more likely to be attained. The best educated and the most cultured men and women have, during all periods and at all ages, acknowledged its power and the righteousness of its cause; never truculently or flamboyantly, and seldom wittingly, yet all the more remarkably and convincingly, they have admitted both its right to exist and its inherent rightness. Most educated and cultured persons, except perhaps the arrogant and the short-sighted, must, from time to time, have experienced a twinge of conscience, a feeling of malaise, a sense of being victims of a senseless snobbery, when they have thought to compare—that is, when they did think to compare—the hard-won correctitude and the strained concentration required to maintain it, the intellectual gymnastics or the subtlety or the relentless logic, and also the high-falutin' imagery of much conventional poetry, with the simple, direct, frank, precise, unstrainedly picturesque, often immediately (as opposed to allusively or exaltedly) poetic language, homely yet dignified, brief yet powerful, of those whom they have called 'the common herd' or 'the uneducated' or 'those yokels' or some other question-begging label.

Confronted with the problem, most scholars and other educated or cultured persons will concede that, on any reckoning, the quantitative importance of the vernacular is not merely considerable but perhaps overwhelming. The vernacular may yet prove to the scoffing sceptics (how very small, relatively, is the 'class' they think they speak for, they seem to have failed even to suspect) that qualitatively, too, it has a comparable importance—or that it will ultimately have that importance.

Many speakers of Standard English—especially those who speak Public School Standard but also those who, in the Dominions, necessarily speak a Modified Standard—are un-aware that a large proportion of their linguistic 'inferiors' would not speak the relevant Standard even if they had the opportunity; some distrust it, some dislike it, some both distrust and dislike it; to them, to 'talk posh' is not a social acquisition but a human derogation. Linguistically they may be right—or wrong; socially they may be well or ill advised, although only a monstrously one-sided person would hold accent to be more important than character; intellectually they may be wrong—or right; morally, no question arises.

Facts speak louder than prejudices. If one dispassionately surveys the general trend of English since it broke free from the yoke of Norman-French and if, further, one concentrates

upon the history of English, both in the British Commonwealth and in the United States of America, one discerns,
perhaps reluctantly but certainly very clearly, an almost
nation-wide 'stream of tendency' away from the elaborate
towards the simple, away from the allusive and indirect towards the direct, away from the remote towards the immediate, away from the artificial towards the natural: and one
perceives that language itself has moved along with it. Ever
since during the War of 1914-1918, language has become more
earthy—and yet, except to those who constitutionally must
wear rose-coloured spectacles, more comforting; more realistic
and simple, yet less subject to vogue and fashion.

This is not the place to deal exhaustively with the shirt-
sleeved language, the friendly, informal, mood-of-the-moment
language, the utterly natural and sheerly personal yet richly
common language that is the vernacular; nor yet fully to
indicate (one cannot yet irrefutably prove) the progress made
by the vernacular; nor again to point to the gigantic strides it
has taken in America (my collaborator may be saying something about this), except merely to record that Ring Lardner
(1885-1933), especially in *You Know Me Al*, 1916—rather less,
Damon Runyon (1884-1946), especially in *Guys and Dolls*,
1932—and, so far the least notably of the three, John Steinbeck
(b. 1902)—have at least indicated the immense potentialities of
the vernacular.

Painfully conscious of the inadequacy of what I have written,
I wish only to add that national, perhaps also international convenience, may speed the acceptance of the vernacular; that the
gains (e.g. simplicity, vigour, sympathy, warm humanity,
accessibility, universality, power to promote general understanding—hence, power for good) would probably outweigh
the losses; and that, even if I thought the reverse to be desirable,
I should still have to admit that 'the vernacular' will probably
end by being synonymous with 'English', and 'English' synonymous with 'the vernacular'. If that happens, there will be
only one kind of English.

POSTSCRIPT
ON THE VERNACULAR

Should the vernacular attain to supremacy, it would inevitably require the lucidity, hence even much of the subtlety, of Standard English; hence, also, much of its variety and, through the inescapable needs of the human spirit, something of its formal beauty. In its very rise to ascendancy, the vernacular would be forced to become rather less illiterate and imprecise. In short, the victory of the vernacular would not be synonymous with the victory of the uneducated, nor yet with that of the barbarism.

I myself prefer that English remain the supple, various, subtle, flexible, almost infinitely adaptable instrument it now is, an instrument even more wonderful than was Attic Greek at its best; and I believe that the creative elect will continue to write such English, the receptive elect to enjoy reading it, despite the predominance of the vernacular; a predominance not at all certain, yet probable rather than merely possible. If the vernacular gain the mastery, it will, I think, retain it. Yet ultimately that victorious vernacular would, I believe, be reshaped to something finer: that, remaining the vernacular and continuing to preclude a competitive Standard English, it would conceivably be transformed into something in some respects superior to the present Standard, in that it would incorporate all the virtues of the vernacular and many, perhaps most, of those of Standard English. The spirit of man is invincible. That spirit would, in its mysterious way, ensure that the spiritual and the emotive needs and activities of mankind should march dauntlessly abreast of its physical and intellectual needs and activities.

ACKNOWLEDGEMENTS

I have to thank the following gentlemen and their publishers for their very generous permission to quote from the poems and verse plays of Mr T. S. Eliot, O.M. (and Messrs Faber & Faber), Mr W. H. Auden (and Messrs Faber & Faber), and Mr Christopher Fry (and The Oxford University Press).

Equally generous permission has been granted by The British Council (the holders of the copyrights) to reprint matter from these *Since* 1939 pamphlets: Mr John Hayward's *Prose Literature*, Mr Henry Reed's *The Novel*, Mr Robert Speaight's *The Drama* and Mr Stephen Spender's *Poetry*. To those writers I am grateful for their very helpful co-operation.

No less generous have been the following contributors to the 'A Decade in Retrospect' symposium, published, during 1950, in *The Month* (and the Editor and Proprietors of that valuable review): Mr Roy Campbell, M. André Simon and Mr F. A. Voigt. They have said—much better than I could have done—some of the things I myself had planned to say.

Finally, I must thank Dr John Hubert Jagger for permission to quote from his *English in the Future* (Messrs Thomas Nelson & Sons), Sir Ernest Gowers, K.C.B., K.B.E., to quote from *Plain Words* (His Majesty's Stationery Office); and especially Professor J. Y. T. Greig, to quote from *Breaking Priscian's Head* (Messrs Routledge & Kegan Paul).

E. P.

PART II

American English

*

CHAPTER ONE

THE CHARACTERISTICS OF AMERICAN ENGLISH AND THEIR ORIGIN

WHAT *is* "the English language"? For that matter, what is "American English"? In a broad sense, the English language is any form of the native language of English-speaking people whose native language is commonly called English—an obviously and absurdly circular definition, of course, but just about the only generally acceptable one; and as for American English, the same definition is equally satisfactory or unsatisfactory if for "the English language" we substitute "American English". Most people would find it hard to define a dog, but no one has any difficulty in identifying one.

Just because of the variety of forms of discourse called English, and because of the human faculty of wonder, it is tempting, in any book on the subject written for English-speaking people, to pay a great deal of attention to the freakish, the idiosyncratic, the bizarre, the obscure, the provincial, and the vestigial. All these things are interesting and illuminating and worth attending to and, in a sense, important; but what is more important than any of them is the normal and the general, and, just because native speakers of any variety of English are so familiar with what is for them normal and general, and unconsciously so sequacious of its unceasing movement, they are likely to be as imperfectly aware of its essential qualities and tendencies as of those of the air they breathe. "Je dis de la prose sans que j'en susse rien." The object of the following section of this book is to help its readers to a clearer sight of what has happened to the English language in America in the last fifty years and why it has happened—a subject that most Americans probably think nothing need be said about, and many Englishmen, perhaps, think the less said about, the better.

A language is a part of a culture (not in the women's-club sense, but in the anthropologist's), and reflects that culture in considerable detail. The most important event of the last hundred and fifty years of Western culture—in some ways, it might be argued, the most important event in human history—is the rapid transformation of an agrarian society (one in which the great majority of men are almost exclusively occupied with the direct production of food—chiefly their own) into a technological one (one in which the application of technology to agriculture liberates from that employment large masses of the population, who are then deflected into the occupation of tending the machines that represent the application of technology to the production of other than agricultural goods). Two peasants out of three leave the plow for the factory.

Largely because a factory takes less space and costs more money than a farm, the application of technology to producing non-agricultural goods leads to increasingly numerous and populous cities, and of this, one important result is the urbanization of culture.

Applied science and the growth of cities, then, have profoundly affected modern Western society and culture and all aspects of that culture, including language. But there is a third influence of more or less equal power, namely, democracy, or the rise of the masses, of which the essential quality is, almost by definition, the heightened influence of the many on almost every aspect of the culture of their society. Democracy is of course complexly related to technology and urbanization, and they are related to each other both as cause and as effect: the order in which I have for convenience introduced the three terms into this discussion is not chronological, but neither would any other order be.

Almost all the changes that have come about, within the last hundred and fifty years and especially within the last fifty, in

Western society, culture, and specifically language, and more specifically in the English language, and yet more specifically in American English (by which I mean, here and elsewhere, the language of the United States), are, I think, chargeable to the direct or indirect influence of one or more of these three forces, with the single qualification that we should include pure science —philosophical science, so to speak—along with technology or applied science, as being partly its parent and partly its child, and as operating on culture sometimes conjointly with technology and sometimes separately.

Of the three forces, at least two, science and democracy, work with less restraint in the United States than in Great Britain; and it is to this fact that I should attribute many of the leading differences between British and American English, especially in the last half century.

I say "especially in the last half century" because even if science and democracy had not advanced beyond the point they had reached in 1900—or in 1800—American English would doubtless differ now, as it differed then, from British English. The chief reasons for such difference as existed in 1900, and still more in 1800, were the difference in physical environment, for example, in climate, terrain, flora and fauna, and density of population; the difference in dominant background and temperament between the British and the American peoples; and the different social and economic and— secondarily and derivatively—political and educational organization.

The first point hardly needs illustration: one need only think of the different senses in which Englishmen and Americans use such words as *robin, daisy, corn, creek, barn*, and *to hunt*, and of the early British immigrants' adoption of a considerable number of American Indian names (and later, Spanish ones) for things unknown in Great Britain. The second point perhaps requires a little more discussion. In the first place, early British immigrants to America were predominantly of the lower and lower-middle classes; their language differed from that of their social betters partly because of the social difference itself, partly because of ignorance, and partly because of jealousy, which can lead to (usually imperfect) imitation, but which can just as well lead to perversely deliberate divagation. In the second place, immigrants are typically misfits, or enterprising, or (commonly) both, and consequently tend to be sturdily self-reliant, opinionated to the point of surliness, and given to innovation, partly from eccentricity, partly from ignorance of old ways, and partly from the irrelevance or insufficiency of those ways under new conditions. The third point is even more familiar than the first; but I will mention one illustration. Some years ago I used to ask college freshmen who had been reading Macaulay's great "third chapter" to write themes comparing some aspect of England in 1685 with the corresponding aspect of America in the 1930's. One of the favorite topics was the country gentleman; and of many—too many—scores of themes that I have read on the subject, not one ever showed any comprehension of the essential differences between the seventeenth-century English squire and the twentieth-century Middle Western American farmer—whose real opposite number was of course the prosperous yeoman.

Here then are six leading influences to which I should attribute the principal differences between British and American English. But there are several more influences, some of them special developments of the six main ones, some of them more or less independent. The first of these is the conservatism of most transplanted languages. This is illustrated not only by the English of the United States, but also by that of Ireland, as well as by the Norse of Iceland, the French of Quebec, and in some ways the Spanish of Latin America. Its coexistence with the contrary tendency to innovation may seem paradoxical, but is undeniable. Further influences are (2) the influence of business and advertising and "efficiency"; (3) the universality, if not of literacy, then at any rate of what we may call quasi-literacy; (4) the somewhat paradoxical bookishness of American culture —its dependence, more than in England, on the printed word; (5) social climbing, proceeding mainly from the exceptional fluidity of American social classes; (6) what I will call, for the want of a better name, puritanism; and (7) the influence of non-British immigrants. To these we might add an eighth, chauvinism, which displays itself in two forms: Anglophobia, and xenophobia generally. Anglophobia—conscious and specific Anglophobia—has greatly decreased since *American Notes* and *Martin Chuzzlewit*, and, so far as it still exists among the populace, tends now to blend with inverted snobbishness. Xenophobia of the more general kind expresses itself, at least in the sphere of language, mainly on a low social and educational plane, in such utterances as "Why don't you talk American?" muttered at UN delegates on trains plying between the Pennsylvania Station in New York and Lake Success.

The characteristics of American English throughout its history, and especially in the last fifty years, may, I think, be explained almost entirely in terms of the action and interaction of these dozen or more factors. They operate in vocabulary, in idiom and syntax and general tone and style, and in pronunciation and even spelling, and under these successive headings (with a certain amount of more or less unavoidable overlapping) I have arranged most of the specific illustrations of my thesis; but certain details, for reasons of convenience, will be given special treatment under the headings "education" and "British and American English". Before proceeding, however, to these topics, I wish to say something of two more general ones: (1) certain special qualities of American culture and the American character, and (2) the several uses and levels of language and their interrelations.

(1) One of the traits of the American character (and hence of American English) owing a good deal to several of the factors named above is a sort of nervous diffidence, leading to an ambivalent attitude toward superiority of any kind (or perhaps toward anything strange, of the merit of which the standardless and drifting mind can not judge). The attitude is half envy and half contempt. In other words, Americans tend perhaps more than Englishmen to forget Gilbert's adjuration not to "treat with virtuous scorn the well connected." The old tag "De gustibus" is generally misunderstood as meaning that anyone's taste is as good as anyone else's, "and probably a damned sight better." But there is one significant exception to this: the prevailing American attitude toward anything that can make

a colorable claim to being "scientific" is paradoxically quite lacking in genuinely scientific scepticism; it is uncritical and credulous and deferential to the degree of superstition. To Comte's three successive stages of the theological, the metaphysical, and the positive, three successive popular or vulgar attitudes correspond very closely: (1) "The Church says so"; (2) "Seen it in print"; (3) "Scientists say ..." *Plus ça change* ... The noise made (in 1950) by Mr Velikovsky's *Worlds in Collision* and by stories about "flying saucers" are cases in point.

Closely related to all this is a sort of "lo here, lo there" attitude that shows itself with regard to language, but also with regard to the arts generally, politics, economics, religion, education, medicine, amusements, clothing, furniture, automobiles, radio receivers, electric refrigerators, gas stoves— almost everything. The attitude proceeds of course from the modern idea of progress, which is in effect that new things are frequent nowadays, that they are often better than old things, and that therefore they are always better. This attitude is certainly not peculiar to America or to the present day; but the exigencies of a uniquely competitive commercial society naturally operate through advertising and other mediums so as to extend the incidence and aggravate the virulence of the disease. The thing has a way of backfiring, of course: if you were anxious above all things else to be up to the minute the day before yesterday, you will almost certainly be conspicuously out of date the day after tomorrow. What "twenty-three, skidoo" is now, "drop dead" will shortly be.

The literary culture of a people is what its members have in common. It shows itself especially in allusion. Among the ancient Greeks it was Homer and Hesiod; among English-speaking people it was for a long time the King James Bible (it was never Shakespeare in the same degree). Today in the United States it is the comic strip and the popular radio program. There are too many things to read (and hear), and there are too many things to read and hear partly because there are so many things to say and so many cheap and easy opportunities of saying them to large audiences. People do not reread or memorize. As a consequence they tend to become tone-deaf to language and careless of it; their attention is almost necessarily limited to the substance of what is said. To a certain extent there is more that needs saying, but even independently of that there has been a decline in the average writer's sense of responsibility and in the average reader's taste and discrimination.

Matthew Arnold long ago heard it across the Atlantic, though its melancholy slow-approaching roar did not make him a pessimist, at any rate in the long run. "We are often told," he said at the end of *The Study of Poetry*, "that an era is opening in which we are to see multitudes of a common sort of readers, and masses of a common sort of literature; that such readers do not want and could not relish anything better than such literature, and that to provide it is becoming a vast and profitable industry. Even if good literature entirely lost currency with the world, it would still be abundantly worth while to continue to enjoy it by oneself. But it never will lose currency with the world, in spite of momentary appearances; it will never lose supremacy. Currency and supremacy are insured to it, not indeed by the world's conscious and deliberate choice, but by something far deeper—by the instinct of self-preservation in humanity." Perhaps Arnold did not mean quite so much that the same good thing will always be esteemed best, as that *some* good thing will be: out of strength cometh forth sweetness. The heart-warming joke in any contest between elegance and barbarism, in language and literature as well as in society, has always been that, if barbarism has won, it has always given rise in the end to a new elegance. The language of Voltaire is in origin bad Latin. But there is a distressing possibility that our barbarism, unlike its predecessors, may not produce a new elegance; for our barbarism is unique in being deliberately cultivated among persons who, thanks to universal "education", are perfectly unaware that they are barbarous. The holy and humble illiteracy of the dark-ages peasant is a far more promising matrix for the rebirth of civilization than the cynical and bombastic semi-literacy of the twentieth-century advertising man. The great danger that threatens the English language in America (and, the more dominant America becomes, in all English-speaking countries) is not the rise of the masses directly: without guidance they would in the end fulfill Arnold's hope; the great danger is that *with misguidance* they will *not* fulfill it, and with misguidance they are abundantly supplied by educated knaves and half-educated fools. Antæus cannot reach his mother the earth through a layer of slime.

(2) The uses and levels of language. By "uses" here I mean spoken and written (and sometimes colloquial and literary, which are not always the same things as spoken and written respectively); by "levels," I mean for the most part educated and uneducated (with full realization that these are both relative terms). Professor H. C. Wyld's doctrine that the literary style must never cut off the roots that bind it to the soil of the contemporary colloquial style must be understood of the *educated* colloquial style, not the uneducated. There is a somewhat similar relation between the educated and the uneducated colloquial styles; but it is interesting to note that the uneducated colloquial style has usually affected the literary only indirectly, through the educated colloquial. One of the things that make the literary (or rather the written) style in the United States in the last fifty years unusual is that, in a unique degree, uneducated people often have important and even admirable, or at least urgent, things to say, and say them in writing—which gets printed. There is here a remarkable kind of short circuit. This is, both directly and indirectly, the effect of universal literacy. The same thing has happened in England, but not to the same extent, because of the greater strength there of social and educational distinctions.

Professor Wyld propounds his thesis in these words (*A History of Modern Colloquial English*, third ed., 1936, p. 188): "The style of Literature is rooted in the life and conversation of the age. From these sources alone can prose renew its life from generation to generation. When Literary prose style loses touch with the spoken language it becomes lifeless and unexpressive, powerless to 'strike the ear, the heart, or the fancy', remote alike from human feeling and from the speech of man because it has never known real life or movement." What interests me here is not so much the truth of the doctrine (which I admit) as the style in which it is expressed. That style is decidedly literary, and not peculiarly or characteristically colloquial at all, as doubtless Professor Wyld intended and knew. We must suppose that in this passage, of all passages, he meant and tried to illustrate his own doctrine, and to write English "rooted in the life and conversation of the age". But he did *not* try to write colloquial English, much less uneducated English; he wrote a highly educated literary English, he knew that he was doing so, and he was not belying his own doctrine, properly understood.

An earlier passage in the same book (p. 157) has an even more important bearing on the subject of these pages. "We may make every possible allowance," says Professor Wyld, "for differences which distinguish the various types of colloquial speech from each other ... and for those differences again which divide the style of uttered speech from that of written prose, ... yet we must recognize that at a given period the language is everywhere one and the same—within the limits of the same dialect—and that written and uttered language ..., from the most familiar and colloquial to the most elevated and carefully finished, are all of a piece; ... they breathe the same general spirit and atmosphere, and express, in divers tones, the same characteristic genius of the age to which they belong."

It is important to recognize the truth of this observation, especially as it applies to American English from 1900 to 1950. It is hard to say whether uneducated speech in America has become, in those fifty years, more familiar, more easy-going, breezier; but certainly all the other uses and levels—educated speech, and both educated and uneducated writing—have become so. This is partly the result of the rise of the masses, but also, I should say, to some extent the result of the relaxation of the educated—their growing confidence that their usage is good usage. So far as this is a sign of increasing civilization, it is all to the good. An almost equally important fact to recognize, however, is the reality of the differences that persist between various uses and levels of language, and the recognition of it is something that Mr H. L. Mencken sometimes seems to me to make too little of (in his incomparably valuable work *The*

American Language, fourth ed., 1936; *Supplement One*, 1945; *Supplement Two*, 1948): he is so eager to establish the occurrence of this or that repellent locution that he is now and then perhaps a little careless whether or not his reader forms an exaggerated impression of its currency or repute.

That speech should and does affect writing is manifestly not a revelation vouchsafed only to Professor Wyld and Mr Mencken; for example, at nearly the same time as their principal pronouncements Professor W. E. Leonard wrote in *American Speech* (vol. 8 (1933), p. 57): "In general every good colloquialism is possible in good prose (or verse), for quite rightly good prose (or verse) is becoming more and more a skilful adaptation of the vigorous, compact, racy idiom of the best spoken speech." The only quarrel I have with this is that it is subject to misinterpretation and even misrepresentation. One should note carefully "good" and "best"—they imply a standard and a judgment. One should note also that Leonard says "skilful adaptation"—not "indiscriminate transference." And finally, one should note "vigorous, compact, racy"; speech may be any one or two of these without being all three, and generally speaking, unless it is all three, little is to be said for its imitation in writing.

There can be no doubt, however, that American English in the last half century (like any language in any period) can and should be considered in many ways as a single entity, subject in its several forms to the same influences, or that the principal influences on that single entity have been colloquialization and vulgarization. (The latter term, I hope, will be understood with no more emotional coloring than I here use it with.) Colloquialization and vulgarization are certainly not the same thing, but they overlap, and together they have in the last fifty years more and more encroached upon and colored what we may call the distinctively traditional and educated literary style. The ultimate reason again is the rise of the masses, who are (not without historical justification) suspicious of intellect and cultivation; and these usually exhibit themselves in a manner of speech (and writing) different from that of the masses. Yesterday the masses neither hoped nor even much wished to understand their betters, and were even disposed to make un-intelligibility a criterion of superiority. My grandfather (born in 1857) has told me of being sent as a child with his father's slave (so that Old Joe might enter a white church) to hear Henry Ward Beecher preach, and of the old man's disappointed exclamation at the end of the sermon: "W'y, *he* ain' no preacher! Ol' Joe un'erstan' every word he say!" Today the masses believe that they can and insist that they shall under-stand, or at least that they shall seem to themselves to do so (though the mysteries of science tend to be an exception, as the mysteries of theology did a few decades ago). That ideally they should is clear; whether they can is dubious. Writers and public speakers, to meet the demands of the new and powerful audience of the uneducated and often stupid, necessarily sim-plify the substance and the manner of their utterance. Now simplicity is a good thing, but it can be overdone, and it is overdone when language is simplified beyond the point that the idea can bear. The bowing and scraping of artists and scholars and men of light and leading generally before Its Majesty the People is not a much prettier spectacle than the same postures before princes and other magnates a few genera-tions ago, and its effect on scholarship and art and science, and light and leading generally, is a good deal worse.

As for language specifically, a literary standard in some ways *is* (or tends to be or should be) "better" than the contemporary spoken standard (to say nothing of the contemporary spoken sub-standard): it is more lucid, more precise, more econom-ical, more euphonious, more richly connotative, more digni-fied, more splendid—all these things because it is more deliber-ate, more calculated. Of course, calculation, or the appearance of it, is or is felt to be, in many colloquial situations, inappropriate to the point of being ludicrous or even offensive; relaxation and ingenuousness (or at least apparent relaxation and ingenuousness) may be more suitable, and in such situa-tions calculation (or at least apparent calculation) is injudici-ous; but that does not mean that, in many other situations, clarity, precision, economy, euphony, etc., are not desirable. Much is heard nowadays of writing as you speak; is there not *something* to be said for speaking as you write? The spoken language constantly and properly modifies the written; but in any civilization rightly so called, the spoken language of the intelligent and educated sections of society modifies and should modify the spoken language of the other sections, and is modified in turn and should be modified by the written language. Lucidity, precision, economy, and the rest, are not everything, even in writing; but relaxation and ingenuousness are not everything, either, even in speech. And further, because some of the qualities in which calculated language tends to excel— clarity, precision, richness of connotation—are in varying degrees especially dependent on tradition, a distinctive written standard should and must exist and should and must be comparatively traditional and conservative—and hence, the variety of human nature being what it is, in some degree aristocratic and exclusive. I have heard it said that the radio program "Information, Please" originated in a conversation between its producer and Mr F. P. Adams, who, on responding automatically with "Antonio" to the question, "What was the name of the Merchant of Venice?", was told by the producer that most people would answer, "Shylock." "Not," said Mr Adams judiciously, "in the circles *I* move in." Whether this anecdote is canonical or not is not important. What is important is that it illustrates, if not the gap between the educated and the uneducated, the gap between the educated and the half-educated—a gap that is, if not wider, in some important ways deeper, and that is seen in language as well as in general knowledge.

CHAPTER TWO

VOCABULARY

EVERY American has some notion of what a staggering number of new words, and new applications of old ones, have entered his language in the last fifty years, on all levels of usage, especially slang and popularized technology. Even the number of these that will probably be more or less permanent, though much smaller, is still very great. No registry of these can possibly be either complete or up to date, and to supply even the beginnings of such a registry is the last thing that this book would pretend to do—partly because that job has been and is being more or less done in other publications and partly because this is a small book, but chiefly because accretions to the vocabulary are the most obvious and familiar kind of change in language and consequently least in need of discussion, or at least of exhaustive enumeration.

The most notable registry of these accretions to American English is to be found in Mr Mencken's *American Language* and its supplements. (The *Dictionary of American English*, though a very valuable work, does not generally attempt to deal with additions since 1900; Berrey and Van Den Bark's *American Thesaurus of Slang* (1942) has the limitation shown by the title, though hardly any other.) Mr Mencken is at great pains to record every revolting freak he can find. It is questionable, I think, whether he has not wasted some of his very valuable time. Many of the neologisms he is at such pains to record are nonce-words, or nearly so: they are commercial speculations, many of them, sometimes naive, sometimes cynical, and these, at least, enjoy virtually no currency at all outside of the shop-signs and telephone directories and house organs in which he has found them. In rejecting them (or rather, for the most part, in ignoring them) the populace shows a sound instinct, even if tempered by dullness. They are popular only in the sense of being, most of them, hopefully designed for the people—not in the sense

BAE

of springing from them, nor even in that of appealing successfully to their fancy. A few catch on and survive; but the
mortality rate is very high. The objection is not a general one
to neologisms, nor yet to the emergence and habilitation of
expressions of genuinely popular or even vulgar origin; the
objection is to almost the opposite: the essential phoniness—
what is more, the cynical phoniness—of such expressions. We
may say of advertising and the allied arts, at least so far as language is concerned, *"Nihil quod tangunt ornant."* The reason
why Mr Mencken welcomes with such warmth, or at least
records with such glee, the thousands of nauseating novelties
to be found in his great book is not, of course, that he has bad
taste; on the contrary, I am bold to say that good taste is conspicuous among Mr Mencken's other virtues, most of which are
rarer than good taste. The reason is rather that he has too much
good taste. As a student of the history of the language, I am of
course grateful to Mr Mencken for spreading his copious flow
of amber over so many flies, and even over so many gilded bugs
that stink and sting; but I do wish he would oftener express
what must be his true feelings. On p. 384 of *Supplement One*
to *The American Language* he speaks of "age and general
acceptance" as "fatuous" tests of propriety. I confess I do not
see what other tests there can be except utility, logic, analogy,
and perhaps euphony, and I hardly think Mr Mencken would
regard any of them as superior except perhaps sometimes
utility—and even Mr Mencken's well-known prejudices
include some good healthy linguistic ones that classify him very
definitely as no complete utilitarian in language. Mr Mencken
is no libertarian either, or at any rate no leveller: no one despises more than he the vulgar and tasteless and affected usages
that he so delightedly records. His occasional semblance of an
open mind is illusory. Mr Mencken's bark, in fact, is a good
deal worse than his bite. For example, he admittedly dislikes
and never uses the very widely accepted (and sometimes quite
useful) American "one ... he" construction, and on p. 384ff. of
The American Language, Supplement One, he lists over fifty
verbs-from-nouns of which he says, they "meet genuine needs,
and deserve to be treated with more seriousness than they

usually get," but at least half of which I cannot imagine Mr Mencken himself treating or using seriously—among them, *to secretary*, *to momentum*, *to baton*, *to architect*, and *to loudspeaker*.

Most neologisms invented by other people tend to be in some degree distasteful or offensive to almost anybody but a completely insensitive and tasteless person or one indiscriminately receptive of novelty for novelty's sake. Essentially we dislike neologisms when and because they proceed (as they usually do) from motives that we dislike or from what we despise as disabilities from which we do not suffer—and sometimes abilities that we envy. Generally speaking, almost the only neologisms that we like are, first, new words for really new things (for example, *television*), and second, inventions that succeed in amusing us without arousing our envy. Among the motives and disabilities that are likely to be despised are greed, mendacity, conceit, affectation, hypocrisy, impudence, timidity, exhibitionism, and either ignorance or learning surpassing our own. No blame should attach to a dislike of neologisms that are perceived or felt to spring from properly detestable qualities or motives. Innovation in language tends to be valuable and admirable according to the linguistic and general intellectual ability of the innovator. *La carrière ouverte aux talents.*

When a neologism, then, both supplies a real gap and is invented by an able (or lucky) person, it is likely to be acceptable and quickly accepted. A good example is *cold war*, in very common—and terribly serious—use in 1950, but very new: according to Mr Lowell Thomas's CBS newscast (an interesting and useful neologism itself) on 3 May 1950, Mr Bernard Baruch (who, incidentally, pronounces his name "buh*rooke*") asserts that Mr H. B. Swope invented the term in 1947 and that he (Baruch) popularized it. A decidedly different kind of neologism, but one equally accepted, is *baby-sitter*—that is, a person (usually a girl in her 'teens) hired to watch children while their parents are "out for the evening". This is interesting (and acceptable) for two reasons: (1) It reflects a number of features of contemporary American culture—urbanization, small families, prosperity leading to "going out for the evening," social climbing, and (somewhat paradoxically) the servantless and yet prosperous household—which in turn reflects industrialization. (The *thing* of course occurs sporadically much earlier and outside of America—one need only think of the Kenwigses; but the *name*, and a frequency of the thing so great that it demands a name, are recent.) (2) The violation it does to idiom and logic, which would require something like "baby-sitter-*with*," proceeds from humor, and from a kind of humor that is a sort of inversion of that illustrated by the now familiar (and rather tiresome) by-words of the pattern of *tripper-upper* (that is, one who trips [someone] up), in which the agential -*er* is repeated at the end of the compound with humorous intent. Again, urbanization and technology are reflected in such an invention as *kitchenette*, which became, very shortly after its invention about 1901 (see *The New Yorker* of 21 August 1937), a normal and unaffected part of every urban American's daily vocabulary—and for that matter, of every urban Englishman's.

The progress of scientific invention affects not only the standard vocabulary, but also that of slang and its congeners, which since 1900 have taken over, for example, "hitting on all four [cylinders]" (that is, "working efficiently") from the language of automobilists, "This is where we came in" (that is, "the same thing all over again") from the "continuous showings" of movie theaters, "wired for sound" (that is, "loud-mouthed") from the early days of the "talkies," and "do a tail spin" ("suffer a sudden and ignominious defeat in a dispute," "lose one's self-possession") and "on the beam" ("working efficiently," etc.) from aviation. On the other hand, technological obsolescence ends the common currency of some terms; for example, *freewheeling*, which, though used for a long time by bicyclists, did not become universally familiar till applied to automobiles, whereupon it had a brief metaphorical use in such senses as "easy-going," "unsystematic," but is seldom heard today because the thing itself went out of use in automobiles after a short life. Again, the reader of a novel of 1920 must know what "runabouts" and "touring cars" are, or rather were; but if he is reading a novel of 1950, he will be better served by "convertible" and "station wagon". And how many people under twenty-five in 1950 could define or even describe a superheterodyne radio receiver, or would think it important to be able to do so? And—to go even further back—what of the cat's-whisker? *Stat nominis umbra.*

Another factor in keeping down the number of technical terms making a permanent place for themselves in the everyday vocabulary is the tendency for words long familiar to be applied in new technical senses, which sometimes become the dominant ones. For example, *(radio) tube, (tobacco) pipe* (this, of course, much earlier), *(chewing) gum, (motor) car.* Again, despite the commonness of *glasses* for *drinking glasses*, the word has almost driven out *spectacles*, the context usually showing clearly which is meant. One invention even displaces another in its influence on the language: *the cars* for *railway train*, now only in rustic use, was common in speech up to 1910 or so, and railway crossing signs up at least to a very few years ago still sometimes read, "Look out for the cars," a warning addressed, certainly, not to the engineer (British, "engine-driver"), but to automobilists—to the operators, that is, of what are normally nowadays meant by "cars".

Again, technical neologisms (in level of usage, often slang or something like it; in form, often abbreviations) sometimes arise only to sink back into virtual disuse just because the things they denote come to displace so largely their predecessors. Once a new process or object, that is, has largely supplanted an old one, there is a tendency to calm down linguistically and apply the old name to the new thing; thus *photo*, recorded from 1863, and *auto*, recorded from 1899, though not exactly obsolete, have been displaced mainly by *picture* and (again) *car*—the former so generally that, when specification is necessary, the full form *photograph* is heard much oftener than *photo. Talkies*, again, speedily lost almost all such currency as it had gained, as soon as nearly all "movies" became "talkies". To some extent this has happened to *(electric) refrigerator*, which is, I think, yielding to *ice-box. Frigidaire* for a while bade fair to become the ordinary term, but for one reason or another failed to acquire

the status (a status flattering but by no means altogether welcome to the original manufacturer) of certain other trade
names—for example, *aspirin*. *Eversharp* (an "automatic" pencil)
has had much the same history. *Kleenex*, on the other hand, is
used pretty loosely for a paper handkerchief no matter by
whom manufactured, and *zipper* (*pace* the B. F. Goodrich Co.
—*Zipper*) even more so in the sense of any interlocking sliding
metallic fastener doing the job of buttons or buckles. More or
less in a class by itself is *vacuum* (pronounced "vackyum") for
vacuum cleaner, so common in familiar speech that a headline-
writer in a Middle Western newspaper can (apparently without
giggling) write "3 [*sic*] Sentenced for Theft of Vacuum."

One of the ways in which science affects the vocabulary is
through its encouragement of regularity and consistency and
system. Traditional practices, in language as anywhere else, are
likely to be inconsistent and even sometimes inconvenient, but
they do enlarge one of the dimensions of life. It is, however,
perhaps rather specially characteristic of Americans today,
under the influence of "efficiency," to prefer neatness and
system and logic. An example of this is the partly successful
effort of a Middle Western newspaper to get people to call the
northern Mississippi Valley "the Upper Midwest" instead of
"the Northwest". It is true that to have two "Northwests" (the
other, sometimes called "the Pacific Northwest," being the
states of Washington and Oregon) is once in a while a little
inconvenient; but the retention, in the Middle Western region,
of the name reminiscent of the old "Northwest Territory" has
a good deal to be said for it. Likewise, the building of a new
library at my university had little sooner established for its
predecessor the flavorful name "Old Library" than that was
given up for "Burton Hall" in (rather economical) honor of an
ex-president of the university. What amounts in part to an
inversion of this (and is yet, in its flouting of tradition, fundamentally the same thing) is illustrated by Mayor LaGuardia's
effort to get his fellow-New Yorkers to call Sixth Avenue "The
Avenue of the Americas"—happily a total failure despite its
rather costly displacement of the traditional name on all street
signs. The common element in the two phenomena is, of

course, the busy-body and perfectionist cutting across of a harmless and established tradition.

Another characteristic of the twentieth-century American vocabulary that can in the main be attributed to the rage for "efficiency" (itself the result partly of science, partly of business) is the vogue of abbreviations of several kinds, chiefly acronyms and "alphabet words." The thing is obviously not new in principle. The fourteenth century yields "Caim" (that is, Cain) from the initial letters of *Carmelites, Augustinians, Jacobins,* and *Minorites,* and from the seventeenth we have "Smectymnuus," as well as "cabal" treated more or less as if formed from the first letters of the names Clifford, Arlington, Buckingham, Ashley, and Lauderdale; and in the nineteenth century, "ess pee gee" and "ess pee see kay" were in general use for the Societies for the Propagation of the Gospel and of Christian Knowledge. But the trick has been greatly extended in the United States since the very early 1930's, perhaps on the special model of *U.S.A.* ("you ess ay"), particularly as applied to governmental agencies, most of which were established by the New Deal or during and after the second world war— *NRA, WPA, PWA, OPA, WPB, ERA,* and the like. These are usually written as they are here, without periods (a new thing in itself) and in capitals, but the pronunciation is of course unaffected, being "en ar ay," etc. The same treatment is given to other classes of expressions, notably the names of colleges, such as *CCNY* ("see see en wye," College of the City of New York), *USC* (University of Southern California), *UCLA* (University of California at Los Angeles), *NYU* (New York University). When such sequences of letters happen to be pronounceable otherwise than as a series of letter-names, they are sometimes so pronounced—for example, "Ascap" (American Society of Composers, Authors, and Publishers), and in that case sometimes occasionally printed as here, in lower case (except for the first letter) instead of capitals. Sometimes, but not always—*CIO* and *AAUP* are conceivably pronounceable, I suppose, but in practice they are always treated just like *AFL* and *MLA.* A painfully silly but unhappily predictable extension of this sort of thing (which is inoffensive when it is accidental) took place in the contrivance of names for the women's branches of most of the armed services of the United States during the second world war—"improvements" on the British"Wrens" (which, as Britons know, finally became official), from "Women's Royal Naval Service," though there was one unaltered borrowing, "Wa(a)c," "Woman's Army (Auxiliary) Corps." The U.S. Navy's "Waves" ("Women Accepted for Volunteer Emergency Service") is bad enough, especially since it deprives the individual Wave of her "Service," but the Coast Guard's "Spars" (from "*Semper PARatus*" the motto of the organization) is worse, and almost exhibits signs of Alexandrian decadence. The Marine Corps, apparently *semper fidelis* to good taste as well as to more urgent obligations, has austerely refrained from adding any comparable puerility to the minor horrors of war, though it enlists women as the other branches do.

Of all the offenses against language for which the advertising spirit can be blamed directly or indirectly, the worst, I think, is that which involves the deliberate corruption of the meaning of established words. Thus *custom-made, custom-built*, has come to be used as if it meant little or nothing more than "expensive." *Exclusive*, again, as applied to clubs, hotels, restaurants, and residential districts, is sometimes only too literally accurate; as applied to shops, it is almost always an empty pretense, extremely few shops excluding any but the impecunious. An only slightly less clear case of deliberate corruption is to be found in the intentionally misleading names under which (till recent governmental regulations partly corrected the situation) comparatively cheap furs were sold—"Hudson seal," for example, being dyed muskrat. The names had long since ceased to deceive anyone, however, which is probably the reason why they were so meekly given up. And anyway, if the writers of advertising for the makers of fur coats are down, they are not out; they now enable their clients to sell unclipped sheep's hides as "mouton." Though this is deceptive, or at least flattering, it is literal and legal; the ingenuity of the drafters of statutes has not yet caught up with the resourcefulness of their friendly enemies in the advertising trade.

Many of the most obvious contrivances of advertising men fortunately just don't get popularly adopted. Perhaps on the model of "The Brain," such sweatily labored appellations as "The Body" and "The Look" have been imposed on movie-stars by their press-agents, but they have a way of dropping out of sight after a few months. So far as I know, "The Bosom" has not yet been used, partly because of popular prudery and partly because of the competition. Scarcely anyone, I should say, uses them even half-seriously—not even the most vacant-minded movie fans, whose vacuity of mind, however, attains so nearly to the absolute that the press-agents can't be blamed for trying. Movie magazines and "columns" have to be seen to be believed. Their appeal is chiefly to the vanity of their readers, and the keynote is the chummy designation of a movie star by his (or perhaps more often her) first name, along with a multiform suggestion that she loves her fans and respects their opinions. It is hard to say whether this sort of thing is more or less distasteful than the virtue-cum-solemnity dodge: "We feel," says an advertising leaflet from my liquor store, warning its customers that Scotch whiskey may get scarcer (or, as we were taught to say during the last war, "be in short supply") because many consumers are buying extraordinary quantities of it—"we feel that it is our duty to advise you regarding this situation so that you can decide what action you wish to take" —which is, being interpreted, "We think we had better tell you about this so that *you* can hoard, too."

It is pleasant to turn from hypocrisy to mere ingenuity, exemplified by a good many advertising "slogans." To be sure, sometimes they backfire, as in *Old Gold*'s "Not a cough in a carload," which I have heard uncharitably and even unjustly perverted by the irreverent, but some of them actually enter into the familiar language—for example, *Ivory Soap*'s "99-44/100 % pure." Another is *Life Buoy Soap*'s "B.O.," widely used, and more or less seriously according to the social and educational status of the user, as a euphemism for the stench of sweat. Another soap's "dish-pan hands" (hands red and rough from washing dishes) is used seriously by only somewhat fewer people than "B.O." It would almost seem as if no advertising appeal were more assured of success in America today than one made to hard-working people's desire to free themselves (chiefly by means of soap) of some of the socially disagreeable by-products of hard work. Without agreeing that the manufacturers of deodorants are mainly inspired by philanthropy, one may agree that they are public benefactors, and that the human impulse they mainly appeal to, though it may show a trace of pretense, is on the whole a thing to thank God on: the determination to smell good is not the loftiest of human concerns (as Mr Bruce Marshall reminds us, St Elizabeth of Hungary probably smelt quite a lot), but it is none the less a gratifying one to other people.

Perhaps in the belief that, if people will sometimes adopt a whole phrase, they are yet more likely to adopt a striking monosyllable, the fashion has arisen of giving monosyllabic names (more or less suggestive of the application) to (especially) detergent powders and "flakes" (for example, *Lux*, *Fab*, *Duz*). There is also some tendency to give prepared breakfast-cereals names ending in *-ies* (for example, *Wheaties*, *Rice Crispies*) probably with the view of appealing to the nursery market, though sometimes it is rather the exhilarating that is apparently meant to be suggested (*Cheerios*) or the invigorating (*Kix*). Some trade-names are a little over-advertised, so that they get imitated to within an inch of the law by competitors. A case in point is *Coke*—now copyrighted by the Coco-Cola Co., as the firm somewhat loudly insists, but contentedly employed none the less by most people with reference equally to Coco-Cola's competitors.

As cheerfulness kept creeping in to Dr Johnson's old schoolmate's philosophy, so humor keeps creeping in (savingly) to the popular attitude toward the triple complex of technology, business, and advertising. Recently at my butcher's I overheard an obviously uneducated customer say, "I want a nice thick sirloin, or a reasonable facsimile thereof." He was not being pretentious; he was being facetious, and partly at the expense of pretentiousness. Where did he pick up the expression? As almost any American over fifteen knows, from its inevitable occurrence in radio and newspaper announcements of prize competitions (especially frequent, for grim reasons, during the depression of the early 'thirties), a condition of participation in which was usually the submission, along with one's entry, of the top of an empty package that had held a tube of the "sponsor's" toothpaste, or what not—such a package, that is, *or* "a reasonable facsimile thereof." *Thereof* seldom occurs outside of statutes, of course, and even *facsimile* is not a part of most people's daily speech; but the expression as a whole has become a counterphrase of stock humor. Again, consider the case of *hamburger* (from Hamburg steak; that is, ground-beef patties), which has given rise to a bizarre development. The final *-er* is probably from the analogy of *wiener*, *frankfurter*, etc., though it may owe something to American analogues of *bedder* or *soccer*. However that may be, the ordinary usage now is *hamburger* for the substance and *a hamburger* for a sandwich filled with a cake of the substance. All this is normal enough; the oddity enters in when the word is taken (sometimes more or less seriously, perhaps, but for the most part humorously) as a compound of *ham* and *burger*, and *burger* taken to mean "sandwich with a broiled or fried filling of any kind." That is, *-burger* has become, in the jargon of the "linguistic analysts," a "bound morpheme." ("Bound" because *-burger* is not used alone.) Despite the presumably universal knowledge that there is no ham in hamburger, we have *cheeseburger*, *oysterburger*, *lobsterburger* (but not yet, so far as I know, *lobsternewburger*, though that blend—both culinary and verbal—will surely occur to someone in the process of time), and even (to swing almost full circle) *steakburger*—where the steak is *not* ground. I should not be surprised if the use of ham as a filling in broiled sandwiches would be forever inhibited by the linguistic problem that it would obviously give rise to. This sort of thing has, even at its worst, a sort of irresponsible playfulness that is almost endearing. Community of subject rather than of form suggests here also *a wimpy* (meaning *a hamburger*), from the name of the voracious and pantophagous dead-beat in Segar's comic strip "Popeye"— and that further suggests *a dagwood* (a multilayered sandwich containing everything in the icebox), from the name of

Dagwood Bumstead in another comic strip, Chic Young's "Dagwood and Blondy."

Comic strips—the Homer and Hesiod and Bible and Shake-speare of the American people—are rich sources of other kinds of popular expressions as well. One of considerable antiquity, as such things go, is "(Caspar) Milquetoast" [sic] in the sense "timid person," derived from the name of the hero (!) of a comparatively early comic strip. Of more recent borrowings. one now known all over the world is *jeep*, which probably originated, like *wimpy*, in Segar's "Popeye," where the jeep was a grotesque and ungainly but engaging little beast distinguished for loyal affection, acute intelligence, and general efficiency and dependability in the advancement of its master's interests. The more recent competitor-allies of comic strips—popular radio programs—furnish another term (like *jeep*, popularized through the medium of military use), namely, *bazooka*, which began, so far I know, as the radio clown Bob Burns's name a few years ago for a sort of hill-billy trombone constructed chiefly of lead pipe and roughly resembling the weapon named for it, both in its appearance and in the position in which it is borne by the operator.

Bazooka brings to mind the multitude of military terms, some official and formal and some even less formal than official, with which hundreds of thousands of temporary soldiers and sometimes millions of civilians became familiar during the last war. Most of them are—not unnaturally—heard far less often than they were from 1941 to 1945 (for instance, *snafu*), though they are still remembered and are, so to speak, stored away in grease and cellophane, but a few, for special reasons, are still in wide use. Of these, I should say that the most prominent is certainly *G.I.*, whose history is complex. It seems to have begun, in the first world war or even earlier, as standing for "galvanized iron," so that *G.I. can* meant in practice "garbage can," most familiar to soldiers as a depository for all kinds of rubbish in barracks. The inspection of barracks necessitates house-cleaning, and house-cleaning includes chucking away rubbish; hence the verb *to G.I.* meaning "to clean up (barracks)," a usage still current, at least in the Army, and still at any rate intelligible to all ex-soldiers. Now some officers in inspecting barracks are fussier than others; and hence "He's very G.I." came to mean that the officer referred to was very fussy about the neatness and cleanness of barracks. Since the same officer was also likely to be fussy about other details of military regulations and proprieties, such as saluting on every possible occasion, calling an officer "G.I." came shortly to be tantamount to calling him a martinet, and "a G.I. Post" be-came almost automatically the name for a military establish-ment where martinets set the tone and embittered the flavor of life. But here a curious complication enters. In or perhaps somewhat before 1940, *G.I.* came also to stand for "general issue" (or, according to some, "Government issue"), applied, for example, to the stout "regulation" shoes supplied by the Quartermaster as distinguished from lighter and more fashion-able ones worn off duty and bought as a private possession by the individual soldier. Since officers buy most of their own clothing (or have it bought for them by the Army) from private dealers, since at any rate it is not usually "G.I.," and since officers are rarer than "enlisted men" (British, "Other Ranks"), *G.I.* easily came to be extended, first as an adjective to anything peculiar to enlisted men or characteristic of them, and then as a noun to the men themselves: "a G.I." came to mean "an enlisted man," and "G.I.'s," enlisted men. All these senses were in use side by side among soldiers in the last war. After the war, in lieu of a "bonus," Congress passed an Act providing for certain privileges (most notably, gratuitous education or vocational training) for all non-professional ex-members of the forces. This Act, with amendments and supple-ments, came to be and still is known as "the G.I. Bill (of Rights)". (At my university, at least, one still hears such questions as "Are you G.I. or Rehab(ilitation)?" This mysteri-ous query, addressed to a student who has served in the war, means, "Are your expenses here being paid under the terms of the 'G.I. Bill,' or under the special provisions for partly dis-abled veterans?") Since the privileges of the G.I. Bill apply to veterans regardless of war-time rank or "grade" (in the American forces a non-commissioned rank is officially not a "rank," but a "grade"), so that a good many Army Air Force ex-colonels, for example, are studying sub-freshman English or Undertaking at public expense, *G.I.* is on occasion extended yet further to the sense "any member or ex-member of the forces," though it is usual to exclude the Navy (except the Marines) and the Coast Guard—*except* with reference to the G.I. Bill.

It would be hard to find a better illustration of how language grows and of how complex and subtle the "rules" of usage can be. And they are none the less "rules" for being accidental and unformulated.

To return to advertising. On a somewhat more serious plane than *B.O.* (but still not without an overtone—I hope—of humor) is such a creation as *novolescence*, meaning—or meant to mean—"keeping one's facilities and amenities up to date," and occurring (I think for the first time) in a Hotel New Yorker advertisement in *Time* (2 October 1950, p. 77). On the whole (assuming an at least semi-humorous intent) it is not so bad as it might be. It is explained and perhaps apologized for in a footnote reading, "Novolescence—a word coined to describe our $2,000,000 improvement program; new decor [*sic*], new furniture, new value." Morphologically, at least, the word is less open to carping than Mr Churchill's *triphibious*.

The influence of radio speakers on the vocabulary is a little hard to distinguish from that of a number of other activities—for example, vaudeville, night-club entertainment, newspapers, and dictating to a stenographer. The noun *M.C.* (pronounced and sometimes spelt "em-cee") and the derivative but undifferentiated verb are older than the radio, and originated in night clubs, but it is the radio that has made them well known, at least in America. The radio, again, is responsible for the frequency, though dictating to a stenographer is probably responsible for the origin, of the practice of inserting the words "quote" and "unquote" (or "end quote") before and after oral quotations—and sometimes, alas, even written ones. The usage of news-service teletype and cables and perhaps of proof-reading, too, probably also has something to do with this. A case similar to these, but different in that it has become a stock device of popular humor, is the insertion of the word "period" at the end of a sentence, as in such an exchange as the following: "Has he got any money to spend on advertising?" "He hasn't got any money, period." Much more offensive than these (so far as they are offensive at all) is the pompous "and I quote" intoned at the beginning of quotations, first (I should say) by Members of Congress and by persons ambitious (quite literally) to succeed them, then by any speaker on the radio, and finally by any public speaker or even writer. In these usages, incidentally, there is an oddly tortuous process beginning in writing, proceeding through a very special kind of speech, and then working its way into speech generally.

Whatever the just distribution of praise or blame for giving rise to the foregoing expressions, the American radio is certainly the origin of "the sixty-four-dollar question" and the new sense of "transcription." The former comes from the radio quiz program "Take It Or Leave It" (renamed "The Sixty-Four-Dollar Question" in the autumn of 1950, *honoris causa*), in which a contestant who has answered his first question may take his reward of two dollars, or leave it and try a second question (for four dollars), and then (on the same conditions) a third for eight dollars, a fourth for sixteen, a fifth for thirty-two, and a sixth and last for sixty-four. Since the questions constantly increase in supposed difficulty, "sixty-four-dollar question" has entered into the popular language in the sense of "momentous or formidable question." I think it will very likely remain in common use for a long time.

The peculiar radio sense of *transcription* has established itself in the following way. Regulations governing the radio in the United States require broadcasts of recordings ("disk," "tape," or "wire"), as distinct from "live" broadcasts, to be announced as such. The radio industry has succeeded in debilitating this wise requirement by two dodges: (1) "Transcribed" and "(radio) transcription" are frequently substituted for "recorded" and "recording"; (2) the required announcement is usually made as inconspicuous as possible. Of the latter device, at least one network program uses a bold and ingenious reversal: the words "Portions [never "parts"] of this broadcast are transcribed" are inserted between two statements calculated to enhance the hearer's valuation of the program, and are chanted in the same orotund and prideful tone and manner, with the result that the law is obeyed but that at the same time the effect (if any) on the hearer is to set up in him a positively favorable attitude toward "transcription."

I have dealt with the radio before newspapers only because so much more is to be said about the latter that the opposite order would be anticlimactic. "All I know," Will Rogers used to say in his pawky way, "is what I read in the papers." The same thing might well be said, in dead earnest, by most Americans (and in a hardly less degree, doubtless, by most Englishmen) today. They should and probably would add, "—and what I hear on the radio," but, partly because the radio is comparatively new and partly because it draws so heavily on newspapers for its usage, the addition is not often important. The American newspaper vocabulary can be illuminatingly divided first into usages originating in headlines and largely or wholly restricted to them, and usages occurring in the main text; and secondly into usages that have and those that have not perceptibly affected non-newspaper practice. Neither classification is rigid, but both have a good deal of practical utility.

First, for headline usage. This has been what it is only during the twentieth century, if so long, and is what it is for four reasons: first, the straining for sensational effect, which leads to a preference for emphatic and vigorous (and hence usually short) words; secondly, inescapable and rigorous mechanical (that is, typographical) considerations of space; thirdly, the increase in the size of the type used in headlines and a corresponding decrease in the practically allowable number and length of sub-heads; fourthly, a number of mainly negative or prohibitory conventions usually forbidding (a) the splitting of a word at the end of a line, (b) ending a line with a preposition or a conjunction, (c) printing a headline (or rather a "head," since most "headlines" run to more than one line of type) lacking in one variety or another (depending on the "style" of the newspaper concerned) of visual balance—a rule that sometimes conflicts with the first, so that "succumbs," for example, may displace "dies"; and (d) printing a headline that is not a sentence—often and even characteristically an elliptical sentence, but still a sentence. The last "rule" (requiring, for example, "Governor Addresses Butchers" rather than "Governor's Speech to Butchers") is perhaps the most constantly and vexatiously operative. It is both a natural development and, within limits, a sound principle, but it has had some unhappy results, not so much in the headline itself, where much may be forgiven, as when they are carried over into the news columns by inexperienced or undiscriminating reporters or "rewrite men" (and compilers of newspaper "style books"). One of those results is the use of as few words as possible in order to make room for the verb. The use of as few words as possible is anything but a bad rule, but some of the applications are unfortunate; for example, the omission of *the* where decency requires it (the newspaper I know best prints regularly, not only in headlines but elsewhere, "University of" for "the University of"). Sometimes, indeed, this mannerism is pernicious not only to decency but to intelligibility; for instance, the very typical newspaper sentence (not a headline) "Only reserved seats will be occupied by alumni," which in English means that the alumni *will occupy nothing but* reserved seats, but in newspaper pidgin means that *no one but alumni will occupy* reserved seats. Another result of insisting on sentence headlines is the tendency to use words vague or misapplied to the point of bafflement. A good example is *area* in the following headline (summer of 1950): "School Told of 4 [*sic*] Basic Family Areas." We learn in welcome elucidation from the following "lead" that what is meant is that a lecturer has told his audience at a "summer school" conducted by Catholic Action what he thinks are the four fundamental *requirements* of a Christian family. *Area*, incidentally, has recently been attaining to increasing currency, partly as a substitute (originally, I think, an Educators' substitute) for *part*, *division*, and partly as a newspaper-headline adjective [*sic*] for something rather larger than *local*—"Area Raid-Warning Set-Up Studied," that is, "a committee is evaluating several suggested systems of giving warning of air raids *in this region*." *Local* itself, in the sense "pertaining to this locality" instead of "pertaining to localities generally," is in origin a piece of American journalese: *cf.* the by-word "Local Boy Makes Good in Big City."

To the requirement that the headline should normally be a sentence (and to the consequent intensification of the exigencies of space) rather than to a straining for sensationalism we may mainly attribute, I think, the special headline vogue of many such short words as the following: (1) *wed(ded)* (for *marry, married*). This is of course an ancient and honorable word, but it has virtually no currency in speech, and little in writing except in newspapers (originally, but, alas, no longer exclusively, in headlines). (2) *rum.* Practically every adult American knows and always has known that *rum* is not a general name for all ardent spirits, but a foreigner drawing his notions of twentieth-century American usage from newspaper headlines during Prohibition would never have guessed it. As usual, *rum* in this sense owed its frequency in headlines to its brevity. Since 1933 there has been less occasion for its use; but even if Repeal had not occurred, I doubt whether the word would ever have attained to serious and general spoken currency in its extended sense (except perhaps in such special combinations as *rum-runner*). This use of *rum* was not original with the headline-writers of 1919-1933: it is recorded by the *Oxford English Dictionary* as occurring in the United States as early as 1858 as an abusive name for all ardent spirits (and *cf.* "Rum, Romanism, and Rebellion" in the Presidential campaign of 1884). It was not, however, in 1919 any longer current in the general sense except among teetotalers and their accomplices, and I suspect that, in using it, headline-writers during Prohibition were sometimes cocking their snoots at the wowsers as well as saving space. (3) *aged.* No one is old in an American newspaper (except sometimes in "feature stories"). Oddly enough, however, precisely opposite alternatives are resorted to according to the situation: in a headline, *aged* (down to about fifty-nine); elsewhere, *elderly* (up to about ninety-one). Thus between brevity and diplomacy, the honors are even. (4) *rap* (v.). This is almost universal headline English (except when it is replaced by the typographically even shorter *hit*) for "reprehend," "reprimand," "censure," "attack (in words)," "decry," etc. ("Mayor Raps Gambling in City"). It has some pungency, perhaps, but more brevity, which is what I think chiefly recommends it to the writers of headlines. (5) *probe* (v.), "investigate," "inquire into"; (n.), "investigation," "(official) inquiry" ("Gas Racket Probe On"—"an investigation into alleged racketeering in gasoline has begun"). (6) *sift*. My impression is that this has recently tended to supplant *probe* as a headline verb—but not as a noun. (7) *flee, fled*, and *speed, sped* (the last not in the sense "exceeded the speed limit," which is always "speeded"). These, like *wed(ded)*, are regular, ancient and reputable parts of the vocabulary, but, again like *wed(ded)*, they are hardly ever heard nowadays in urban colloquial speech and hardly ever seen except in newspapers (originally, I imagine, in headlines, but now elsewhere as well). (9) The last example is perhaps scarcely worth mentioning because of its (happy) rarity, but it presents some rather specially interesting and in a way characteristic aspects. The financial editor of a certain American newspaper of considerable circulation has for years expressed the idea that shares on the stock market have not varied much during the day by writing, "Stocks Trod Narrow Path" (or sometimes, for variety, "Lane"). Since American newspaper headlines are nowadays always in the present tense (except in certain special cases, of which this is not one), it is obvious that the writer imagines that a verb exists whose principal parts are "trod," "trod" (or, for all I know, "trodded"), "trodden" (or perhaps "trod" or "trodded"). The ultimate explanation is probably a combination of the headline-writer's desperate need for short words with the obsolescence of the verb *tread* in urban colloquial American English. The painful effect is that I have several times seen, and once or twice heard, the blunder imitated by well-meaning people within the editor's orbit.

Almost the only place I know of where what might be called the title headline holds its own against the sentence headline is the obituary pages of some newspapers, including notably *The New York Times*, where it is the almost invariable form, and where, for example, I saw, in the summer of 1950, "Dr X. Y.

Z——, A Psychiatrist, 57." To be sure, in the very next column was "Arthur B. C——, 74, Tore Down Houses," which (a) is a sentence, and (b) seems uncharitably and unseasonably reproachful; but since about the only alternative in the style here usual would have been "Arthur B. C——, 74, Housewrecker," one sees that the copy-reader here used a sentence not because he had forgotten or was rebelling against the peculiar rule of his department, but as an incidental result of a humane desire to write a headline that would sound as little as possible like "Aged Man Wanted for Dynamiting."

The direct influence of newspaper headlines is slight in everyone's speech and in educated writing; it does show itself in the formal writing of the uneducated, who are by no means unaware that the written standard differs from the spoken and by no means willing to seem ignorant of the difference. Accordingly, when they write, for example, letters to the editor, they are likely to resort to models of writing; and since the only models of writing they know really well are newspapers, and especially headlines, it is not surprising that *rap*, *wed*, *rum*, *sift*, etc., turn up in their writing. On the other hand, even the speech of the same class has been perceptibly (though not very importantly) affected by certain usages found not so much in headlines as in news stories, especially in sensational newspapers. A good example is *cohort* in the sense "follower" rather than "set of followers," a usage resulting from a false inference based on the plural *cohorts*. Again, the popular mind is sometimes rather surprisingly and almost perversely inclined to attach more precise and specific meanings to newspaper words and phrases than was originally intended: I have known "oil king" to be taken quite solemnly as indicating an almost statutorily exact financial superiority to "oil baron". I have also heard *sex-fiend* used with the same naive assumption that it is a perfectly normal and unaffected word with a clear and definite meaning.

One irritating affectation that has long been common in newspapers without the excuse of brevity, that is now equally common on the radio, and that is unhappily beginning to be heard in the speech even of more or less well educated people, is "the nation's capital." Presumably this completely unnatural expression originated as a piece of "elegant variation" for "Washington, D.C." (the "D.C." being sometimes necessary to prevent confusion with the State of Washington—which of course should have been named something else in the first place); but one wonders why "the national capital," which, though clumsy, at least accords with normal prose idiom, would not have answered just as well. (We still, thank God, do not say "the nation's debt.") Again, inferior newspapers are partly to blame for spreading, and perhaps also for originating, a number of queer but very widely current malapropisms— notably *flaunt* for *flout* and *comprise* for *compose* ("The club is comprised of retired farmers"). Note that *flaunt* and *comprise*, and perhaps *flout* also, are literary rather than colloquial words; hence my suspicion of newspaper origin. The illiterate *predominate(ly)* for *predominant(ly)* is perhaps also partly the fault of second-rate newspapers; certainly it is common in them. But for the most part, such similarity as there is between the vocabulary of the newspapers and that of uneducated colloquial speech is owing to the influence of the latter on the former, not the other way round. Students a hundred years from now will be much mistaken if they assume that the popular speech of 1950 can be reconstructed from contemporary newspapers, and the more weight they give to the flashiest parts of newspaper vocabulary the more mistaken they will be. For example, such deliberate and artificial coinages as Mr Walter Winchell's *infanticipating* simply do not occur in the normal speech or writing of any social or educational class, and the same is true of *Time*'s mass-produced imitations—*cinemactress* and the like, which defeat some (though they may further others) of their own presumptive ends (or can it be that the *Time*ly writers are sometimes pulling the *Time*ly editor's leg?) when carried to the length of such unpronounceable blends as "GOPolitician" (though instances of this sort have appeared in *Time* less often in the last few years). Even in the realm of the standard vocabulary, journalistic usage neither resembles nor modifies speech so much as one might expect; *Time*, for example, entitles its movie-review section "Cinema," as do a number of newspapers, but in any kind of American speech except the jocose or affected or otherwise highly special, the word is *never* heard. It might almost be said that the only journalistic word to become really and generally current in speech is *cheesecake* (first a newspaper photograph, and then a display in the flesh, of women's legs); and that did not begin in the language printed in newspapers, but in the technical slang of newspaper photographers and reporters. (I suppose the origin of the application is in the idea of a fancy and rather too filling and possibly unearned dessert—or as the British would say, "sweet.")

Newspaper vocabulary, then, in the sense of words and uses originating in newspapers and springing out of the special problems of newspapers, has had comparatively small influence; but on the other hand, newspapers have certainly added to the currency—even the colloquial currency—of a large number of words and uses of very various origin, whose common element is recent and excessive popularity in the wrong places. Consider the following list: *adjust* (v. i.), *angle* (n.), *author* (v.), *bottleneck, brief* (v.), *constructive, -conscious* (e.g., "race-conscious"), *contact* (v.), *education*(al), *engineer*(ing), *home* and *homemaker, implement* (v.), *inferiority complex* (and *superiority complex*), *-inspired* (e.g., "Kremlin-inspired rumor"; *cf.* "police-described suicide-attempt"; this might be called the newspaper-extended participle), *integrate, know-how* (n.), *level* (n.), *-minded* (e.g., "air-minded"), *negative, outstanding, over-all* (a., especially in "over-all picture"), *process* (v.), *proposition* (n.), *science* (and *scientific* and *scientist*), *screen* (v., "sort," "classify," "select"), *service* (v.), *set-up* (n.), *sincere* and *sincerity, streamline*(d), *swell* (a.) and *lousy, teen-age* (a.), and *youth* (both collective, meaning "young people," "adolescents," and singular, with *a*, meaning "a (very) young man").

I think it is safe to say that if an historical novelist of fifty or a hundred years from now should wish to give his readers a fairly realistic illusion of the flavor of the everyday American English of 1950 (especially the half-educated variety), he could adopt no more economical means than to sprinkle his dialogue with the foregoing thirty-odd expressions. Those of them that have not originated within the twentieth century have at any rate attained within that time to their eminent and unquestionable position as vogue-words, counterwords, or current jargon. I should say that newspapers, in the strict sense of the word, are originally responsible for only two of these, *angle* ("aspect," "point of view," "special interest") and *-inspired* and the like (as in "Kremlin-inspired rumor," that is, one instigated by the government of the U.S.S.R.), though they are probably in part chargeable with the adjective *teen-age* and with *youth* in both the senses mentioned above (both senses are certainly of respectable antiquity, but neither has been used for a long time in unaffected speech or writing). Only if housewives' magazines are newspapers can newspapers be primarily blamed for the sentimental genteelisms *home* ("house," "dwelling") and *homemaker* ("housewife," "housekeeper"); and the verb *to author* probably owes its (rather limited) currency very specifically to *Variety*, the *jongleurs'* trade journal. Industry, commerce, and advertising, in various degrees and combinations, are the source of *constructive* (as a weasel word for "favorable [criticism]"), *to contact*, *negative* ("critical," "censorious," "captious," "pessimistic," "not sycophantish"), *science* (and *scientific* and *scientist*) vaguely used, *set-up* ("system," "arrangement," "disposition of parts"—originally a machinists' word), *engineer(ing)* (as extended in, for example, "sales engineer" and "human engineering"), *bottleneck, know-how, to service, streamline(d)* (as in such extended senses as "make [made] simpler or more efficient or both"), and *to process* (though for the extension of this last from things to men, the Army and Navy during the last war, I think, are chiefly responsible). They are quite certainly so for *to brief* ("to furnish with preliminary information"), and probably for the noun *level* in its intrusive and superfluous uses, though this has been extended yet further and more foolishly by the Educators ("I wish to prepare myself for teaching history on the high school level"—that is, "I want to teach history in high school"). And not only by the Educators. I find, for example, in a newspaper story about the draft published in the autumn of 1950 a sentence beginning "A young man, on reaching the age level of say eighteen ...," where *level* obviously contributes precisely nothing to the meaning. It is rapidly becoming very like what is called in Chinese grammar a "numerative." *To screen* meaning "to examine and classify (a number of entities) with a view to selecting the most suitable for some purpose" comes partly from "personnel engineers" and their opposite numbers in the Army and Navy and partly from newspaper headlines. I predict that it will lead to the increasing dominance of *to film* over an older sense of *to screen*—"to make a movie of (a play or novel or the like)." Its origin (in the screening of gravel) is fairly obvious. At least four of the expressions in the foregoing list can be attributed at any rate in the main to the jargon of Educators, "social workers," popular psychologists, etc.: *adjust* (for "adjust oneself"), *race-conscious* and the like, *to integrate*, and things like *air-minded*. From another kind of psychology comes *inferiority complex*, bringing with it *superiority complex*. Diplomacy, I suppose, is chiefly responsible for *to implement*. The Educators (in connivance with commerce and advertising) must take most of the blame for corrupting *education* so far as to make it stand for training in anything from Greek to garbage collecting, and for anything from instruction to propaganda, as well as for getting people to say "educational" when they mean nothing more than "informative" or "enlightening." *Outstanding* (for both "excellent" and "prominent"), *over-all* for "general," and *proposition* for almost anything can perhaps not be fathered on anyone in particular, nor can *sincere*, which I can hardly bring myself to use at all. Of the whole list, the only ones that are not in some measure offensive (to me) are also the only ones that can be called slang and the only ones of genuinely popular origin—*swell* and *lousy*. These thirty-some words and uses are not, of course, all twentieth-century or all American in either origin or exclusive currency, nor, for the most part, are they offensive because they violate any principle of logic or analogy, and not all of them, I will admit, are altogether superfluous or indefensible; they are offensive in one degree or another because they are used too much, and by the wrong people. One's aversion to them, that is, if one feels any, is a "conditioned response," and very

possibly in a decade or two everyone's responses will be
differently conditioned. But for that matter, anyone's understanding of or feeling for any part of any language is a
conditioned response; and my responses are so unalterably
conditioned that when I hear these expressions I cannot help
echoing Sir Alan Herbert's "What a word!"

Counterwords are related in a number of ways to euphemism: both owe some of their currency to newspapers, or perhaps, in the case of euphemism, rather to the more general
factors of universal quasi-literacy and the mass-publication and
circulation of printed matter (though euphemism essentially is
admittedly very ancient, as indeed its name must remind us);
both tend to be vague; and both are tinged with timidity or
dishonesty. Euphemism may for some purposes be usefully
divided into euphemism proper (which operates mainly in the
spheres of obscenity both sexual and excrementitious, profanity in the broad sense, and death and illness) and what may be
better called grandiloquence. The difference is mainly one of
degree, but it is important if only because, though euphemism
proper is waning, grandiloquence, on the other hand, or at any
rate one kind of grandiloquence, is growing. Euphemism
proper is indeed in a hopeful stage of decline in America. Once
in my childhood I heard a minister make the Prodigal Son fain
to fill his stomach with the husks that the swine did eat, and
another say that immediately, while Peter yet spake, the
rooster crew. (*Cock*, incidentally, is the only word specifying
the male sex in animals that has not come back, like *bull*, *boar*,
stallion, into almost universal use, and even it may now be
used in most circles without causing visible distress; and cock-
roaches are not so often docked of their first syllable as they
used to be.) The reverend gentlemen's pontifical bowdleriza-
tion of the Scriptures in public reading reflected, of course,
their own spoken and written usage, but such usage seems more
and more outmoded. The growing frankness of American
writing in the last fifty years, and only less of American speech
(not that speech has gone less far, but that it had less far to go),
reflecting the growing freedom of thought and manners,
has been accompanied—at first sight rather oddly—by a

considerable increase in church membership, especially among Protestants (most of whom it would be more accurate to call non-Catholics). The freedom of manners and the frankness of speech, to be sure, are not found exclusively or even typically among the new church-members, but there is certainly a considerable overlapping. (The same is true of drinking.) This is probably to be attributed mainly to galloping consumption in non-Catholic theology: the new church membership, I suspect, is to be found less in the conventicles of hot gospellers than in "institutional churches" and "community churches" (many of them undenominational) serving as social centers, where traditional theology has been displaced by what one of the best teachers I have ever known—Canon Wedel of Washington—has recently called "The Christianity of Main Street."

The reaction against euphemism is so strong that it sometimes proceeds to the point of dysphemism. It is to this that I should mainly attribute *the hell* ("What the hell," "The hell with it"); the unidiomatic or at least unhistorical use of the definite article here results chiefly, I think, from the "tough" or dysphemistic substitution of *hell* for *devil* in phrases where *the* had become fixed. It illustrates a really increased toughness in the spoken language, and is therein different from the increased appearance of four-letter words in print, this being only a belated record of old habits of speech. (Joyce and Lawrence were printing some of these words a good deal earlier in the century, we know, but not in America, and not generally in England.) Mr Ernest Hemingway in *Across the River and Into the Trees* (1950), printed and widely sold in the United States, uses two of the four-letter words, but represents a third—usually felt to be the most shocking—by a spelt-out initial (and once by an inexact but alliterating synonym). Another dodge for the same word is a slight distortion. What is interesting and important here is not the continued, entirely usual avoidance of the word itself, but the novel appearance of plain suggestions of it—so plain that probably no reader over twelve misses the point.

Among the several public uses of language there is a sort of hierarchy of purity. Generally speaking, the more numerous and more various the readers or hearers, the more fumigated the vocabulary. The order of purity (beginning with the purest) is as follows:

1. Radio
2. Movies
3. Popular magazines
4. Popular newspapers
5. Other magazines
6. Other newspapers
7. Books (especially novels)
8. Broadway plays

Television is rapidly moving up (if it *is* up) the list, as televised movies made before the purification of Hollywood under Mr Hays come to be more and more thoughtfully selected. Numbers 3 and 4 sometimes exchange places, as do numbers 5 and 6, and 7 and 8.

This, clearly, is almost entirely a matter of the language used, not of what is suggested or even represented. The radio and the movies, to be sure, are usually excessively and ludicrously careful to avoid touchy subjects (except, manifestly, what D. H. Lawrence called "permissible pornography"), but many popular newspapers and magazines are anything but that.

Educated writing has naturally been subject to the same influences (science, urbanization, democracy) as other forms of language, but it also rather specially reflects (as, to a smaller degree, educated speech does) the displacement of the genteel style by the style of well-bred ease. I should define the genteel as the ill-bred trying to seem well bred, and not too confident that it is fooling anybody. It shows itself in syntax as well as in vocabulary: it is so fearful of splitting an infinitive that it says "really to have been known"; it is so fearful of saying *will* for *shall* that it says *shall* for *will*. Its insecurity, when extended from syntax to vocabulary, goes further, and confounds both the moral and the linguistic, and the puritanical and the upper-class. But its heyday is past: not for a long time have I heard *limb* for *leg*, or seen "d——n" for "damn," and *bitch* in its canine sense is today pretty generally inoffensive. (This is true despite the young woman, or, as she would say, lady, that I heard of not long ago, who blushed on a distinguished professor's uttering the word to her of the mother of some pups they were looking at, and then said that she didn't really mind at all—it was only that she had never before heard the word applied to a dog.) The secondary meaning of *bitch*, incidentally, has undergone a queer development: it is rather freely used, not for "whore," but for "virago" or "spiteful woman" or "captious and overbearing woman," and next for "overbearing man," and finally for "difficult problem or situation"—all of these proceeding, I am pretty sure, not from *bitch* meaning "whore," but partly from *bitch* meaning "virago" and the like, and partly from *son of a bitch* meaning not literally "bastard," but "disagreeable (and especially overbearing) man"—a use itself proceeding from the indiscriminate and unimaginative ascription of illegitimate birth to anybody one doesn't like. A yet further, stranger, and, I think, commoner development is that of *bitch* into a verb, meaning "complain," which has become so common that I doubt whether it offends anyone. That *bitch* is hardly ever used in American today for "whore" or "unchaste woman" is owing not directly to squeamishness, but to the frequency and vagueness and essential thoughtlessness and innocence of its common uses.

Profanity—real profanity—is a good deal commoner both in print and in most speech than it was two or three decades ago: *darn(ed)* and *hail Columbia* and *goodness gracious* and suchlike sarcenet surety for one's oaths have largely given way to their undisguised originals, though for some reason or other the printed form of *God-damn(ed)* still often retains the gossamer veil of *goddam*.

A good deal is to be said, I think, for the genteel tradition, even on its squeamish and taboo side: it did show a love of excellence, even though the nature of the excellence was misconceived. But self-conscious vulgarity is not the only alternative to self-conscious genteelism, whose displacement by the style of well-bred ease as the norm of educated writing is a heartening sign of a maturing culture. Some genteelisms, unfortunately, became so well established in the genteel era that they have remained, even under a more honest regimen, perfectly unaffected parts of the speech of people who are not consciously affected or squeamish at all. A good example is calling a pregnant woman an *expectant mother*, a monstrosity for which newspapers are probably in the main responsible, though most of them now freely use the words *pregnant* and *pregnancy*.

Newspapers in general have shown a commendable bold-ness in the last decade or two, though they have usually had to be prodded. In the last few years, for example, owing almost entirely to Dr Thomas Parran of the U.S. Public Health Ser-vice, most newspapers and magazines have taken bravely to printing "syphilis" and "gonorrhœa" instead of "social dis-eases" and the like. Note, however, that *pox* and *clap* have not been restored to decorous usage; indeed, many Americans to-day would not understand *pox*, and do not know why small-pox is so called. Here the habit of euphemism (of the mystify-ing variety) has apparently worked irreparable harm. *Rape* is also used now and then in newspapers, though less often in headlines than its brevity must make copy-readers wish; there, *attack* and *assault* are still the usual substitutes, and have taken on much of the titillative power of *rape* (as of course euphem-isms ineluctably do, on the Norfolk-Howard principle). "Girl Slugged and Assaulted; Critical" does not mean that the Common Law has been so far modified by statute in the United States that a beating has ceased to be legally an assault, nor yet that the young woman has been merely moved to pro-nounce a discriminating or censorious judgment; it means that she was knocked on the head and raped, and is in danger of her life.

Some expressions used to be thought so shocking that even in disguise they were, and sometimes still are, avoided in writ-ing and in public speech. The growing freedom of manners is partly, but only partly, responsible for the weakening, in the case of certain words, of the vestigial nervousness that used to be stimulated by one kind of disguise, phonetic distortion. This is chiefly represented by *nerts*, whose very wide currency today in comparatively decorous use can hardly be explained except by supposing that decorous people, seeing through the distortion and yet unable to imagine that the word, even distorted, could possibly have attained to public currency in its anatomical sense, have taken to using it innocently in both forms as an inherently meaningless exclamation. The process has perhaps been facilitated by the currency of another (fairly old) sense, as in "That was nuts for him," that is, "the perfectly adapted opportunity or situation for him". A partly similar case is *bull*, especially as in *bull session*. Another kind of disguise is best exemplified by "S.O.B.," which up to a few years ago was hardly more generally acceptable than the full form, but which has now pretty much lost its terrors, except when they are deliberately revivified for ulterior ends. In 1949 the President of the United States (who is a Baptist) unluckily permitted himself to be quoted by the newspapers as referring to someone as an "S.O.B." This outraged the moral sensibilities of countless Republicans (whose silent voices, in the improbable event of Senator Taft's having been the hero of the incident, would have been nobly replaced by those of an equal number of virtuous Democrats). But at least the newspapers of all parties did report the episode, in full, and often with open merriment—merriment shared, I feel sure, by a good many more readers than were honestly scandalized, and in a ratio much more in favor of open merriment than would have been true fifty or even twenty or thirty years ago. Another instance of disguise by initials is *P.D.Q.* ("pretty damned quick"), which, though once very common, has, since the very early 1930's, practically ceased to be heard because *damn(ed)* has come in that time to be very generally regarded as innocuous.

The flight from euphemism has been pretty general, and surprisingly rapid. Only in the last few years has it been safe for most American newspapers to print the word *homosexual*, just as only in the last few years has it been safe for them to say anything at all about the subject in any but the vaguest and most allusive way. It is interesting to note that none of the colloquial synonyms have come into newspaper use, except *pansy* now and then—and even that probably only when the writer thinks it means "sissy"; *fairy*, in the last few years, has become so well

known in the sense "homosexual" that nervous speakers and
writers tend to avoid the word almost altogether. I dare say
that *Iolanthe* would hardly be performed today in America (by
an American company) without the emendation of a couple of
passages of dialogue. The old taboo still attaches, that is, to the
expressions in any way irregular (including euphemisms) but
hardly any longer to the idea itself or to the public mention of
it by its formal name; and the time is past when a decidedly
liberated professor of psychology in a large urban university,
in referring to homosexuality in animals, would feel constrained (as one did in my hearing twenty years ago) to say in
a lecture, "wrong [*sic*] sex habits in rats."

Euphemism in the narrow sense, then, is going out of
fashion; but its twin brother grandiloquence is in some ways
more vigorous than ever. Of the several principal and enduring
influences on American English, democracy (or rather its illegitimate extension) is chiefly to blame for this melancholy
fact. Commerce and advertising naturally find their account in
abetting the damnable tendency to avoid, in every sort of
public utterance, any word or statement that can conceivably
hurt anybody's feelings—a tendency that has even led to, and
perhaps partly proceeded from, a regrettable extension of the
law of libel: *The New Yorker* for 7 October 1950 (p. 23) mentions, for example, an award of damages to someone who had
been publicly called a "swashbuckling opportunist" and a
"boastful ruffian." I cannot help feeling that in this respect the
age of Milton and Salmasius was healthier. There are, I conceive,
a good many people whose feelings *ought* to be hurt. And this
pussyfooting is recent: Mark Twain, who died only forty years
ago, wrote at least two books that no American publisher
would dare issue today. But the increasingly prevalent practice
is that of mutual flattery. The classic example (much older than
the twentieth century) is the thoughtless and indiscriminate use
of *lady* and *gentleman* (though more the former than the latter)
with the result that the collocation "ladies and men" is frequent
even today. (This may, to be sure, sometimes proceed at least
partly from motives in themselves creditable, but it is hard to
think that these are mainly operative when the one term or the

other is habitually applied to oneself.) On the other hand, perhaps the "habitually" takes away the reproach; certainly many expressions pretentious or affected or otherwise objectionable in origin do at length establish themselves in the innocent and natural usage of quite unpretentious and unaffected people who are at the same time unquestionably well educated. *Dear*, for example, is seldom heard nowadays in urban use in America in the sense "costly" (and *costly* is itself hardly more common in ordinary speech). The usual word is *expensive*—originally much too imposing and weighty a word for most people's private affairs, but now established beyond a doubt as the ordinary and unaffected word. The same thing is perhaps on the way to happening with *finance(s)* and *financial*. For perhaps somewhat the same reason, *hall* has largely supplanted *corridor* and *passage* and also *entrance* or *entry* (the last of these, incidentally, not in common British use today in this sense). The fact remains that the attitude *originally* shown by *expensive* for *dear*, and by *finances* for *money* and the like, as applied to one's own concerns, is exactly the opposite of that shown by the Chinese "my miserable hovel," etc. The Chinese has no objection to exaggerating honorifically and grandiloquently the amenities of his neighbor's house, but avoids doing so to those of his own, to such an extent that he does just the opposite. The Chinese are a highly civilized people. And most Americans today, if they live in a flat, call it an apartment—and much more generally than thirty years ago. The virtual disappearance of *flat* I should attribute not so much to the vaguely swank French *appartement* as to the use of *flat* in *cold-water flat*, that is, one in which the plumbing system is not designed to furnish hot water—accordingly, mean and squalid quarters.

Negro for *nigger* is not exactly euphemistic or grandiloquent, but it is close enough to both to be mentioned here, and important enough to be mentioned somewhere, for American Negroes have had noticeable success in recent years in reducing the frequency with which *nigger* is seen and even heard, especially in the North. In one instance, at least, this has backfired: a brand of canned oysters (from Mississippi) that used to be "Niggerhead" has for the last two or three years been

"Negrohead." A case related in certain partial and complex but fairly clear ways both to *Negro* for *nigger* and to euphemism and grandiloquence is the altogether laudable rehabilitation, during the last fifty years, of *Jew* (n.) and *Jewish* (a.) for *Hebrew* —even and indeed especially in the usage of Jews themselves. There is still some tendency to say "Jewish man," "Jewish girl," etc., rather than simply "Jew"; and most Jews, or at least many, dislike *Jewess* (as most Negroes dislike *Negress*).

The *draftee* of the first world war became the *selectee* of the second. On what is possibly the eve of the third, I have seen *inductee* in newspapers, but so far, at least, this seems to apply to "selectees" only during and perhaps shortly after their induction into the Army. This succession supplies a perfect example of a new euphemism's displacing an old and weakened one, for the plain English word, of course, is *conscript*. It is doubtful, I think, whether a conscript finds his experiences in the Army much less irksome because he undergoes them as a draftee or a selectee (or because the obstacle course he runs in Basic Training is now called a "confidence course"). And yet perhaps he may, if we are to judge from parallels in grandiloquent substitutes for the names of certain civilian occupations, some of whose followers have tried with some success to get people to call them by new and fancy and, presumably, flattering names. The standard example, and one of the most successful, is *mortician* for *undertaker*, but even that has had only a very partial success: in the most recent telephone directory in my own city, it is not even listed; *Undertakers*, though it refers the bereaved and the curious to *Funeral Directors* for the listings, is at least present. *Funeral director* is in some obvious ways inferior to *undertaker*, but it is almost infinitely preferable to *mortician*. To judge from the listings, *mortuary* has more standing than *mortician* among the undertakers themselves, but I doubt whether this is true of people in general, who seem to me to say "the undertaker's." Far worse, however, than *mortuary*, is *funeral home*, which has, happily, even less popular and colloquial currency but which appears in a large minority of the listings. *Casket*, on the other hand, which came in earlier than *mortician*, is (probably for that reason) actually commoner than *coffin*, I should say, even in unaffected use. But to balance this, I have the impression that *pass away* for *die* has not had such good luck, and is heard less often than it was earlier in the century.

The history of *realtor* is set forth by Mr Mencken in the fourth edition of *The American Language* (and in *Supplement One*). It was invented in 1915, and is legally restricted to members of the societies united in the National Association of Real Estate Boards, who are very jealous of its assumption by schismatics—so jealous, in fact, that my impression is that the word is seldom used by people in general, either exactly or inexactly. *Public relations counsel* for *press-agent* originated (again according to Mr Mencken) sometime between 1919 and 1923, though *public relations* by itself seems to have been in use somewhat earlier, and the main objection, I should say, is to that part of the phrase rather than to *counsel*. For no good reason clear to me, the office in charge of publicity at one American university has recently been calling itself the "Department of University Relations." The shortened form may have been contrived from good motives, but it is obviously misleading, if only because the university has many "relations" that are not with the "public"—notably with other universities, at least some relations with which are the function of a quite different office. Corn-cutters have managed to get themselves pretty generally called chiropodists, but barbers are now universally barbers and not tonsorial artists, as they often yearned to be a few decades ago. Names of the two kinds exemplified by *beautician* (hair-dresser) and *sanitation engineer* (garbage collector—British, "dustman") seldom occur outside of shop-signs and the like except in derisive use. On the whole, grandiloquent names for vocations tend to get themselves popularly adopted only when either convention or common sense produces in the popular mind at least some faint associations of dignity with the vocation in question.

Two expressions remain that might be called (like some discussed above) either euphemistic or grandiloquent. Both have to do with drinking. Neither is new or exclusively American, but their almost complete habilation is both. These are *alcoholic* (n.) for *drunkard*, and *bar* for *saloon*. The history of the latter is especially freakish, for *bar*, which has gained its present universal currency in America since the repeal of Prohibition, got that currency from the desire on the part of the liquor trade to soothe their alarmed enemies in 1933 into believing that, even though the Noble Experiment was over, "The saloon would not come back." In point of fact, of course, the "bar" of 1950 is essentially indistinguishable from the "saloon" of 1918, though its appointments are sometimes more luxurious and though one is now likely to see as many women in it as men. (And there is no longer any "free lunch.") What makes the development especially interesting—and, so far as I know, unique—is that *saloon* itself was in origin what might be called a euphemism-by-curtailment for *bar*, the full form being *saloon bar*—that is, "bar fitted out like a parlor," "bar for ladies and gentlemen"—"posh bar," in short. And that has not been the last act in the comedy: many bars, and by no means all of them the best ones, now prefer to call themselves "cocktail lounges," which properly means just about what *saloon bar* originally meant.

"The phrase would be more germane to the matter, if we could carry cannon by our sides; I would it might be hangers till then."

Grandiloquence, especially in the names of vocations, easily suggests the subject of titles and honorifics. The use of "Honorable" before the name of almost any man in public life is still common, as it has been for many decades, in *The Congressional Record*, newspapers, and political speeches, but in hardly any other widely public uses of language. It is perhaps less frequent generally than it used to be, as is certainly the nineteenth-century bestowal of military titles on resolute civilians, a practice that is virtually extinct, though a good many demobilized war-time Brigadier Generals (British, "Brigadiers") get their friends or at least their employees to continue the use of the title. In much the same way, any lawyer that has ever sat on a bench, even that of police magistrate, expects to be called "Judge" for the rest of his life (though sometimes the same title is familiarly used of elderly lawyers who have never been even police magistrates—but this is only the jocose magniloquence of affection). "Acting Deputy Assistant Under Secretary of the Interior and Mrs Smith" continues in full force. *Professor* is decidedly less often heard, if not so much less often seen, than it used to be. This is true (at least in cities) not only of its application to high school principals and school superintendents and to teachers of music and dancing and even less academic persons, but also of its more or less legitimate use. In most respectable American colleges and universities teachers of all ranks most commonly speak of and to each other as "Mister," except when intimacy justifies substituting something more familiar. The (real) professors that would still like to be professored are usually willing to settle for "Doctor," and there is some tendency for "Doctor" to be used, even by academic people with good taste, of and to exceptionally distinguished professors, though it is hard to see why, considering that there are probably more doctors that are not professors than there are professors that are not doctors, at least in the principal universities. *Doctor* is also applied quite legally to an even greater variety of paramedical operatives than in 1900, and a large minority of Protestant ministers (especially non-Anglican), particularly in cities, not only really are doctors (*honoris causa*, to be sure) but expect to be so called. It is almost safe to say that most Protestant ministers would by now have assumed the title, or been decorated with it by acclamation, if it were not for the very wide use of *Reverend*, found pretty awfully far up the social and educational scale as an exact analogue of the Catholic *Father*. A minister's wife of my (distant) acquaintance calls her husband "Revvy." She does not herself, however, expect to be called "Mrs Reverend Smith," which, like "Mrs Colonel Jones" and "Mrs Judge Brown" and "Mrs Doctor Robinson," was still common in America in the nineteenth century. These expressions are still heard, but only in the backwoods and in what might be called backwoods enclaves in cities. Protestant churches are prolific sources of drearily arch coinages, such as the pretty widely used "minister of music" (choirmaster), which the inventor presumably regarded with fondness as a rather cute blend of the two senses of *minister*; and the society of young "church workers" at a certain Anglican cathedral is called, I regret to say, "Canonaides," but so far as I know this has not been copied. The revivalistic sects have supplied *Singspiration* (a song service preliminary to a sermon), and from more or less the same soil sprang *scofflaw*, which won first prize in a competition conducted in 1924 to find a denigrating name for buyers of liquor under Prohibition. It not only failed to get into the dictionaries; its principal currency (while it had any) was derisive of the state of mind that produced it. Another competition, in 1942, designed to find a sentimental substitute for *mother-in-law*, was won by *kin-mother*, which had even less success, if less be possible.

There have been various occasions in this chapter to mention instances of contemporary American slang, but it will not be amiss to say a word or two in general characterization of it. I cannot help feeling that the slang of 1950 is tougher than that of the earlier part of the century, and if so, the causes are doubtless urbanization and the generally increasing toughness of manners. The feeling may, however, be in part an illusion springing from the associations one is likely to make between the old-fashioned and the innocent: *poker-face* may once have seemed as grim as *dead-pan*, and *a slowpoke* as cutting a piece of urban scorn as *a square;* and *corny* and *character* are perhaps not more knowingly and raffishly contemptuous than their nineteenth-century equivalents. One piece of slang very common in the last decade or so that is interesting and typical in several ways is *sharp* meaning pleasingly alert or original (as of a piece of repartee), or modish, or both. It originated, I suspect, in Harlem, and at first seems to have applied to men's clothing (from the sharp creases in new trousers?). Since the first year or two of its general currency it has been heard oftenest, I should say, from sophisticated people, who use it with an overtone of somewhat superior amusement both at the word and at the thing described, as who should say, "I never use this word so in serious approval, nor do I seriously approve of the thing I am applying it to." It is a commonplace, but an important one, that most slang comes into the general vocabulary from what might be called the margins of society, and the rule continues to hold good in America today. The reason is probably in part the natural necessity of strange names for strange things, in part the frequent occasion for mystifying the Gentiles, in part the strong fraternal and clannish feeling usual among members of close corporations, and in part the often exceptional degree of mental liveliness exhibited by people who live more or less precarious lives. Almost every occupation or status that could be called marginal continues to make characteristic contributions from its special language, first usually to general slang, from which some of them rise into general colloquial speech, and some few into formal written usage (few, that is, relatively; absolutely, many). Of these occupations or statuses the principal legitimate ones are in the realm of popular entertainment. In roughly the order in which they have begun their contributions to the language, these are vaudeville and the circus, sports (especially, in America, baseball), the movies, jazz music, and radio, only the last three, naturally, having made most or all of their contributions in the present century. The illegitimate occupations most prolific of words and phrases taken over into the general language are those of the gambler and of the gangster, to which should be added the cants of prison life and of tramps so far as those are distinct from criminals' language generally (not that tramps are necessarily criminals). Several of these have been illustrated earlier in this chapter, and countless further examples of most of them will readily occur to any American —and to many Englishmen—living today. It would be so obvious as to be hardly worth saying that the occupations more or less new in the present century have made the greatest number of recent contributions, if there were not one exception, namely, crime, which I should say has been drawn on more heavily than it used to be—a fact that is merely a part of the growing toughness of manners and speech generally. Somewhat paradoxically at first sight, this criminals' language, however new much of it may be to most law-abiding people, is characteristically older than most of the other lingoes: the extraordinary antiquity, conservativeness, and uniformity of cant is a commonplace observation among students of the subject. Indeed, just because of its original purpose and continued utility—the mystification of honest folk—cant tends not to get recorded till late in its life, so that much of it is doubtless older, sometimes very much older, than can be proved.

But some of the borrowings from the language of crime (especially gangsters, in the 'twenties) are not obviously either old or new or even obviously of criminal origin, and have, furthermore, spread so far that they are now often used with hardly any thought of their provenience and have even become almost literary—*to be put on the* (or *a*) *spot*, for example, and even *to take the rap*. *To take for a ride*, on the other hand, I should say had not quite got to the same point. Such phrases, it will be noticed, are for the most part slang or canting rather *as phrases* than in the sense that they are composed of slang or canting words; their status, that is, proceeds from their provenience and the resultant connotation of the combination. The same thing is more or less true of a number of other phrases not of criminal origin, but still in various degrees what I have called marginal: *Oh, yeah?* (generally tough-guy rather than specifically gangster); *sez you* (probably Harlem, or perhaps rather stage-Harlem)—both of these, by the way, are now decidedly dated and "corny." *We wuz robbed* ("we've been abused or overreached or cheated") comes very specifically from the ritual ululation of the Brooklyn Dodgers' fellow-citizens on the frequent occasion of "Dem Bums'" having lost a baseball game. A current mannerism that seems even less essentially slang and that none the less is so in connotation and tone and shade of meaning is the peculiar use of *so* at the beginning of a rejoinder (for example, "I'll have to pay for it? So I'll have to pay for it!") with some such implication as "don't get excited," or "what of it," or "just stop and think of it and you'll see it isn't important," or "if I'm not worrying, why should you?" It is closely related to the rather earlier and now somewhat *démodé* "So what?" I suspect that the original source of both is the language of the New York streets, with sub-auditions of a Yiddish idiom. All these expressions are or have recently been very common, some contain neither slang words nor sub-standard grammar, and none contain both; and yet all of them come unmistakably from the speech of people whose usage generally is sub-standard, and all of them have or have had a slangy or canting connotation or association. Even the position of a word in a sentence may alter its meaning and connotation in the direction of slang or at least pure colloquialism; for example, *certainly* in "He certainly works hard," which even *means* something different from "Certainly he works hard," besides being at home in a different kind and even on a different level of discourse. At such a point it becomes very hard to draw the line between slang and a cliché, and between a cliché and an idiom.

CHAPTER THREE

IDIOM AND SYNTAX

CHANGES in vocabulary are conspicuous and definable, and partly for that reason it is arguable that they are not in all senses the most important ones. The opposite of this is true of changes in tone or style, which is quite as much a matter of syntax and idiom and word order and sentence length, to mention only some of the factors, as of vocabulary in the narrow sense. Sometimes, indeed, as we have just seen, the tone is a matter of provenience and connotation and allusion. Certainly the tone of American English has changed in the last fifty years on almost all levels and in almost all uses, and for the most part in the same general direction; and certainly that change has not been solely or even perhaps mainly in vocabulary.

In discussing different levels and uses of language—that is, the different standards—we may set up a number of dichotomies according to the particular question at issue: literary and colloquial, written and spoken, formal and informal, educated and uneducated, upper-class and lower-class, urban and rustic, up-to-date and old-fashioned, affected and natural. Even those of the foregoing pairs that may seem to be most nearly convertible—for example, "literary and colloquial" and "written and spoken"—are not quite so for all purposes. "Colloquial" is an especially dangerous word: too many people imagine that it means "slipshod" or "provincial" or "slangy" or "illiterate" or what not. Properly, it means none of these—though the common misconceptions of it have the partial justification that it does certainly, in some degree or other, overlap with every one of those terms, even once in a while the last. But the important thing to realize is usually that the colloquial usage of the educated urban member of the upper classes is in most ways much closer to his literary usage (or at least to his literary standard) than it is to the colloquial usage of the uneducated rustic member of the lower classes. In other words, the most important distinctions are not between literary and colloquial generally, and even less between written and spoken, but rather between educated and uneducated, urban and rustic, upper-class and lower-class: they are social and educational. It is not hard to see why this should be true. Since most writing—most published writing, at any rate—is done by comparatively educated persons who live in cities and belong, say, to the upper half of society, it is natural that their written style (mainly colloquial in origin) should come to set the standard of literary style, at the same time that it does not cease to resemble that of their speech.

Assuming that there are such things as good and bad English, the worst is not socially and educationally the lowest, but the next to the lowest, or perhaps the next above that. The lowest often has the strength and dignity of the elemental, the honest, and the unassuming. The worst English is the lowest on the way up, adulterated by diffidence or affectation and tricked out with spurious ornament: it must be worse before it can be better: it must crave ornament and refinement before it can distinguish the true from the false. The best collection I am acquainted with of the writing of contemporary uneducated Americans is in Professor C. C. Fries's *American English Grammar* (1940). Here we find some conscious though false "refinement," but we find much more of pretty faithful transcription of the writers' spoken usage—as much, probably, as could be gathered from any available source except perhaps recordings of "candid microphone" radio programs. The syntax of this language when it is not standard (as in fact it is most of the time) tends to be analogical and analytic in a peculiar way. A good example of this is what might be called the vulgar genitive relative construction: "That's the man that I knew his father" for "That's the man whose father I knew," a construction almost universal in uneducated speech, which firmly avoids *whose* as a relative pronoun, though it uses it freely as an interrogative. Note also the typical *that* instead of *who* or *whom.* The lowest usage here shares with the highest the preference of the relative *that* to *who* in most restrictive (defining) clauses: *who* as a general substitute for *that* comes in on a higher, but not the highest, level (especially written), and *whom* for *who*, on the half-educated level.

This construction is typical of the kinds that there is more or less equal occasion for in speech and in writing and that are accordingly illustrated amply in Professor Fries's materials. But there are other constructions equally typical of uneducated speech that are not likely to appear in what little uneducated writing has been published, just because the situations in which they occur do not normally confront the writer. One of the most notable and typical of these is the use of *this* in the very special sense of "the person or thing concerned in the anecdote I am about to relate": where the literary language might begin with "A certain girl," and the educated colloquial with "There was a girl that," the uneducated colloquial today will usually say, "There was this girl, see?" Though this use of *this* some- what resembles the use of *these* in such a phrase as "one of these new cigarette-lighters" (that is, "a cigarette-lighter of the well- known new kind"), it is not quite the same thing logically, and, what is more important, it is a very different thing socially: thousands of educated Americans who use the latter freely in familiar speech would not think of using the former seriously anywhere. Another and less marked but abstractly even more unreasonable social difference is to be seen in certain elliptical constructions, where, generally speaking, both educated and uneducated speech are elliptical, but where educated speech makes a more thorough job of it.

Educated (or urban): "[*Do you*] know any good reason why not?"

Uneducated (or rustic): "[*Do*] you know any good reason why not?" *The New Yorker* often uses the latter in mockery, especially in its "editorial comments" appended to blunders or fatuities quoted from newspapers. A somewhat parallel case (though here the difference is between British and American expressions) is the frequent British "I don't think" for the almost universal American "I don't think so."

One piece of uneducated syntax that I think is more com- mon among recent immigrants and their children than among other Americans is the avoidance of the pluperfect, especially in conditional clasues; for example, "If I wasn't tired last night, I wouldn't have gone home so early." "If I didn't hear his voice when I met him yesterday, I'd never have recognized him." This comes mainly, I suspect, from the speakers' adhering to the syntax of their native languages, in some of which the construction may well be less unidiomatic, or the distinction less clear.

Most of these expressions, even such as are more or less substandard, are at least natural. Even in comparison with educated speech and the literary standard, uneducated and half-educated speakers often speak not badly and even write not badly so long as they stick to familiar syntax. Their trouble comes when they try, for one reason or another, to rise above themselves and write (without sufficient guidance) otherwise than they speak. Naturally, the models they attempt to follow are written models, and most available written models have been produced by relatively educated people, whose language (especially written) differs from that of their imitators in the variety and resourcefulness of its syntax more fundamentally than in vocabulary (at least in treatments of the same subject). Consider the following expressions:

1. Any student who falls below average will be put on probation.
2. Those students who fall, etc.
3. Such students as fall, etc.

Anyone, educated or uneducated, would probably use no. 1 in speech, and might use no. 1 or no. 2 in writing; no. 3 is likely to be used only by educated persons, and mainly in writing. The uneducated or the half-educated, when they try to sound "literary," are likely to attempt no. 3, but they often come to grief with the comparatively unfamiliar construction and wind up with "Such students who fall below average will be put on probation." And imperfect education is found in strange places: I have seen that sentence, and two or three others like it on the same page, in the catalogue of quite a respectable college (whose teaching staff would probably say that their registrar was not really one of them). But the native habitat of the animal is the "letters to the editor" columns of all but first-class newspapers. (The fact that the construction was once standard English—"of swich licour of which vertu engendred is the flour"—is beside the point: the multiple negative ("He nevere yet no vilenye ne sayde … unto no maner wight") and the double comparative and superlative ("more rawer breath," "most unkindest cut") were also once standard English.)

A construction frequent in half-educated speech, but rare both above and below that plane, is the use of *may have* for *might have* as in such an unintentional oxymoron as "He may have done it, but I'm sure he didn't." This comes about from having been taught that historical English idiom *does* prefer *may have* to *might have* in, for example, "He may (might) have done it, but I don't think he could have." The insufficiently instructed or attentive learner, that is, in an effort to avoid a venial and inconspicuous and more or less "natural" error, falls into a grave and glaring and unnatural one. This is exactly like saying "between you and I" because one has got it into one's head that one must not say "me and him could do it." Another case of the same thing is what The New Yorker calls "the omnipotent *whom*" ("The man whom the police believe is guilty refuses to confess").

Another construction resulting from imperfect observation and analysis and occurring very commonly in half-educated and then in uneducated writing is illustrated by the following quotation (slightly but not essentially altered) from a reputable urban American newspaper of 1950: "The conferences will be held in whatever city in which he happens to be conducting salesmen's meetings." This could not originate either in educated usage or in uneducated speech; it is perfectly typical of half-educated writing. It is, clearly a conflation of "… in the (*or* any) city in which he happens to be conducting salesmen's meetings" and "… in whatever city he happens to conducting salesmen's meetings in." In educated usage, either would appear; in uneducated usage, the most likely form would be "… in the (*or* any *or* whatever) city he happens to be conducting salesmen's meetings." Only half-educated writing (imitated in uneducated writing) combines two factors: (1) fear of the final preposition, and (2) realization of the necessity of a preposition somewhere.

The fear of the final preposition sometimes expresses itself by simple omission, as in the following quotation (like the last, verbally but not formally changed) from an American detective story published in 1950: "He might well have frozen to death in the crevice Marston had left him." This omission of "in" after "him" (or alternatively of "where" after "crevice"), fortified by the by-word "go places (and do things)," is, I think, a good deal commoner, at any rate in educated speech and writing, than it was fifty years ago. But this construction comes only in part, I believe, from the same causes as the very similar one last exemplified. In part it has pursued (if I am right) a devious but in some ways characteristic path—from educated speech through careless educated writing, half-educated writing (where it is extended), half-educated speech, uneducated speech, educated speech, and finally (now in its extended form) back to educated writing again. Of the alternatives "This is a good place to stop at" and "This is a good place at which to stop," natural and unaffected usage—written and spoken, educated and uneducated—prefers the first. On all levels of language, then, the habit is established, not so much of ending with *at* as of avoiding the medial *at which*. In short sentences, this gives no difficulty. But some sentences are long —most typically in educated usage, especially written. By the time an educated speaker or even writer has approached the end of such a sentence as "This is a good place to take up the whole question at issue between the liberals and the conservatives at," he is almost sure to have so far lost sight of the syntax of his sentence as to omit the *at*—and he is so accustomed to avoiding the medial *at which* that he does not insert it. This sort of thing, occurring in a generally literate style, does not make an illiterate impression even when it is noticed. And it is seldom noticed—except by that assiduous but inaccurate noticer, the half-educated writer and speaker, who, skittish of *at which*, and holding as an article of faith the schoolma'am's prohibition of ending a sentence with a "preposition" (it is not really a preposition here at all, but an adverb), seizes with glad cries on his illusory salvation, and writes (and says), "This is a good place to stop." Indeed, he even says, "This is a good place to eat." But this is not the end. Uneducated speech constantly modifies educated speech (especially in twentieth-century America), and educated speech modifies educated writing; and the final result is the sort of thing exemplified in the quotation introducing this discussion.

The construction just dealt with illustrates in a modest way a very important fact about the relation in America today between uneducated usage (especially speech) and educated (especially writing): more markedly, I think, than fifty years ago, and more markedly than in England today, the prevailing stream of influence is from the bottom up rather than from the top down. In some important ways, what has changed in literary usage is not so much style itself as the status or prestige of various kinds of style already existent. Mr Ernest Hemingway's style (in his tough vein, not his sentimental) is not so new as it may seem; what is new is its acceptance as a tolerable and even suitable style for writing that educated people will take seriously as literature. And even Mr Hemingway's style, I suspect, is tolerated rather than admired by many people who seem or even profess to admire it. They believe that Mr Hemingway has so much that is important and interesting to say, that they indulge him in his manner of saying it. The same thing applied to Theodore Dreiser and, longer ago, to Carlyle (not that the three styles resemble each other in any other way). But some people appear to admire it for its own sake. In a review of Mr Hemingway's *Across the River and Into the Trees* in *The New York Times Book Review* for 10 September 1950, Mr John O'Hara (himself a novelist) calls Mr Hemingway the "outstanding" writer since Shakespeare. Here, as usual, it is hard to tell whether "outstanding" means "important" or "excellent" or both. Whichever he means, Mr O'Hara thus settles the business of Molière, Milton, Swift, Voltaire, Goethe, Tolstoy, Dostoyevsky, Proust, Rolland, Joyce, Gide, and Mann. (One could think of others.) Whatever Mr Hemingway's virtues as a writer (and I suppose that a writer's virtues include his style even in a fairly narrow sense, and even in Mr O'Hara's opinion), this estimate is typical of a common feature of contemporary American culture, and to some extent of twentieth-century Western culture generally—namely, a sort of mentally dyspeptic rejection of a cultural tradition so massive that it seems to defy assimilation—a rejection accompanied by a search for a new and lighter diet. To change the figure, one yearns for a new heaven and a new earth.

Mr Hemingway's style, to be sure, is not typical of that of his contemporaries (Mr O'Hara will not allow me to say "his peers") among American novelists, most of whom have broken a good deal less sharply with the literary tradition. But this fact is usually apparent only when the novelist is speaking "editorially," that is, in his own person as narrator and conductor of the action or commentator on it, not when he is writing dialogue of stream-of-consciousness; and one notable way in which the typical novel of today differs from that of some decades ago is that it uses a larger proportion of these two forms, especially the latter. Further, it is obvious and notorious that novelists have increasingly tended both to simulate, when writing in these forms, the actual daily spoken language of people like their characters, and also to deal with the life of "the common man"—the latter even when, and perhaps particularly when, the common man is not the reader contemplated, as in serious novels he usually is not. In short, most American novels today are both more naturalistic and more "proletarian" than their predecessors of half a century ago. But there are further effects. The novel is the normal and dominant literary form of the present century even more than it was of the last; and to the extent that people tend to regard the language of the normal and dominant literary form of their day as exhibiting the norm of language generally, or at least of literary language generally, they tend to conform their speech, or at least their writing, to it. The final result then is that, though the general idea of a standard and even of a literary standard does not disappear, that standard today under the influence of the contemporary novel tends to approximate more and more closely to the spoken language (or what passes for it) of the uneducated. What we have later in speech is the reflection of a reflection. The secondary reflection, to be sure, is less important than might be supposed. It is easy for people who regularly read books to overestimate the circulation (and hence at least the direct influence on the language of the uneducated) of even the best-selling novels and other books; they have little notion, even in an age when almost everybody can and to some extent does read and write, of the immense semi-literate majority, whose continuing influence on "the" language is incalculably great. Like the plankton of the ocean, it supports and sustains the life that lies above it and swims amidst it. (It should be remembered, however, that a fish is a nobler creature than plankton.) "The people" more than ever before supply or are thought to supply the language of literature, but they don't read the literature; and I think it not altogether fanciful to suggest that dialogue in novels meant to be naturalistic and proletarian may some day become as conventional and as unlike its original model as the language of pastoral poetry became unlike that of real shepherds.

There are, however, novelists that write elegantly, and poets —more than for at least a long time—that write learnedly and even pedantically; but these novelists are read by a much smaller fraction of the population, even, than read Mr Hemingway, and the poets by a smaller fraction still, and they are correspondingly untypical and uninfluential.

But if the uneducated do not read poetry or novels—even Mr Hemingway's—they do read newspapers, and newspaper usage does affect theirs. It is commoner than it used to be, for example, in uneducated and half-educated speech as well as writing, to specify automatically and superfluously the country in which some great and famous city lies: my barber relates to me, on my every visit to his shop, a new episode from his (mostly fictitious) adventures, after the Liberation, in "Pairse-Frants." Such a specification would sometimes be appropriate in the neighbourhood of Paris, Kentucky; elsewhere (and there is quite a lot of "elsewhere") it strikes one as provincial and intrusive. Its frequency owes most, I think, to the date-lines of newspaper stories, but something, perhaps, to national pride.

Again, the verb *protest*, even in the language of educated people, has almost entirely supplanted *protest against*, probably because of newspaper headlines (though possibly also from the parsimony of writers of querulous telegrams to Congressmen). It still seems illiterate to me, but I must confess that few people, even literate ones, seem to agree with me. Other newspaper, especially headline, influences on at least the uneducated language, particularly in writing, have been mentioned in the preceding chapter; but on syntax and on usage generally, at least two of the most conspicuous and characteristic tricks of the twentieth-century American newspaper have had (happily) almost no influence at all. The first of these, at least, one might expect to have had a good deal. Almost the only principle of elegance, or rather of richness and flexibility of language, comprehended and admired by the uneducated is that of the avoidance of repetition. As might be expected, the principle is misunderstood and, in the writing read and admired by the uneducated, misapplied: the supposition comes to be (1) that to repeat a word is always bad, and (2) that the only way to avoid repetition is to use a synonym. Newspapers feed this superstition with common food even in their ordinary news stories, but with a continual feast of dainties only in sports writing, especially in accounts of baseball games and prize-fights. One single to left field or one left hook differeth from another in glory; but the difference on earth being less than it doubtless will be in heaven, and such difference as there is not being always easy to convey in words, the temptation to call a ball a *sphere*, a plate a *sack*, and a knockout a *sleeping pill*, on, at the latest, the eighteenth occasion for mentioning them in a single story, is almost irresistible, particularly to the writer (or radio announcer) celebrating his silver jubilee in his vocation. The customary reader of these Homeric exercises, however, seldom imitates their style, perhaps because he thinks it beyond his reach (as it usually is). And yet a few of the classical kennings have attained to a certain colloquial currency—for example, *slap-happy* for *punch-drunk* (both, by the way, excellent phrases, though the former is superfluous and shows, perhaps, the strain of contrivance).

This sort of thing, though mainly twentieth-century and characteristically American, is not exclusively either: cricket and soccer matches are so recounted, and were before 1900, as were baseball games. But there is another and superficially similar newspaper practice that I think comes somewhat closer to being peculiarly American and twentieth-century. It is, if possible, even less truly colloquial in origin and likewise in currency. This is the omnibus sentence using "elegant variation" like the sports-writer's, but chiefly for the purpose of saving space and sentences rather than to keep up interest by giving an illusion of variety. "Mrs LoRette Pift, 33, was found with her throat fatally slashed in her concrete-basement home at 4128 Whittier Avenue early this morning. The recently divorced mother of 5 was last seen by her neighbors early last evening talking on her front steps with her unemployed campcook ex-husband Meshach, 47. Police are looking for the 220-pound former sailor, who was divorced from the prematurely gray ex-beauty operator last May." The reason why this sort of thing is not imitated in popular speech is not that the populace don't admire it, but that they can't do it, at least without an uncolloquial amount of reflection.

These devices are not usual in all parts of American newspapers; they are not usual, for example, in editorials (British, "leading articles"). But even here there has been a change. Certainly American newspaper editorials do less thundering than they used to do. This is chiefly because of mass circulation: a new class of readers must be appealed to—readers who read less, who read worse, who are stimulated by the spirit of the times to think well of themselves and to make no apologies and acknowledge no superiors, and who (and this, at least, is healthy) increasingly distrust gobbledygook and double-talk. It is neither their fault nor the newspapers' if they do not always distinguish gobbledygook from the style demanded by dignity or complexity or both; it is the fault of their genes and their schooling.

A very special case of journalese is the style of *Time* (or should one write "TIME"?), which began publication in 1923. By style here I mean language in a rather narrow sense as distinct from manner. The manner of *Time* combines oddly, even in a single sentence, the arch, the flip, and the hieratic. Of its style the leading features are the participial opening, inversion of subject and verb, descriptions used like titles ("World Historian Toynbee"), the omission of *the*, asyndeton (the omission of *and*), occasional preference of the possessive case to *of*-phrases ("at week's end"), the ferreting out of a few impudently recherché words (for example, *tycoon*, about the only one that has caught on), and two kinds of blends—pronounceable but seldom pronounced (*cinemactress*) and unpronounceable (*GOPolitician*). Such "raciness" as it has is usually of the dismal *ersatz* variety; it is the very reverse of the colloquial. "If it were God's will," said Pantagruel of one of the more hideous of Panurge's incomprehensible gibberishes, "we would all speak so with our tailes." Happily, the only person who probably ever did speak so had to, and he was just reading aloud (presumably through the normal orifice)—the narrator for the radio and movie "March of Time." Some of these devices are not original with *Time*, but others of them are at least mainly so, and are, alas, no longer peculiar to it, though fortunately even these are little imitated in writing except in (generally inferior) newspapers, and in speech hardly at all. That the style of *Time* (or *Time*style) has not been more widely and closely imitated than it has been is probably by no means ungratifying to its proprietors; its continued uniqueness is worth money to them. And I simply do not believe that any writer for *Time* writes that way either to his fiancée or to his milkman—or even to his boss.

Of all *Time*'s mannerisms, I find habitual asyndeton uniquely irritating; have we, for God's sake, not enough time to write "and"? A close second is the omission of *the*. This is an altogether different thing from *The New Yorker*'s omission of *a* at the beginning of such "Talk-of-the-Town" items as "Fellow we know came in yesterday." *Time*'s ellipsis originates in the (or a) written language; *The New Yorker*'s in the spoken, where the *a* is not consciously and deliberately omitted at all—it is thought but not uttered, because it gets thought before the breath reaches the larynx. The style of widely read periodicals does and should reflect and does and sometimes should modify ordinary speech; but there are writers on current American English who cannot tell the difference between *Time's* omitted *the* (which is completely uncolloquial in both origin and currency) and *The New Yorker's* omitted *a* (which is genuinely colloquial in both).

As for *The New Yorker* generally, I suppose it is indecorous to conduct a love affair in public, especially a one-sided one with a magazine, but I cannot conceal my passion. *The New Yorker*, it seems to me, has, ever since it began (in 1925), not only steadfastly published the most uniformly civilized English written today in America; it not only holds its contributors of non-colloquial and non-"dialectal" material to a norm as close to that of Fowler's *Modern English Usage* as is sensible in America; it not only uses (especially in "Talk of the Town") a style so entirely that of well-bred ease tempered by subtle mockery of various kinds of sub-standard American English that more than one writer of college textbooks on English composition has quite missed the point: it also defends the language by publishing now and then Mr Frank Sullivan on clichés and Mr A. J. Liebling on "The Wayward Press," and, between times, by means of quotations from contemporary writing, does more than its share to paint in properly black and odious colors the foolish dangling participle and "the omnipotent *whom*." And in another department of linguistic interest, it has recorded the almost uniquely admirable exhibitions of several varieties of sub-standard usage to be found in Mr Leonard Ross's "Hyman Kaplan" (recent immigrant from Central or Eastern Europe), and in Mr Arthur Kober's "Bella Gross" (second-generation American in the Bronx) and "Benny Greenspan" (the same transplanted to Hollywood).

The radio has not very much affected general usage independently of newspapers and movies (except perhaps in giving some non-radio currency to "and I quote," etc., discussed in Chapter Two), chiefly because its language is largely modeled on theirs. It has, however, probably hastened the more or less colloquial adoption of some newspaper usages by thrusting them daily upon the ear rather than the eye. Further, though

the style of newscasts is identical with that of newspapers, the
style of commercials and to some extent that of soap-operas
(I hope my British readers will understand all three of these
terms) is sometimes a partly new blend of the more or less
formal written and the informal spoken styles, and also (what
is not the same thing) of the educated and the uneducated. The
former of these combinations, to be sure, is not new: it is as old
as the drama. But the drama—even modern realistic drama—is
not for the most part written for the uneducated, whereas
most radio scripts are. And even when a script like the admirable "Line-Up" (CBS) seriously tries to reproduce real speech
(usually uneducated) with absolute or at least highly convincing fidelity, it sometimes fails to do so for the reason that time
is money, especially on the radio. The stage, again, has
long been accustomed to this; but the radio intensifies it. Besides "and I quote" and the like, I can think of no specially radio
mannerism that has got much beyond the radio except the
back-scratching repetition (especially in the vocative) of a
speaker's full name: "This is X. LaVon Klunker again, la'ies
and gen'lemen. La'ies and gen'lemen, that was Honor'ble
Aristides Q. Slumpf, giving us his reactions on the latest
election figures. Aristides Q. Slumpf is known as the Elder
Statesman of Squeehawk County. *Thank* you, Aristides Q.
Slumpf."

"Thank *you*, X. LaVon Klunker—King, if I may say so, of
News Announcers." Even these fatuities, of course (and, so help
me God, nothing is invented but the names), have not become
and probably never will become really colloquial, but they are
sometimes heard in public speech off the radio.

One of the most important and characteristic traits of
American English in the present century, in almost all uses and
on almost all levels, is a sort of overlay of what might be called
the international lingua franca. Most of the immigrants of the
last hundred years have been of other than English stock, speaking other languages than English. They have affected the
vocabulary of American English perhaps surprisingly little; its
idiom and syntax, I think, a good deal. Their children and
grandchildren (and by infection their children's and grand-

children's playmates), though they acquire a perfectly native vocabulary and (for the most part) pronunciation, are very shaky in many matters such as the idiomatic use of prepositions, so that they say, for example, "in a method" on the analogy of "in a way" or "in a fashion." This kind of speech is almost an anticipation, in some features, of Basic English: it is unallusive and tuneless; its syntax is highly analogical; it prefers constructions readily translatable without formal alteration into other languages; it shies away from real and apparent oddities and anomalies (for example, *out of pocket, far to seek*); its vocabulary is simplified and at the same time analytical, so that verbosity sometimes results (*male bird* and *female bird* for *cock* and *hen*, *lack of self-confidence* for *diffidence* or *timidity*); it tends to be blind to the meaning of old compounds and to supplant them with new ones, sometimes made up of essentially the same elements (for example, *sheep herder* for *shepherd*). In short, though not (at its best) unidiomatic to the point of being exactly "incorrect" or broken, it is unidiomatic in every broader sense. It interacts with half-educated journalese: plenty of fairly well-educated Americans think "it comes natural" is as illiterate as "he speaks natural," and as for journalese, one does not have to look through many issues of most American newspapers before coming upon a perfectly sound English phrase put cautiously into deprecating quotation marks: for example (headline), "Grocers' Convention Delegates 'at Odds.' "

If we combine this international-lingua-franca English at its worst with the lower forms of journalism (especially headlines) and the most hideous features of Basic English, and add a generous portion of gobbledygook, we get something fearfully close to George Orwell's Newspeak.

CHAPTER FOUR

PRONUNCIATION AND SPELLING; DIALECTS

EVERY speaker of English knows that his language varies in its pronunciation from person to person and from region to region. Like every language, it has varied so throughout history and tends to vary increasingly, though there are always strong counter-currents that may halt or even reverse the stream. One instance of this is that the pronunciation of English in America, so far from becoming more various in the twentieth century, has become more uniform. But in the first place, it has by no means become completely so; in the second place, as a whole it still differs strikingly from British pronunciation; and in the third place, differences in pronunciation, because they normally appear only in speech and not in writing, are more likely than any other feature of language to be misunderstood and even relatively unknown. For these reasons, as well as because of the intrinsic interest of the subject, I mean to deal with American pronunciation at some length despite its having changed so little since 1900 that it may seem to fall outside of the proper subject of this book.

Pronunciation generally is a highly complex subject, which most people fail to analyse, chiefly because almost none of the most important differences between two modes of pronunciation are indicated by conventional spelling. Some, indeed, are not indicated even by so precise a notation as that of the International Phonetic Association (IPA) and can hardly be more than roughly indicated by any practical printed notation whatever: strictly speaking, any book dealing with pronunciation should be accompanied by phonograph records. Most speakers of English assume that, for the most part, the conventional spelling indicates or even determines *the* "correct" pronunciation. The conventional spelling, and even the roughly phonetic respelling of most dictionaries, are interpreted in each region according to the habits of pronunciation there current, and accordingly many real differences in pronunciation are either unknown to many people or ignored or underestimated by them.

I am not speaking here of words over which even educated speakers in a single region may disagree as to which syllable is to be stressed ("*adult*," "*adult*"), or as to whether a vowel is "long" or "short" ("apparaytus," "apparattus"), or as to whether a consonant is "voiced" or "voiceless"—for instance, as to whether the first *s* in *persist* hisses ("perssist") or buzzes ("perzist"). I am not speaking at the moment, in fact, even of such conspicuous and well-known regional differences as the dropping or the sounding of *r* before consonants and at the ends of sentences, nor yet of the American "uh(r)" for the British "ah(r)" as in *clerk*. When I speak of the Kentucky Derby, I pronounce it "duhrrby." (I write two *r*'s here and elsewhere to indicate the retained and fully sounded *r*; most Englishmen and many Americans would be misled by a single *r*.) When I speak of the Epsom Downs Derby, I pronounce it "dahrrby." I would never think of saying "dahby," any more than I would think of imitating the Southern British intonation. Likewise, I say "suhthurrk" for *Southwark*, but not "suhthuk"; "buhrrkly" (Hills, California), but (Bishop) "bahrrkly" (but not "bahkly"). This set of practices, which is representative of the usage of educated Americans who "pronounce their *r*'s," suggests a distinction made habitually and more or less unconsciously—a distinction between the quality of vowels and such a point as "dropping the *r*."

What I do mean here by pronunciation is mainly (1) the vowel system (which will be explained shortly), (2) the degree of distinctness in the enunciation of certain consonants, and (3) intonation. Most speakers perceive differences in all three of these to some degree, but fail to analyse them and hence to simulate successfully any other dialect than their own.

By "vowel system" I mean the set of varieties—rather subtle varieties, for the most part—of vowels and diphthongs characteristic of each dialect. For example, most Englishmen pronounce *oh* and *ay* with something closer to a diphthong ("*oh*-oo" and "*eh*-ee") than most Americans; and again, most Americans, at least in the West, pronounce *not* with something nearly or quite identical with "naht" rather than with most Englishmen's much closer approach to "nawt." Such correspondences are pretty regular within each dialect, and the differences appear in anybody's natural speech quite automatically. They are seldom indicated at all in dictionary "keys to pronunciation." (It is this fact that makes most "pronouncing dictionaries" generally useful to almost any speaker of English.) Even within the United States the vowel system varies rather widely, but this variation is mainly geographical rather than social or educational, with the result that all but the most extreme varieties are heard by most Americans with tolerance and even with pleasure, or at worst with good-humored amusement.

The degree of distinctness in the enunciation of certain consonants other than *r*—particularly *t* between vowels—also varies geographically, but varies socially and educationally as well, educated speech being as a rule more distinct than uneducated. Curiously enough, however, the very speakers that are most likely to make "pri'y" out of "pritty" (*pretty*) become overprecise, at least about unstressed vowels, when they have occasion to speak publicly; they imagine that the ordinary (unstressed) pronunciations of *a* and *the* before consonants (in *all* dialects and at *all* levels)—namely, "uh" and "thuh"—are slovenly, and unsuitable for ceremonial occasions, and consequently they substitute "ay" and "thee," in accordance with the spelling.

The third factor of dialectal difference in pronunciation is intonation—the "tune" of speech—which cannot be intelligibly represented by any mere alphabet, however minutely discriminating, and only awkwardly by musical notation. Of all the differences, this is the hardest to analyse or to simulate. It shows up, of course, much more in whole sentences than in isolated words, in which, indeed, it is often scarcely evident at all. In the United States today, intonation is a good deal more uniform than the other two elements, both in all regions and among all classes; and by the same token, it usually distinguishes very sharply such varieties of British and American speech as are otherwise much alike.

To deal with the whole subject of American dialects in a chapter on pronunciation would be quite improper in a more comprehensive book than this one. Those dialects do differ, or at least their colloquial forms differ, in vocabulary and even in syntax and idiom, as is made amply clear in the parts so far published of *The Linguistic Atlas of the United States and Canada*. But a number of facts make proper the restriction of my treatment of the subject to pronunciation: (1) The other differences *are* almost wholly colloquial. (2) They are much smaller than corresponding differences among British local (especially rustic) dialects, and scarcely ever prevent mutual understanding. (3) They are becoming steadily smaller. (4) They are much harder than differences in pronunciation to generalize about, particularly because some of them are sometimes greater among the varieties of a single main dialect than among the main dialects themselves. (5) Differences in pronunciation, though smaller than formerly, are still much more general and more marked than other differences. (6) The pronunciation of no single American dialect possesses or is likely to gain the same unique measure of prestige enjoyed in England by that of the class dialect sometimes called "Received Standard," "Received Pronunciation," or "Public School Standard," which is a special development of the regional dialect of Southeastern England. This remains true, however similar American dialects are in other ways in educated and especially literary usage. It is consequently more important to deal in some detail with differences in pronunciation even in a short discussion of American English than it might be in one of British English.

Before naming and describing the principal American dialects (by which I mean, here and subsequently, dialectal pronunciations) I will take the precaution of saying what I do *not* mean by the word dialect (except once or twice, on which occasions I put the word between quotation marks). I do not mean the brogue or patois of the comic stage Irishman or

Negro or what not, and I do not mean the unidiomatic English of (mostly) recent immigrants and, to some extent, their children. Of American dialects in the sense in which I am here using the term, there are three: the Eastern (New York City and its environs, and parts of New England), the Southern (the South generally), and what is variously called Northern, General American, and Western (the rest of the country). In the following pages I shall use "Western" as, in my opinion, on the whole the most convenient, but it must be observed that as I use it it does not mean exclusively or even typically "Far-Western."

Very broadly speaking, Eastern and Southern share the dropped r with each other and with Southern British as against Western, and Eastern and Western share a system of vowels and diphthongs, especially certain of the latter, with each other as against Southern. There are a good many qualifying exceptions of a number of kinds to these generalizations, but as generalizations they are sound. The resemblance of Eastern and Southern American to Southern British and of Western American to Northern British and to Irish English (mainly in the treatment of r) used to be explained by the hypothesis that the English-speaking settlers of Western America were mainly of other than Southern British stock. But this seems to be unacceptable because of other than linguistic evidence, and students of the subject now more commonly take another view—briefly, that the retained r of Western American and non-Southern British English is a relic of a feature that in the seventeenth century was found wherever English was spoken, including Southern England; that Southern England subsequently dropped the r; that Eastern and Southern America (that is, the Atlantic seaboard), being in close and continuous contact with the mother country and especially with London and Oxford and Cambridge, did likewise; and that Western America, lacking that contact, preserved the seventeenth-century r. This at any rate accords with the odd but none the less indisputably general tendency of transplanted speech to be more conservative in some ways than the speech of the home country and of regions in contact with it; and if it is true (and it seems to be), then Western American English is in certain respects the most archaic English dialect spoken today by very large numbers of people. The theory gains some plausibility from the consideration that both the earlier and the later British immigrants speaking this or that particular British dialect were usually so scattered in America that that fact alone would probably have ironed out the most conspicuous imported differences in pronunciation even without assistance from the extreme mobility of the American population.

As for proportions among the three main American dialects, of ten Americans in 1950 roughly seven speak Western, two Southern, and one Eastern. Western is slowly spreading, as it has been doing for some time, especially at the expense of Eastern. At the same time the New York variety of Eastern, so far as it has resisted this encroachment on its territory, shows some tendency, especially on the lower levels, to become more sharply differentiated, in an almost opposite direction, from the easterly New England variety: a Concord farmer and a Broadway newsboy, that is, though they are both likely to speak Eastern—that is, though they will drop their r's without using Southern vowels and diphthongs—use pronunciations quite different from each other in certain other respects.

This will be enlarged on presently; but first it will be well to illustrate some of the leading differences among the three main dialects:

Eastern American (and Southern British): I see a bigguh rand bettuh cow fuhthuh ron [*almost* rawn] and ovuh.

Southern American: Ah [*sometimes* I] see a bigguh rand [*sometimes* and] bettuh [—*and then something between* cow *and* kyow—*almost* keh-oo] fuhthuh ron [*almost* rawn; *sometimes also* on *or almost* awn; *sometimes again* furrthuh ron (*almost* rawn), *and yet again* furrthuh on (*almost* awn)] and ovuh.

Western American: I see a biggerr and betterr cow furrtherr ahn and overr.

I have tried to show by these examples (1) that Eastern American agrees with Southern British in all the points covered; (2) that Southern American typically agrees with both in the treatment of r, but that it sometimes disagrees on this point in every possible way (even opposite ones, according to the subdialect and the individual speaker), except in pretty uniformly dropping final *r* in an unstressed syllable at the end of a sentence; (3) that Southern American stands alone (among the four dialects mentioned) in often substituting "ah" for "eye" (*I*)—which is really a diphthong, "ah-ee"—and in using, even oftener, something like the vowel of *fat* for "ah" as the first element of *ow*—which is really another diphthong, "ah-oo"; (4) that Western American stands alone in making out of *on* something closer to "ahn" than to "awn"; and (5) that Western American stands alone in never dropping an *r* anywhere (that is, it stands alone in America; it agrees in this respect with some non-Southern British dialects).

As to the dropped *r*, two special points should be made. (1) By writing *bigger and* with retained *r* in two ways—"bigguh rand" and "biggerr and"—I have tried to suggest a subtle difference that really exists, namely, that *r* retained before a vowel outside of Western American tends to be slightly trilled, to be a true consonant, and to attach itself to the *following* vowel; whereas *r* in Western American tends in all positions to be untrilled and to be almost or quite a vowel rather than a true consonant. The Western American pronunciation of the verb *err*, that is, is more accurately described as a single sound—a vowel—than as a vowel followed by a consonant. (2) This Western *r* is indeed so much a vowel that it tends first to form a diphthong with a preceding vowel and secondarily to "darken" it, with the result that speakers of other dialects sometimes represent the—or a—Western pronunciation of *very* and *American* as "vurry" and "Amurrican." (*Per contra*, the Southern British pronunciations of the same words use an *r* that is so decidedly a (trilled) consonant that they suggest to at least Western Americans the spellings "veddy" and "Ameddican.") And the Western *r* becomes less a consonant at the same time that it becomes more a vowel; hence such monosyllabic pronunciations as "worrnt" for *warrant*.

One prominent feature of much Southern American speech that is not represented above is the pronunciation of "short *e*" ("eh") before nasals (*n*, *m*, or *ng*) almost like "short *i*" ("ih"), so that, for example, *pen* becomes almost indistinguishable from *pin*, and *enemy* is heard as "innimy." Southern Englishmen sometimes sound (at least to non-Southern American ears) as if they were doing nearly the same thing; and if their "short *e*" does not come quite so close to "short *i*" as the Southern American's sometimes does, they appear to compensate, so to speak, by not limiting the substitution to the "short *e*" before nasals. Something more will be said about this in Chapter Six.

In all American dialects, "long *i*" ("ah-ee") and *ow* ("ah-oo") tend to become reduced respectively to "uh" and "ah" when unstressed, as in "uh *doo*" for "I *do*" and "are *age*" for "our *age*." Southern American, as we have already seen, commonly makes "ah" out of "ah-ee" even in stressed positions ("*Ah* doo" for "*I* do"). To generalize, there is a tendency here to drop the second element of the diphthong. In the popular speech of New York City, perhaps especially among the children of recent immigrants from parts of eastern Europe, there is an exactly contrary tendency in stressed syllables— namely, to separate and lengthen the two elements of diphthongs and to give the second element more stress than it has in other dialects, so that the effect on the ear is almost that of two successive and equally syllabic vowels; for example, *cow* becomes "cah oo" rather than "*cah*-oo," and *buy*, "bah ee" rather than "*bah*-ee." A yet further modification appears when another vowel follows immediately: a diphthong ending in "ee" develops a parasitic *y* sound, and one ending in "oo" a parasitic *w* sound. For example: *fire* becomes "fie yuh(r)" instead of "*fie*-uh(r)," *annoyer* becomes "uhnoi yuh(r)" instead of "uh*noi*-uh(r)," and *hour* becomes "ow wuh(r)" instead of "*ow*-uh(r)." The same thing happens to the quasi-diphthongs *ay* (as in *pay 'em*), and *oh* (as in *poet*). For that matter, it happens even when "ee" or "oo" is not part of a diphthong, but a wholly independent vowel: *see 'em* ("see yum" for "*see*-um") and *truest* ("troo wist" for "*troo*-ist"). I find this kind of sound extraordinarily grating, as I think most Americans do who do not utter it: it is, I believe, one of the few exceptions to the general truth that most Americans (whatever may be true, according to G. B. Shaw, of Englishmen)

278 BRITISH AND AMERICAN ENGLISH SINCE 1900

can hear other Americans speak without loathing and
despising them.

Another familiar feature of the pronunciation of New York
City that, like the last, is most frequent (I believe) in the language of the children of recent immigrants (and in this case, of
the immigrants themselves) is what might be called "intrusive
g." It appears between the sound usually written *ng* and a
following vowel, whether in the next word or in the next syllable of the same one. The classic example (and it *is* classic) is
"Long Guyland" for *Long Island*. Even in the face of Mr
Mencken's formidable disagreement, I am inclined to accept
the opinion of a number of my Jewish friends that the feature
originated in Yiddish (or rather in one style of Yiddish pronunciation), though it is now heard from the lips of many
Gentile New Yorkers. "Long Guyland" is of course not the
only example of the phenomenon: it occurs, for instance,
between the participial ending *-ing* and a following indefinite
article, so that we get "I'm buying ga car."

This treatment of *ng* suggests another detail of pronunciation
that may seem to be and that yet is not exactly the opposite,
namely, "dropping one's *g*'s." What is so called is inaccurately
so called. When one "drops one's *g*'s" (as in *singin'*), what one
really does is not to *drop* any sound at all, but to *substitute* one
sound for another—in this case, to substitute *n* for what is
usually *written* with *ng* but is none the less not the sound of *n*
plus the sound of *g*. The sound is actually as much a single one
as *n* by itself is, or *m*, and conceiving it as *n* plus *g*, or the sound
substituted for it as *ng* minus *g*, is nothing but an accidental
result of a convention of spelling. (Readers may test the truth
of these statements by observing that though *singer* does not
rime with *sinner*, neither does it rime with *finger*—which
really has a *g* sound in it. The letters *ng*, that is, denote two
sounds in *finger* but only one in *singer*.) Certain other aspects of
the "dropped *g*" will be mentioned in Chapter Six; but this is
a more appropriate place in which to mention an associated
phenomenon less commonly observed. This is the fact that
when one "drops the *g*" one also (in contemporary urban
American usage) "darkens" or obscures the preceding vowel,

whereas one never does so when one does not "drop the g." To illustrate—*battin'* (in the kind of speech just mentioned) sounds exactly like *batten*, and not like *bat in; batting*, on the other hand, is always "bat-ing," never "bat-'ng." "Bat-'ng," in fact, occurs in no pronunciation known to me, though "bat in" does occur in some rustic American and provincial British speech, and was probably a mid-stage in all dialects in which *battin'* is now identical with *batten*.

To return to the pronunciation of New York City and its environs, another feature of that pronunciation is most notable (and perhaps, among some speakers, found only) in the word *bottle*. Most Americans, I think, pronounce the *t* here less distinctly than most Englishmen (at least educated ones), but the New Yorker often goes further: he partly or entirely replaces the *t* by what phoneticians call the "glottal stop" (produced by momentarily closing the gap between the vocal cords, as *t* is produced by momentarily closing the gap between the tip of the tongue and the front of the palate, or *p* by closing the gap between the lips). I often heard Westerners in the American Army during the last war amusing themselves by getting fellow-soldiers from New York to "say *bottle*." The sound is seldom heard elsewhere in America, but it is common in some varieties of British (especially Scottish) speech, and is heard there much more generally than in a single word.

I have mentioned incidentally above the more or less general American tendency to enunciate *t* (and I will add *d*) between vowels less clearly than most Englishmen do, so that *pretty* comes out as something closer to "pri'y" than to "pritty," and *ladies* is almost "la'ies." There is a closely parallel and almost as general tendency to slur *n* in the same position, so that, for example, *any* sounds something like "eh-ee" with a slightly nasalized "eh." "[Have you] got any ties?" thus becomes "guh eh-ee ties?" (or, in some Southern speech, "tahz"). The parallel is not accidental: *t*, *d*, and *n* are produced with the tip of the tongue in the same position—too tense a position, and one requiring too much energy, for a sloppy speaker.

This is more or less general American in its incidence; I find myself constantly reverting to the speech of New York City.

There was, in the middle 1940's, a vogue among more or less sophisticated young people for jocosely substituting *er* with retained *r* ("uhrr") for any stressed vowel ("The berse is merd as herl"—"The boss is mad as hell"). This probably owed something to the *nuts-nerts* model (see Chapter Two), but more, perhaps, to the alleged habit of New Yorkers (especially Brooklyners) of saying *coil* for *curl* and *curl* for *coil*. Expert opinion is divided as to whether the interchange actually occurs, or whether the same sound, rather—a kind of "uh-ee" rather than "oh-ee" (*oi*)—is not used in both classes of words, being apprehended by speakers of other dialects as *oi* when *er* is expected, and vice versa. I suspect that the truth is that the latter analysis is correct for the *origin* of the phenomenon, but that now, in the mouths of some speakers, the interchange actually occurs. Whatever happens, it happens only in stressed syllables. The "uh-ee," incidentally, is not limited to vulgar or uneducated or slovenly speakers: a Latin teacher of mine, for example, who was unmistakably a lady and, what is more, a learned lady, always said "Vuh-eegil." She did *not* say "Voi-gil" or speak of his use of the active and passive verses in his epic voice. And "uh-ee" for *er* is heard not only in New York but also sporadically in some parts of the South, though this is hardly true of *oi* ("oh-ee" rather than "uh-ee") for *er* and certainly not of *er* for *oi*.

I have twice mentioned the fairly general tolerance by most Americans today of other pronunciations than their own. The chief beneficiary of this tolerance is the Southern dialect, which (except perhaps for some of its peculiar diphthongs) is widely regarded in other parts of the country with affectionate indulgence tempered by amused condescension, especially when it is heard from a young and attractive woman. The affection is felt at least equally in the South itself, and without the qualification. I am inclined to think that at least one reason for this state of affairs is that the North (including East and West) still has a guilty conscience about having won the Civil War and the South a feeling of self-pity for having lost it. Eastern speech, on the other hand, particularly if also obviously educated, enjoys, outside of its own territory, less popular favor, mainly because of the reputed and to some extent real cultural primacy of New York City and New England, which excites envy disguised as contempt. (The attitude toward educated Southern British—though not towards Cockney—is much the same, and for the same reason.) The ignorant American outside of the East is likely to be less favorably, if not less deeply, impressed by the Harvard accent than by the Harvard vocabulary—or what he takes for it. The reason why he sometimes still (though less than formerly) admires "ten-dollar words" at the same time that he resents what might be called a ten-dollar accent is that he half-consciously realizes that the former are more frequently acquired by individual effort than the latter, and hence (at least theoretically) more nearly within his own grasp if he would but make the effort. In one very notable recent instance, to be sure, plain Western Americans tolerated, at least, a pronunciation that many of them would ordinarily have thought snobbish and affected—Mr Roosevelt's. But this was a highly special case, in which the plain Western Americans were so well pleased with what was said and with the speaker's convincing (and probably genuine) appearance of good will that for once they could and did forgive—and even admire, and acknowledge to themselves that they admired— the Dutchess County-Groton-Harvard pronunciation. It was not Mr Roosevelt's admirers, even in the West, that made fun of "agane and agane and agane" and "I hate waw." Indeed, it is probable that those pronunciations were commonest among their deriders. I should not be surprised if many an Eastern Isolationist member of the American Association of Manufacturers schooled himself to say, between 1939 and 1941, "agen" and "worr," at the same time that he innocently continued saying "agane'st" and "wawlike." And yet Eastern speech, despite a certain amount of Western low-brow suspicion and dislike, does enjoy real prestige (as does Southern, for emotional reasons already set forth); witness the adoption by many Westerners (usually social climbers) of *often* with a *t*, "eyether," and "tomahto," all of them natural to many Easterners of all classes. But the principal proof, I should say, is to be found in the fact that Westerners moving to the East or the South often adjust their pronunciation in time (not infrequently in a remarkably short time) to that of their new neighbors, whereas the transplanted Easterner or Southerner much oftener apparently undertakes to love and cherish his till death them do part.

This is not, of course, true without exception, and was probably less true a few decades ago. My grandfather, whose childhood was spent partly in eastern Massachusetts and partly in the District of Columbia, but who moved to the Middle West (in 1880) as a very young man, had stopped "dropping his r's" at least by his fifties. As often happens, however, there were some vestigial remains; he persisted in the "intrusive r" ("papa rand mama," "Victoria rour Queen"), which develops only in the speech of people who "drop their r's" or once dropped them. Contrariwise, there is some tendency for even people who cling generally to their native dialect in a strange land to adopt unconsciously their new neighbors' pronunciation of proper names widely used in the region; a friend of mine, for example (from a suburb of Boston) took his M.A. at Ha'va'd but his B.A. at Darrtmouth. A partly parallel case is that of *Concord*, Mass., and *concord* meaning "peace." They are obviously the same word, but they are almost always pronounced differently: *Concord* always sounds exactly like *conquered* (the natural development); *concord* shows the influence of the spelling in being usually "con cord" or "cong cord." And the circumstances in which other words than proper names are added to one's vocabulary may affect the pronunciation; *monastery*, for example, which I learned early and at home, I pronounce—as I do most words like it (*secretary*, for example)—with four syllables in the regular and general American fashion (another respect, incidentally, in which American English is more archaic than British English), but give only three to *baptistery* and *presbytery*, which I learned later and from an Englishman. There is also a certain amount of conscious tinkering among the socially ambitious even without migration from one part of the country to the other. I will confess that, at an age when I perhaps ought to have known better, I deliberately replaced my native "ah" (as in *odd*) with the sound between "ah" and "aw" that is usual in such words outside of Western American English, and that earlier I schooled myself (with the assistance, in this case, of my school teachers) to say "tyoon" instead of "toon." The latter manipulation, though earlier and more defensible, was less successful than the former: I sometimes catch myself saying "tyoo," but I never—well, hardly ever—say "fawther." But whatever the lamentable facts in my case, what seems to be tinkering is not always that: for example, a friend of mine from Indiana (where the dialect is in some places a modified Southern) does not, indeed, substitute "yoo" for "oo" in *too*, but does substitute a vowel superficially like it but really closer to the German *ü* or French *u*. This is not tinkering at all, but a native feature, honestly come by.

In a few particular words, pronunciations in origin not merely dialectal but decidedly local have become universal, but only in special senses, while for the other meanings some relatively standard pronunciation is used. For example, *cuss* and *bust* have acquired meanings different from *curse* and *burst* (pronounced with or without the retained *r* according to the speaker's practice) and are used by the same speakers, with the result that *bust* and *burst*, at least, are probably thought of by many people as altogether distinct words. Indeed, from one point of view they may be said to have become so. The *nuts-nerts* complex probably owes a sort of perverted debt to these models. Again, in Great Britain, *ass*, contrary to regular historical development, has the vowel of *fat* at least as commonly as it has that of *father*, for the reason that the latter pronunciation makes the word practically indistinguishable from the Southern British pronunciation of *arse*. In America the problem is different and more complex: here, *ar* came in certain localities not only to drop the *r* but also to substitute the vowel of *fat* for that of *father* in words like *arse* (for example, "passel" and "passley" for *parcel* and *parsley*), so that instead of *ass*'s taking on the pronunciation of *arse*, *arse* took on that of *ass*. The problem has been met differently in America, too: instead of altering the pronunciation, Americans—over-dainty Americans and those taught by them—don't say *ass* (in its proper sense) at all. I have actually heard a minister make the Lord ask Balaam why he had smitten his donkey. Ordinarily, however, the verbal prestige of the Authorized Version prevents such indecent liberties.

The pronunciation of foreign words varies widely, mostly according to the social and educational status of the speaker. On the lower levels no effort whatever is usually made to approximate the native pronunciation: in the liquor trade, *Noilly Prat* rimes with *doily mat*, and *crème de menthe* and *crème de cacao* are "cream de mint" and "cream de cocoa" (these of course might almost be called partial translations rather than pronunciations). This habit of Anglicization is very old, and was once universal and entirely respectable; indeed, it could be argued that "cream de cocoa" is preferable to "vallay" for *valet* or "Callay" for *Calais*, both of which are commoner in America than in England because of the stronger oral tradition of culture in the mother country and the greater confidence likely to be felt by educated people there in the soundness of that tradition and in their acquaintance with it. The fact remains that both in England and (even more, perhaps) in America educated people tend more than they once did to try to approximate the native pronunciation of all except the oldest and most familiar loan words. But Latin, at least in America, is a special case. As "Old English" says, "They pronounce Latin like furriners nowadays." The so-called "Roman" pronunciation of Latin, first introduced into American schools a little after 1870, is now practically the only one taught there. The proportion of the population even slightly acquainted with Latin is small and growing smaller (as is the degree of its acquaintance), but it is influential. When such persons have occasion to use a Latin expression in speech, they are more and more likely to pronounce it in the "Roman" fashion. This probably accounts for "dahta" and "strahta" (and perhaps partly and indirectly for "datta" and "stratta"); and the accident of identical sound between "Roman" *ae* and English "long *i*" and between "Roman" *i* and anglicized *ae* has produced hopeless confusion between *alumni* and *alumnae* in both speech and writing. *Societas Philosophiae*, the motto of Phi

Beta Kappa, which the founders at William and Mary in 1776 certainly pronounced "so *sigh* a tass fill a *soffy* ee," is now usually "*soky* a tahs fill oh *sofy* eye." Another frequent academic phrase that is for no good reason usually given a "Roman" pronunciation is *cum laude*, which is certainly oftener "coom louduh" than "come lawdy" even in the mouths of people who ought to know better. In the pronunciation of the names of Greek letters (not that Greek is nowadays much more studied than Swahili, but that college fraternities, etc., make the names of the letters quite widely familiar) a curious compromise or blend is almost universal; *Phi Beta Kappa*, for example, is nowadays almost never either "fee bayta kahpa" or "fie beeta kappa," but "fie bayta kappa." *Alpha Phi*, on the other hand, always has "fee," never "fie."

The radio, especially through some of the better news programs broadcast over national networks, has done a good deal toward establishing more or less "correct" pronunciations of many foreign proper names. This is partly owing to the wide use of Professor W. Cabell Greet's book on the subject, but sometimes partly also to the foreign residence (during the war) and general alertness, knowledgeableness, and cultivation of some of the news commentators, such as Mr Raymond Swing, Mr Edward Murrow, and Mr Elmer Davis. Otherwise, I don't think the radio has had much effect on popular pronunciation, though it very possibly will in the course of time. At least on programs nationally broadcast, a moderate variety of the Western dialect preponderates over Eastern and Southern even more, I should say, than it does among the population at large: and among most kinds of professional broadcasters a speech that is at least distinct and incisive is widely cultivated, for obvious reasons. One would expect, then, that the radio would gradually lead to a standard of popular speech more uniform, more widely Western, and more distinct; but broadcasting has been going on for so short a time, and other kinds of speech than that described are still so frequently broadcast, and there are so many more influences than that of the radio, and people are so inattentive, that the process is and will be very slow. Or rather, it is and will be very slow except perhaps in settling a few specific cases of alternative pronunciation like that involving *ration*. This word was, at least in the Middle West, most commonly pronounced "raytion" during the first world war; it is now (at least there) much more commonly pronounced "rassion." The change (which was not established till the latter part of the last war) was, I think, largely owing to the influence of the radio, which probably picked up "rassion" from British practice.

A much older, more pervasive, more characteristic, and more powerful influence on American speech is that of "spelling pronunciation," that is, pronunciation based on an assumption mentioned earlier in this chapter—that spelling regularly indicates and even determines *the* "correct" pronunciation of a word. Such an assumption is naturally characteristic of the culture of a people who have for a time and in some degree been cut off from an ancient and continuous oral tradition; when they start hungering and thirsting after knowledge, they are inevitably driven to books rather than to teachers, and, when also to teachers, then to teachers themselves dependent on books. The spelling bee is still a flourishing American institution, and what might be called the big leagues even get in to news reels, the radio, and television. American culture, in short, is in some ways more bookish than British culture, and though "Seen it in print!" is less of a crusher in a dispute than it used to be, the assumption behind it is still common. And this bookishness often takes a specifically orthographical form. Newspapers may and do safely reflect their own tastes and those of their readers with the grossest and vilest perversions of vocabulary and syntax and idiom, but they misspell only at the risk of being put in their place by letters to the editor from readers whose vigilance and complacency are likely to be directly proportional to their ignorance of everything but spelling. Indeed, newspapers sometimes provoke the same kind of censure when they chance to spell correctly one of several words of which an *incorrect* spelling has become fixed in the popular imagination as the right one: *wiener*, for example, and *sacrilegious*, which the popular imagination is firmly convinced should be *weiner* and *sacreligious*. As for the prepositions *till* and *round*, even most newspaper writers themselves seem to be quite sure that these are no better than colloquial contractions of *until* and *around*, and they accordingly spell them almost always *'til* and *'round*, and probably feel quite folksy when they descend to writing them.

The schoolma'am, then, has convinced the American people of the supreme importance of orthography, but what is important, of course, in the spoken language is that she has also convinced them of the reasonableness of pronouncing as you spell. An example of one of the effects as well as of the limitations to which it is subject is to be found in the words *creek* and *breeches*. The standard pronunciations are respectively "creak" and "britches," but a good many people, brought up on the provincial "crick" and then learning that prestige attaches to saying "creak," make the generalization that the best pronunciation accords automatically with the spelling, and conscientiously acquire also the pronunciation "breaches," reserving "britches" for jocular use, and even coming sometimes to think of it and spell it as a different word. Incidentally, nothing whatever justifies calling the short *i* standard in one word and provincial in the other except social convention. That is decidedly not the same thing, however, as saying that social convention doesn't count; it counts for almost everything. Another analogical spelling pronunciation very commonly heard is *brooch* riming with *hooch* instead of with *coach*. Spelling pronunciation and the schoolma'am influence have also doubtless had a good deal to do with depressing the social status of "dropping one's g's," a practice once common in very high social and educational circles indeed, and one that normal phonetic development would otherwise by this time probably have made universal. "Huntin', shootin', and fishin'," I believe, are much less common today among "county" Englishmen than they used to be, and in America scarcely any educated person outside of certain Southern regions any longer "drops his *g's*"— *in formal public speech.* In familiar speech, or at least domestic speech, on the other hand, my impression is decidedly that the only people that *never* "drop their *g's*" are the same people as never say "punkin" for *pumpkin* but also, alas, never say

288 BRITISH AND AMERICAN ENGLISH SINCE 1900

"hankerchiff" for *handkerchief*, but instead rime it solemnly and relentlessly with "land per chief." The "dropped *g*," in short, is heard often (in special circumstances) at the top of the social and educational scale, almost always at the bottom, but seldom in the middle. The explanation is easy; it is that in some ways culture at both top and bottom is oral and auditory, whereas at the middle it is visual. We have already seen a parallel in the sphere of euphemism.

A few relatively new or at least recently habilitated words give trouble when they come to be spelt because they don't fit general spelling conventions. *Busses-buses* is a case in point; and how is one to spell the past tense of *to pal around with?* Most writers seem to prefer "palled" to "paled." I am driven to suggest that the best spelling would be "chummed."

What has happened to poor old Simplified Spelling (or Speling), so much heard of forty years ago? Perhaps it has been taken up by the wrong people—the proprietors of Bar-B-Q stands, the impresarios of New Burlesk Every Nite, and the champions of revised frate rates. *Nite* also appears on *hi(gh)way* signs (for a not altogether unacceptable reason), and *sox* is almost universal (quite so in the names of baseball teams). A reputable currency is enjoyed by *(al)tho*, *thoro* and its compounds, and *thru*; the same is even truer of words like *program(me)*, *catalog(ue)*, and *cigaret(te)* (though not among makers of cigarettes): but that's about all. Even apart from the dislocation that would be produced by a general reform of English spelling, and from the impossibility of getting the enthusiasts for it to agree on a system, the English-speaking peoples, particularly Americans for reasons mentioned above, take a perverted pride in the intricate and mysterious anomalies of the spelling of their language; it makes them feel superior to foreigners.

CHAPTER FIVE

THE TEACHING OF ENGLISH;
EDUCATION AND "EDUCATION"

To deal, with some approach to adequacy, with the English language in America in the last fifty years, one must deal with the teaching of English there and then; and to deal at all with that, one must talk about contemporary American education generally. Now, in order to talk sensibly about education, one must talk about man's nature and about his environment—that is, the world and society; and in order to talk sensibly about man's nature and environment, one must distinguish first between the mutable and the immutable, and secondly between the actual and the potential. American Educators (and Educatrices) sometimes speak and oftener act as if they were the first—and the most disturbing fact is that they sometimes apparently *believe* that they are the first—to discover and to give due consideration to the facts (1) that labor productive of the necessities or supposed necessities of all men's continued physical existence is necessarily anterior to every other human activity; (2) that the conditions of human existence and society—*any* society—require that that labor should be the principal occupation of the majority; (3) that that majority are entitled (if anyone is "entitled" to anything) to as full and rich an enjoyment of life as they are capable of—in other words, that all men, *as* men, have dignity if any man has; and (4) that society and the state and education should take full account of that fact. But the Educators, I conceive, make two mistakes: first, their premises are incomplete; secondly, their inferences are faulty. The habit of trained reflection would complete the premises; a knowledge of history would perfect the inferences.

The missing premise is that, however paradoxical it may seem and however "unjust" it may be, the majority of men have always been and will always be enabled to enhance and enrich their enjoyment of life and leisure *only* by the exceptional labor of exceptional men, and that exceptional men can perform and could have performed that exceptional labor *only* by liberation from ordinary labor—that is, by access to what is properly called leisure. The leisure class (in this sense) is the old-age insurance, the life insurance, even, of the human race. Like all life insurance, it postpones present goods to future ones; like all life insurance, it comes dear; and like all life insurance, it's worth it. There must be (in this sense) a leisure class: and it must be, if it is to do its job, selected for brains.

As for the faulty inferences, let us first get the immediately relevant facts straight. Most Americans, including most American college graduates, speak and write their own language like navvies. (The fact that the same is true of most Englishmen in an almost equal degree is sad, but not the immediately important thing.) The English-speaking navvy's English, for the navvy's ordinary purposes, is not so bad—not nearly so bad—as it might be, but it is bad enough. It is not getting better. It is, furthermore, becoming gradually the standard of usage that it is unnecessary and even imprudent to surpass. This situation is bad enough (at least in the long run) for the navvy, but it is worse for society as a whole. Navvies are necessary, their occupation is honorable, and they have their rights, but the more navvies and navvy-like members a society has, and the more influential they are, the less civilized the society.

The average English teacher in the average American college will testify that many or even most of his students, when he gets them, cannot speak distinctly, cannot spell correctly (that is, conventionally), cannot punctuate intelligently, cannot understand or correctly use any but the most elementary words for the most elemental things, cannot distinguish a sentence from a phrase (that is, a proposition from a noise), cannot analyse or understand any piece of syntax in any considerable degree complex, and cannot express an idea—or conceive that it can be expressed—in any but the first way that happens to occur to them. Further, when the English teacher has done with them, they are not much improved. Still further, the teacher knows it. And what is more, the defect is by no means confined to the average young American's proficiency in his own language, but extends to his general knowledge and to his attitude toward knowledge.

How has this come about? Is it new? Is it likely to get better?

It came about directly and at first from a refusal to recognize —or at least to admit openly—that most men are less intelligent and less educable than a few—a refusal accompanied by an insistence on none the less going through the motions of giving the many the education that only the few could absorb. But the fact that the many could not absorb and even did not desire it (once they found how hard it was) became shortly inescapable. At this point there were two paths to take: (1) One could give up the assumption and the pretense that they did desire it and could absorb it, and make such provisions for the occupation of their time till the age of fourteen or eighteen or twenty-two as might seem best for them and for society, reserving *and preserving* for the able few the education that only the able few can receive; (2) one could go off the gold standard —one could, that is, equate a liberal education with the amount and kind of education that all children would accept and could receive. In other words, one could make the following series of propositions: (i) Gold is more precious than brass. (ii) Some people are allergic to gold. (iii) Brass looks quite a lot like gold. (iv) Almost no one is allergic to brass. (v) People want *something* shiny. (vi) They are displeased to be informed, not so much indeed that they are allergic to gold as that gold is more precious than brass, or even different from it. (vii) These people are numerous and irascible and increasingly powerful. (viii) It would therefore be prudent to give them brass and call it gold.

It was this latter course that was chosen in America. It was chosen when a choice had to be made—that is, at about the beginning of the twentieth century.

It has had, naturally, further effects. Most Americans regard education as primarily the duty of the state, and accordingly the great majority of American children go to the schools of the state, that is, the public schools (answering to the British council schools, formerly board schools). The majority is still greater if we count with the public schools the church schools, mainly Roman Catholic, most of which certainly resemble the public schools more closely than they do most of the "private" schools (which answer partly to the "public" and partly to the proprietary schools of Great Britain). Most Americans furthermore believe that both their own social status and their children's chances in life depend largely on the length of time they can keep their children in school, and the percentage of children that enter high school has risen from about ten in 1900 to about seventy-five in 1950. Most American parents, again, like most parents everywhere and always, believe or think they believe that their children are at least as intelligent and educable as their neighbors' children. Being what they regard as democrats, they also believe that it is the duty of the state to keep their children in school for at least the average length of time, to advance them regularly from grade to grade, and to stand all or most of the cost, irrespective of what or how much the children can or do learn. Between 1890 and 1920 the normal or ideal (though not the average) period of schooling rose from six or eight years to ten or twelve; since 1920 it has risen from ten or twelve to fourteen or sixteen. This should mean that most young people of eighteen in 1950 should be about twice as well educated as their grandparents in 1890. They aren't. It should mean at least that more young people of twenty or twenty-two should be as well educated as those persons who went to college during the 1890's. Again, they aren't. What it does mean is that more money is spent on more people who take longer to learn less.

If this were all, the situation would not be so bad. The United States is rich enough to exempt from productive labor a larger and larger fraction of its citizens for the first eighteen years of their lives and even for the first twenty-two, regardless of what or how much they learn during that time. It would be possible to occupy, in other pursuits than those of productive labor, the time of *all* children above the grade of imbecile up to either of those ages profitably both to themselves and to society. It is not so occupied.

But suppose it isn't? Are not the ablest children, at least, and more and more of them, given more and better education?

No.

The reason for this is complex but clear. In the face of the conditions described above, brass began to be tendered for gold, and to be accepted eagerly *as* gold by the majority. But the majority were dimly and yet uncomfortably aware that gold existed and that the minority throve on it. Being aware of that fact, they were also jealously resentful of it. Furthermore, it had come to be regarded as the primary function of the public schools to keep all children off the streets and out of trouble with the police till the labor market should be ready to absorb them. Children and teachers being what they are, it became practically necessary for teachers to purchase their safety, if not their comfort, by occupying the children's time as agreeably as possible to the children. Doubtless life at every age should be as agreeable as is practical, but children have a forgivable and even endearing way of underestimating the degree to which it is practical. The immediate result was that school work became less irksome and laborious. That is not quite the same thing as saying that it became less serious and valuable, but it is near enough; and in any event, it *did* quickly become less serious and valuable: the "straight A" report card became easier and easier to get, and hence more and more commonly got. The next step was for the Smiths to begin to make nasty inquiries into why Johnny Smith was not bringing home so many A's as Jimmy Jones, who was obviously, in the Smiths' eyes, a cretin, whereas Johnny was just as obviously cut out for a financier, or at least an inventor. The fault could not possibly be in Johnny, who, though of course boy, all boy, was an angel as well as a genius, or in the American public school system, which was Democracy in Action; it must therefore be in the third factor, Johnny's teacher. She must be incompetent, or at least she must be lacking in an understanding of Johnny's personality. What do we feed these nincompoops at the public trough for, anyway? Besides, if they could do anything else, they wouldn't be teaching; *you* know—"Those who can, do;

those who can't, teach." And what the hell is the matter with that School Board?

Unfortunately, Johnny's teacher may indeed be incompetent, and less detectably so than she would be at most other occupations. The chances are pretty good, however, that she is not incompetent (at least by nature) and that she has taken to teaching mainly, at any rate, because she likes to teach. The chances are even better that she understands Johnny's personality only too well and that Johnny is neither a genius nor an angel, and better still that there is quite a lot the matter with the school board. But Johnny's teacher knows which side her bread is buttered on—and how thinly and precariously; and besides, having had her nerves fairly well shattered by Johnny and his playmates from nine to three, she is not eager to subject them to her Principal in his office from three to five and to Mr and Mrs Smith at the Parents' and Teachers' Association meeting from seven to nine. After all, she must keep fresh in order to correct papers from ten to one, and then get lots of sleep so that she will not be too tired in June to go to Summer School and take the six "credits" in Education on which her next salary increase of fifty dollars a year depends, as well as her record for Showing an Interest in Professional Growth.

When she goes to Summer School, she is usually at least theoretically free to choose whether she shall study the subject she teaches or something else. In practice she is likely to study something else. For this there are three reasons: (1) Ignorant as she may be of her subject, she knows more about it than her average pupil can or will learn. (2) She knows that her Principal is more likely to recommend to the school board an increase in her so-called salary if she studies something else. (3) She has, and wishes to retain, self-respect, which entails respect for the way she earns her living; and respect for the way she earns her living is a lesson that she requires help with. The result of these three considerations is that she studies Education.

Just what Education is (as distinct from education) is not easy to explain to an Englishman or a Frenchman or a German. It is, furthermore, not unembarrassing. Originally it was and essentially it still professes to be the study of the history, "philosophy," and methods of education and instruction (the Educators do not usually distinguish), as well as of "administering" schools. Each of these branches has become an academic and professional specialty (British, "speciality") or "major" or *Hauptfach*; one may take a Ph. D. with a major in Educational Administration and a minor in Educational Psychology just as if they were Latin and Greek or Chemistry and Physics. The teacher coming to Summer School at the nearest university has already "had a good many courses" (that is, received a good deal of officially accredited formal instruction) in these mysteries, as a condition of "getting her certificate" (that is, being certified as a legally employable teacher). But she has ordinarily also already received her bachelor's degree—usually not in arts, but in "Science" or "Education" or "the Science of Education". In order to get her next year's fifty dollars, she must work toward a master's degree—again, not in arts (though it is in some places officially and technically in arts), but in Education. (Incidentally, her training has probably left her ignorant of the history of this meaning of "arts.") She accordingly registers as a student of Education in the graduate school.

In the graduate school *alone* (as distinct from the undergraduate teachers' college or college of education, as it is variously called, through which our teacher has already passed), one American university (and it is not exceptional) "offers" *two hundred and forty* "courses" in Education. These are divided into the following classes and sub-classes: (1) Agricultural Education (13 courses); (2) Art Education (8 courses); (3) Curriculum and Instruction: (a) General (21 courses); (b) Elementary Education (19 courses); (c) Secondary Education (36 courses); (d) Higher Education (7 courses); (4) Educational Administration: (a) General (9 courses); (b) Elementary Education (1 course—something wrong here); (c) Secondary Education (7 courses); (d) Higher Education (4 courses); (5) Educational Psychology: (a) General (36 courses—repeat, 36); (b) Elementary Education (1 course—something wrong again); (c) Secondary Education (2 courses); (d) Higher Education (4 courses); (6) Physical Education (32 courses, not subclassified—the mind evidently changes between three and thirty, but not the body); (7) History and Philosophy of Education (13 courses); (8) Home Economics Education (12 courses); (9) Industrial Education, (15 courses).

Seated before this table prepared in the presence (and by the hands) of them that trouble her, and having in remembrance where and in what subject her Principal or Superintendent took his Doctor's degree (by whose title she had jolly well better address him), and recalling Johnny's ineptitude and intractability, Johnny's teacher "takes," not usually further courses in her subject, but further courses in Education. In the following autumn she returns to Johnny, armed (the word is apt) not with more knowledge of algebra, or Latin, or history, or chemistry, or even Spanish, but with more devices for keeping Johnny from throwing spit-balls at her. Her head has long since been anointed with axle-grease, and her cup is full.

Johnny's teacher, obviously, is not to blame for this cloud-capped tower and gorgeous palace of science. Even her teachers in the teachers' colleges are not ultimately to blame for it, nor is it *quite* so bad as I have (I hope) made it sound. Many teachers doubtless can and do profit even from bad instruction in the history and objects and methods of education; some conventional methods of instruction doubtless are antiquated; and, confronted with the facts of American society in the twentieth century, even wise and learned and disinterested men would doubtless have erected a fabric of advanced training for teachers in some ways resembling the present one.

In some ways, but not in many. The teachers' colleges are what they are mainly because the educational system generally is what it is. But there is an increasing amount of what might be called re-infection: the general effect of the teachers' colleges is to make the educational system in turn yet worse by assuring parents, teachers, and children that, if all is not yet as it should be in the schools, all we need to make it so is more of the same. And the effect is intensified by the appalling fact that, as the years go on, more and more Educators are themselves necessarily the product of schools formed and governed by Educators, and actually believe what they say.

And what do they say? If we are to judge from the results,

they seem to say approximately this: (1) The main function and object of education is to keep all children in school as long as possible and in the company of children of their own age, and to prevent their getting their feelings hurt. (2) To these ends, the curriculum and the standard of performance must be determined by the dullest and least promising and most sullen and unbiddable children of the worst-educated parents. (3) Better still, there should be *no* standard of performance and no prescribed curriculum: each child should study what he likes and "compete with his own abilities," not with other children, and should be given his certificate or his diploma regardless of what he has studied or what he has learnt.

" 'What *is* a Caucus-race?' said Alice ... 'Why,' said the Dodo, 'the best way to explain it is to do it.' ... First it marked out a race-course, in a sort of circle, ('the exact shape doesn't matter,' it said,) and then all the party were placed along the course, here and there. There was no 'One, two, three, and away,' but they began running when they liked, and left off when they liked, so that it was not easy to know when the race was over. However, when they had been running half an hour or so ... the Dodo suddenly called out 'The race is over!' and they all crowded round it, panting, and asking, 'But who has won?' This question the Dodo could not answer without a great deal of thought, and it sat for a long time with one finger pressed upon its forehead (the position in which you usually see Shakespeare, in the pictures of him), while the rest waited in silence. At last the Dodo said, '*Everybody* has won, and all must have prizes.' "

(4) Children are too sensitive and tender and immature to be made to study any harder than they want to, or to study at all any subject they don't want to study; but they are not too immature to be allowed to decide for themselves what they shall study and how hard. This is what is called Preparation for Life in a Democratic Society. (5) America being a democracy, its education should be democratic; and the way to get a democratic education is to pay attention exclusively to average and below-average children (who, after all, make up the majority), and to make it not only difficult but as nearly impossible as can

be for superior children to get a superior education unless their parents (a) know a good education when they see one, and (b) can afford it. (6) If they can afford it, they may send their children to private schools; but private schools, of course, are snobbish and undemocratic, and—for that reason—are only tolerated anyway. And it won't be long before they are brought into line: inflation is playing hob with their endowments as well as with the incomes of many of their patrons. (7) Anybody can teach anything. He needn't know anything about it; he need only know How to Teach It. It is quite irrelevant that his teachers at the university (outside of the teachers' college), not having taken the requisite courses in Education, couldn't get a job in any high school in the state. (8) No one, not even a parent, should teach anyone anything— not even the alphabet or table manners or driving an automobile—unless he (a) is a professional teacher, and (b) has Taken a Course in How to Teach It. (9) No subject of instruction is more valuable than any other. (10) No subject of instruction not valuable or comprehensible to the average child should be taught to any child. (11) No subject should be taught to anyone that the average child cannot be easily made to see will directly increase his share of bread and circuses. Latin is a good example. Shakespeare had small Latin and less Greek (never mind who said it and from the heights of what learning); therefore "extravagant and erring spirit" means "spendthrift and mistaken state of mind." Well, maybe it doesn't; but who wants to read Shakespeare anyway? Give me a good comic book any time. Of course, a fellow ought to read *some* heavy stuff; if he doesn't, he can't be a Leader in his Community. But what's the matter with Dale Carnegie, if you want heavy stuff? (12) You got a tooth-ache, you go to a dentist; you want your motor tuned up, you go to a garage mechanic; you want to know something about education, you go to an Educator. It stands to reason Educators are people that know a lot about education. Educators are modern, snappy guys just like me and you. High-type men. Democratic, too; not like those stuck-up moth-eaten old mossbacks they got over there at the college that read Shakespeare and Latin and all that crap. *You* know—

wayny-weedy-weeky and to-be-or-not-to-be-that-is-the-question. Know what they make a year? *Well!* And even these scientis' ain't always so practical, either; *you* know—electricons and stuff. Why don't they get wise to their selves? You want *my* opinion? Any scientis' spends his time in a college, he ain't got much on the ball. If he had, he'd get out and invent a new-type carburetor or something, *I* always say. (13) What if your kid *don't* read so good, that don't mean he ain't smart. The Principal up at the high school, he told me that just means the kid ain't got *verbal* intelligence, but he's got *real* intelligence all right. Don't tell *me* that kid ain't got intelligence; jever watch him box my kid? My kid don't outsmart him more 'n half two-thirds the time. Say, 'd I tell you the crack my kid pulled on his old lady last night? Like to batted his ears down, but *jeez* it was smart; afterwards I went out in the kitchen and laughed fit to bust.

This may be laid down as an iron law of American education hitherto: the longer the normal duration of schooling, the lower the standard of attainment, or, to use the Educators' word, Achievement. (A friend of mine was told last year that his daughter, by getting A's in all her subjects, was "over-achieving." She was also Impairing her Status as a Member of the Group; what shall it profit a girl if she gain a knowledge of algebra and lose her A in Democratic Citizenship?) The more normal it has become to have twelve years of schooling in-stead of eight, the worse the last four have got—for everybody. That may be because most children should leave school at fourteen, but I am inclined to think that it is not and that they should not, and that the reason for the deterioration of the American secondary school is the failure to segregate fourteen-year-old children with brains and educate them, leaving what that great and genuine democrat Thomas Jefferson called, in precisely this connection, *the trash* to be, for as many years as their parents think genteel and the state thinks wise, restrained, amused, and so far as possible instructed in their duty in that state of life to which it shall please God to call them. And just possibly to be educated, a little; certainly everyone should have the opportunity of learning everything he can learn about everything. The trouble with the present state of affairs is that no one in the average public school has much opportunity of learning or encouragement to learn much more about anything than his dullest classmates can and will learn, or anything about anything that his dullest classmates can and will learn nothing about. It might be remarked that this principle is not carried over to the selection of the football team, membership in which is on the contrary very strictly a matter of native genius and demonstrated competence; and no one thinks that undemocratic or unjust.

The iron law I have spoken of will remain iron until the segregation I have spoken of is effected. As I have already suggested, the first year of high school would in my opinion be perhaps early enough for the segregation to be made. For one or more of several possible reasons the primary schools—the first six or eight years, with pupils from five or six years old to twelve or fourteen—do not seem to be so bad as they might be; indeed, I will be generous and say that they may be better than they used to be in somewhat more ways than they are worse. If this is true (and I at least hope it is), I should guess that the main reason why they are at any rate not worse than they are is partly that everyone still admits (1) that all normal very young children must learn a good many quite definite things, and (2) that they must in practice learn them by continual drill, and partly that methods of instruction are more important in the early years of schooling than they are in the later ones, if only because very young children cannot be expected to take consciously much of a hand in their own education. A fourteen-year-old child can perhaps be justly blamed for taking the attitude of "Learn me, dern yuh!"; an eight-year-old child hardly can be.

The colleges, too, are at least potentially not so bad as they might be. In fact, they are not even *actually* so bad as that: in most colleges, or at any rate in the good ones, of which there are really quite a lot, many applicants still are excluded and many students still are dropped for the excellent reason that they cannot or do not meet the competition. That is, there still *is* competition in the colleges, and at least moderate success in

it is still sought and admired, and failure still feared and despised. Competition does not engender the noblest of motives
for the attainment of learning or anything else, but it does
engender strikingly effectual ones. If it were stiffer, it would
be yet more effectual. It would also incidentally supply one of
the conditions for making Democratic Education into democratic education. In my own university I am proud to say that
at least the speed at which the standards of admission and performance tend to deteriorate has been checked by the establish-
ment, in the middle 1930's, of what is called the General
College, to which are relegated the least-promising products of
the secondary schools for a two-year "terminal" curriculum in
"general" education culminating in the degree of "Associate
in Arts," with the resulting diminution almost to zero of
letters from Indignant Parents and Taxpayers inquiring why
their children should be excluded from the state university.

The weakest link is the secondary schools. It is not hard to
see why, if the reasons I have suggested for the primary
schools' not being so bad as they might be are sound. "I have
a curious job," Mr Sholto Douglas wrote to Mr A. J. A.
Symons, who quotes the passage in *The Quest for Corvo*
(1934; Penguin Books edition, 1940, p. 112). "I am in charge of
a lad of seventeen. He learned to read and write at the age of
seven. He was then given a ten-year holiday. Now I am called
in. The depths of his ignorance are abysmal. At first I thought
that I could not endure. But I have come to be interested immensely ... I hope to travel far with him." With a couple of
immaterial modifications, probably every teacher of college
freshmen in the United States today would echo all but the
last two sentences of that quotation with references to most of
his students; and the fact that he would also echo the last two
sentences with reference to a saving remnant is all that pre-
serves his self-respect and even his sanity. Some few public
schools, even secondary schools, are, to be sure, as good as the
best private ones, but unhappily these are almost all of them in
well-to-do and more or less fashionable districts (notably on
Long Island) where practically all the parents are so uniformly
able and willing to pay high taxes for schools and so

uniformly appreciative of what good schools are that they do not need to send their children to private schools. (Not that *all* private schools are good, any more than all public ones are bad.) For the most part, even when the teachers could and would like to do a better job (and very often they could and would), social pressure and the structure of the machine prevent their exacting from superior children even a standard of performance that average children could meet.

The inferior children set the standard; the average children suffer for it; the superior children, and society at large, suffer yet more. The Phi Beta Kappa *Key Reporter* for the autumn of 1950 says of a booklet entitled *Education of the Gifted*, published by the Educational Policies Commission of the National Educational Association, and prepared by a subcommittee whose chairman was President Conant of Harvard University, that the booklet "states that ten per cent of a high school graduating class is gifted and one per cent highly gifted." I confess that I am a little dubious of the validity of this degree of precision, but let it pass. To continue, "Of these *only half* go on to college. The reasons for this *waste of brain power* are *lack of funds*, lack of encouragement and recognition from parents and teachers, and lack of incentive (because of the *American tendency to belittle exceptional ability* and the *failure to require high ability for positions of leadership*). The commission recommends early recognition of gifted youth and *special education* for them. ... The top ten per cent should be encouraged to get college education and the top one per cent education beyond ... college. ... *Scholarships should be provided for needy gifted students* ...and funds should be allocated for the study of the psychology of the specially gifted." [Italics mine.]

The failure to have done long since and as a matter of course what that report recommends (which is essentially what Jefferson contemplated when he designed an educational system for Virginia), the unwillingness to do it, the belief that it is, as Mr Mencken would say, against God and morals to do it, is the measure of Democratic Education in the United States in the twentieth century. The deficiency, I repeat, is not fundamentally the fault of the teachers or even of the teachers' colleges, but of ideas pervading American society in the twentieth century, which presents the teachers with a formidable and hitherto unsolved problem; and the teachers cannot be blamed for preferring the semblance of a solution to a confession of despair. It is easy to determine the degree of a child's knowledge of how to conjugate a French verb in the past definite; it is not easy to determine the degree of his Social Consciousness. That is not to say that Social Consciousness, or rather social consciousness, may not be more important than French verbs; it is only to say that French verbs can be taught and the success of the teaching measured, whereas Social Consciousness, if it can be "taught" at all, can *not* be measured. What the Educators do is to try to "teach" it and pretend to measure it. They spend so much time doing both that the French verbs get lost in the shuffle, and any consequent uneasiness is assuaged by the assurance that French verbs aren't important anyway. And besides, plenty of children who are demonstrably unable or unwilling to learn French verbs are not *demonstrably* incapable of having their Social Consciousness improved by "teaching." "And while we are at it, it would be just as well to discourage the able children from learning French verbs even if they want to; their success will inspire envy and embarrassment in the other children, and vanity and impracticality in the able ones. And now that we no longer try to teach French, there is room in the curriculum for Advanced Social Consciousness in the third year of high school and for a Seminar in Social Consciousness in the fourth. We can't put *that* in right away because no teacher here has taken the Teachers' College course (Curriculum and Instruction 321b) in How to Organize Seminars in Social Consciousness on the Senior High School Level in Communities of Less than Ten Thousand, but next year we can do it."

Newman, I seem to remember, long ago had some pointed things to say about a system of education that, "professing to do so much, does so little for the mind."

The teaching of English in America in the twentieth century, or more precisely, the performance exacted of students of English, has inevitably shared in this gradual deterioration.

Stenographers, to be sure, if not their bosses, are still expected to be able to spell conventionally and punctuate illuminatingly and maintain, most of the time, some degree of grammatical concord; and there is of course at any moment a point beyond which no one may in practice and with impunity push the corruption of the vocabulary. There is also still a good deal of old-fashioned arbitrary and "authoritarian" teaching of traditional usage; teaching that is often undiscriminating and unhistorical, but that none the less has the virtues as well as the vices of conservatism; teaching that at least tends in effect, whatever it means to do, to preserve the continuous intelligibility of language as well as its ulterior values, which depend almost entirely on association—which depends in turn almost entirely on tradition and convention. American neo-grammarians of the present day (I suppose they would prefer to be called the New Grammar Boys) often sound as if they thought that continuous intelligibility and what I will venture to call by the quaint name of beauty were nugatory and even positively un-- desirable qualities in language. And like the Educators, they sometimes sound as if they thought they had discovered a previously unknown fact—in their case, that language has changed and that most of the changes have come from the bottom up—from which they almost seem to infer that change, especially when effected by uneducated people, is in itself desirable.

Yet another discovery of theirs, made every year or two by a new champion of Democratic Education and regularly proclaimed in yet another article or book, is that usage determines "correctness"—that the "rules" are conventional, not rational; relative, not absolute. These pronouncements usually exhibit several family resemblances: (1) They treat as if on the same plane (a) ending a sentence with a preposition, (b) saying "It's me," and (c) saying "ain't." As one would suppose most civilized English-speaking people had long known, *a* is and always has been sound literary as well as colloquial English, *b* is and long has been as usual in the familiar speech of the crustiest linguistic tory as of everybody else, and *c* is "correct" from the standpoint of navvies. (2) They (the Discoverers, not the navvies) regard any counsel to master and observe the "rules" about *shall* and *will* as a lesion of the majesty of the people because these are not a part of (at least the Western) American vernacular. (3) They imagine that the teacher of traditional literary and colloquial English considers an analogy used as a teaching device identical both with a law and with a reason; for example, they fail to perceive that it is neither pedantic nor purblind nor ineffectual to clarify a pupil's comprehending and assist his memorizing the "taboo" about *he ain't* by pointing out that *ain't* may be regarded as a conflated contraction of *am not* and *have not*, and that *am* and *have* are not used (outside of pidgin English and possibly Gullah) in the third person singular—not even in the pupil's vernacular. A dull teacher, of course, may go further, and bring in abstract logic; and so may any teacher's dull pupil—or dull critic. (4) They themselves are sedulous to avoid, in their declarations of independence, every usage whose tabooing they decry. It is this last point that seems to me often to convict them of muddle-headedness or insincerity or antidemocracy or all three, for it implies that what is not good enough for them is quite good enough for their pupils. Their pupils, I submit, should at least be given the refusal of a high standard of usage, as members of a civilized society—I had almost said, as children of God. Many even of the duller children are by no means always so unwilling as their pastors and masters fancy to believe that their language can be improved, to wish to improve it, and to look to their teachers for assistance. It is no more clearly wise or fair to recommend—and to teach only, and to everybody— a minimum standard of language than a minimum standard of table manners or bodily cleanliness; it is mental subsistence farming. But the hungry sheep look up....

These Modernists not only make discoveries and draw inferences; they give advice. The principal pieces of advice are as follows: (1) *Write naturally*. Of course one should write naturally, in the same sense and the same degree as that in which one should sing or walk or drive a car or play golf or eat peas naturally. (2) *A peculiarly literary style is as bad in a note to one's milkman as a peculiarly colloquial one in a critical essay.* Even leaving aside the perhaps dubious validity of this generalization, I submit that whereas no one needs much teaching in order to write an effective note to his milkman, anyone needs quite a lot of teaching in order to write an effective critical essay; that in any society that can be called civilized, some people do write critical essays; that it is an important function of any civilized educational system to train quite a lot of people to write critical essays, even if most of those people use that training afterwards only as an aid to distinguishing the good critical essays of other people from the bad ones; and that one of the best ways of accomplishing both those ends is to make as many people as possible write critical essays and revise them under competent criticism.

On these counsels of perfection the New Grammar Boys are generally agreed. When they come to recommending models of style and standards of usage, they split up into three schools of thought, as follows: (1) Determine the average standard (if possible by statistical methods), and then try not to rise above it. (This is the proposal of the Committee on Applying the Technique of the Kinsey Report to the English Language.) (2) Determine the average standard of Congressmen or millionaires or newspaper columnists or successful evangelists, and then try not to rise above *it*; after all, they are the Leaders of Our National Life. (This principle has not yet been extended to prize-fighters, baseball players, and movie directors, but that's being worked on.) (3) Model your style on that of popular journalism. (This is the austere, or High-Church, school of thought. It supplies specimens of the models it recommends in a good many of the collections of "freshman readings," of which several hundreds have been published in the last thirty years as substitutes for literature. Some of them make quite a lot of money.)

The Advanced Thinkers among the New Grammar Boys have recently discovered what they have not, so far as I know, called the Modern Quadrivium; only (to be charitable) because they have not thought of it. It is called Communications (or Communication or the Communication Arts). It combines instruction and practice in Listening, Speaking, Reading, and

Writing. These four arts are all included in a course whose students meet three or four times a week for thirty weeks. The fact that long experience shows that the average American college freshman of the present day is not and apparently cannot be taught to *write* decent English in that amount of time is apparently regarded as irrelevant.

No one, obviously, would deny, or for that matter ever has denied, that the ability to listen and read intelligently and speak intelligibly is at least as important as the ability to write intelligibly, let alone interestingly and elegantly, or that some formal instruction in some of these "skills" (to use the word now in vogue among the faithful) is desirable and possible for some people. But there are a number of things that the New Grammar Boys and the Educators do not sufficiently consider. Some of them are (1) that even at the worst, writing lends itself to real teaching in a degree in which reading, listening, and even speaking do not. (2) Apparently everyone agrees that most American college freshmen today are not decently proficient in these "skills"; otherwise why undertake to teach them the rudiments when they get to college? (3) Since they are not proficient in them, why not work at improving the high schools' average performance? (4) If the high schools' average performance cannot in practice be improved, why not segregate promising students (*regardless of their parents' means*) and really prepare them for genuine college work? (5) As for the rest, why hope to get better results in teaching them one competency by trying to teach them three more in the same amount of time?

The teaching of English in American colleges today is what it is because the teaching of English and almost everything else in most American secondary schools is what it is; and that is what it is because the American educational system is what it is; and that is what it is because American society today is what it is; and American society today is in many ways not essentially democratic at all—it is plutocratic.

CHAPTER SIX

BRITISH AND AMERICAN ENGLISH: SOME FINAL OBSERVATIONS

IN the preceding chapters I have tried to deal with American English so far as seemed practical without reference to British English. Again so far as seemed practical, I have tried to deal separately and successively with vocabulary, syntax and idiom and tone and style, and pronunciation. As my readers will realize, it has not everywhere been practical to hold rigorously to any of these divisions or classifications of my subject, or at least has not everywhere seemed so to me.

Similar limitations apply to the present chapter; so far as seemed practical I have reserved for it the discussion of certain fundamental and characteristic differences between British and American English in the twentieth century—but *only* so far as it seemed so; and likewise, within it I have, so far as seemed practical, dealt separately and successively with vocabulary, idiom (etc.), and pronunciation—but again, *only* so far as it seemed so.

In the first place, British and American English undoubtedly are different, and Englishmen and Americans undoubtedly know it. Of most of the kinds of differences, there are many examples that are universally notorious, but this understanding has its limits, as we shall shortly see. But before we do that, let us try to characterize British and American English in a very general way. American English, especially today, might be called, I think, in comparison with British English, a smart-aleck language. Perhaps it would be more accurate as well as more up to date to call it a wise-guy language: a wise guy is tougher than a smart aleck and has come into prominence, though hardly into existence, more recently; and similarly, the difference of American English of the twentieth century from British English, though it is fundamentally of the same kind as it was in the nineteenth, has tended to deviate from greater "smartness" to greater toughness. Another way of saying it is to say that British English has more *frein* and American English more *élan*. Yet another is to say that British English is stuffy and American English bumptious.

These characterizations, I think, would be approved by most observers as coinciding with their own general impressions; but the accuracy of these general impressions has a good many limitations among both Englishmen and Americans. One British writer of detective stories, for example, widely and deservedly popular both at home and in America, is almost notorious for his distortions and exaggerations and sometimes apparently deliberate and downright inventions of American slang. But British misconceptions are probably oftener quite innocent: the best-known instance, I suppose, is Mr Chamberlain's notion that one could get at the meaning of *jitterbug* through *jittery* or *the jitters*. To match this in America, we have the comic stage Englishman with his oh-I-say-by-Jove-doncha-know-this-is-bally-bloody, and on what I trust is a higher level, the notion (in which I must confess I shared till recently) that what an American calls quotation marks were *always* called inverted commas by an Englishman. (They aren't.)

These inaccurate impressions sometimes lead on both sides, especially in matters of pronunciation, to false and deplorable charges of affectation. For example, many educated Englishmen say "iss-you," and most Englishmen educated or uneducated say "hoss-tile." To most Americans, who say "ish-oo" and "hoss-till" or "hoss-t'l," the usual British pronunciations seem affected; they are not. Likewise, to many Englishmen the usual American pronunciations seem slovenly or ignorant; they are not. A sort of converse of this is true, *mutatis mutandis*, of the quadrisyllabic American "secretary" for British "secret'ry." To be sure, certain national pronunciations, especially in America, may begin as affectations or at any rate as spelling pronunciations, and yet become so widely accepted as to be used by persons who cannot possibly be charged with affectation; they merely say what they have always heard—for example, the (more or less) "French" pronunciation of *valet*, very common in America even among quite well-educated people.

Another kind of misconception that I think is widely prevalent is the common British notion that American English is more vulgar and slovenly than it is and the common American notion that British English is more cultivated and precise and generally "high-toned" than it is. The reason for the British notion is perhaps partly the exaggerations of British journalists and other writers who have travelled in America, from Dickens and Mrs Trollope on down; partly, in recent years, American "talkies" (especially of the gangster variety) as well as the vulgar speech of many American soldiers in England from 1941 onwards (by no means always enlisted men— British, "Other Ranks"); and partly the fact that American prosperity has sent to England many tourists who have more money than taste. The reason for the corresponding American notion (in which I probably share) is that most British travellers in America come, I should say, from a higher social and educational class than most American travellers in England. It is even harder for an American to be free of this notion if he is, like me, an academic person who is well acquainted with the lower as well as the upper reaches of his countrymen's language but who has never visited England, whose acquaintance with Englishmen is almost wholly limited to the educated, and who is not likely to have read much vulgar British writing. Though elegance has, I am pretty sure, more prestige in England than it has in America, British vulgarity probably plunges as low as American (I have seen some indications of it); and in general I suspect that average British usage is not so choice as many Americans think, nor average American usage so vulgar as many Englishmen think.

Turning to vocabulary specifically, one of the most familiar differences is American *vacation* for British *holiday*. The situation is complex but clear and explicable, and explicable, furthermore, in terms of the differences between British and American life. In medieval and even seventeenth-century England and Europe generally, it is safe to say that most people did not annually leave off their regular employment for a stretch of two or three weeks, but this was partly compensated for and made unnecessary by the customary cessation at least from heavy agricultural labor on the very frequent holy days of obligation (whose frequency was one of Luther's minor complaints). Naturally, therefore, *holy day*—that is, *holiday*—came to be the normal name for a day of rest. But some holy days came in batches—at Christmas and Easter, for example, and consequently *holiday* might sometimes be extended to any ecclesiastically enjoined period of rest, even one lasting beyond a single day. Finally the feature of ecclesiastical injunction ceased to be thought of as essential, with the result that the word is used as it is used in England today. *Vacation* existed in England in much the same sense as the latest one of *holiday*, but it originated in, and tended—and tends—to be mainly restricted to, intermissions between the stated terms of the courts of law and the universities, when they are "vacated." In America, the situation in the seventeenth century and even in the eighteenth was quite different. There, or at any rate in New England, holy days, and the whole cycle of the Christian year, were frowned on and left unobserved as being unscriptural and corrupt and Romish and carnal, and hence another name had to be found for other days or periods of rest than "the Lord's day." It was found in an extension of *vacation* from judges and lawyers and tutors and undergraduates to everybody else (when, that is, New Englanders began to get shiftless enough to stop working once in a while). Then at about the same time or perhaps a little later, common American usage took over *holiday* in the secondary, restricted, and partly secularized sense of a single day, other than Sunday, set apart for observance by abstaining from work. The result is the present usual difference on this point between British and American usage. I hope I shall not sound chauvinistic or provincial if I say that the American usage seems to me less likely to be ambiguous.

Differences in the conditions of political life are significantly reflected by certain differences between the British and American use of *office* and *politician*. In *The American Union* (1948; Pelican Books, 1950, p. 76), by Mr H. G. Nicholas, an

Englishman, is a reference to the United States Congress as one "whose members were expressly debarred from holding any *office*"—a usage common in America in the eighteenth century (see Article I, Section 6, of the Federal Constitution) and usual in England today as then with reference to the House of Commons, but likely to be puzzling to Americans today, who, for good reasons, include Congressmen among "office holders." Again, *politician*, a harmless and useful and even mildly honorific word in England today, is likely to have a sinister ring to Americans, who, when they call a friend that, smile. Their nearest synonym (and it is not very near, or really very common as a synonym in speech or unaffected writing) is *statesman*, which owes such extended currency as it has partly to the pejoration of *politician* (and of *politics*) and partly to our national habit of grandiloquence.

The State suggests the Church, and here again different institutions bring about different expressions. The "Protestant Episcopal Church in the United States of America" is inevitably an offshoot of the Church of England (as most Americans more or less understand), but no less inevitably it has a completely different position with reference to the state, and an only less completely different one in the popular mind. Consequently, though rectors, vicars, curates, archdeacons, canons, chapters, matins, and evensong do exist in the United States, most of the words are not very familiar among non-Anglicans—that is, among about ninety-eight per cent of the population. But a more common and important difference in the ecclesiastical vocabulary, and one reflecting more broadly the ecclesiastical history of the United States, is to be found in the use of *clergyman, minister, parson, pastor,* and *preacher*. With certain exceptions on both sides, the common usage may be shown by the following table:

	British	*American*
clergyman	One in Anglican orders	Any "minister of religion," including Jewish rabbis
minister	A dissenting minister (usually)	A Protestant minister or clergyman

	British	American
parson	Rector (and more loosely, any incumbent) of an Anglican parish church (and more loosely still, equals *clergyman*)	Rustic or jocose synonym of *minister*, and almost specifically non-Anglican (or Roman Catholic or Jewish)
pastor	In ordinary use, almost exclusively nonconformist and literal	(1) Any minister of religion (except Roman Catholics and Jews), even one who performs no strictly pastoral functions. (2) The principal priest in a Roman Catholic parish.
preacher	The clergyman or minister preaching at a particular service (usually)	Familiar and sometimes mildly contemptuous for any Protestant minister (especially non-Anglican)

Priest, except among some Anglicans, almost always means a Roman Catholic priest in America, even to the occasional exclusion, sometimes by the Orthodox themselves, of the married Eastern Orthodox clergy.

One more oddity of the American ecclesiastical vocabulary, heard mostly from others than Anglicans and Roman Catholics, is *services* for a *single* religious service: "I went to services last Sunday" doesn't necessarily or even usually mean I went to more than one, nor does "The body will lie in state before the services" mean that there are going to be two funerals. I should guess—but only guess—that this began with sentences like "There will be services at eleven and eight in the winter, but only at eleven in the summer."

When we come to slang and familiar speech generally, we come to that department of the vocabulary in which British and American differences are naturally greater than anywhere else, just as they are greater in the colloquial language generally than in the literary. This fact, together with the short life of much slang, would make it absurd to attempt anything more than the

smallest sampling in a short book, but one or two characteristic specimens may be given that have also some degree of
ulterior significance or interest. (1) British *swanky* more or less
equals American *classy*, but not in the usage of those many
Americans who sometimes say *swank*; and such is the prestige
among them, of British usage, as well as the social connotation
of *classy*, that they, at least, hardly say *classy* except in mockery.
In other words, *swank* is swank, but *classy* is not classy. Americans who are too sophisticated to say *classy* but afraid to say
swank say *ritzy* or *snazzy*. (2) Differences in slang and in familiar speech generally can lead to curious misapprehensions. For
example, *The New Yorker* for 7 October 1950 reports that *The
Daily Racing Form* sent a reporter a few days before that date to
"cover" what was advertised as "an exhibition of British book-
making" at the British Book Centre in New York. Such misapprehensions have a redoubled comic potential when they
happen to involve an expression that is more or less indecorous
in one country and completely innocuous in the other. The
Englishman's *knocked up* startles the American, but the American's *bug* and *bum* startle (or used to startle) the Englishman.
American soldiers who came into contact with British soldiers
during the last war were made happy by the British Army
term "compassionate leave" (American, "emergency leave"),
and particularly delighted in depriving it of its first syllable;
and there is a line in *Trial by Jury* that I have known to make
Americans jump.

Even the best published guides to Englishmen's and Americans' mutual understanding sometimes say things that are inaccurate or at least misleading—for example, Mr Mencken's
American Language (and its supplements) and Mr H. W.
Horwill's *Dictionary of Modern American Usage* (Oxford University Press, 1935; second edition, 1943). Mr Mencken says
or appears to say, for instance (*Supplement One*, p. 525), that
American practice, unlike British, universally gives the title
doctor to surgeons, dentists, and druggists. This is true of surgeons and dentists, whose universal possession of diplomas of
M.D. and D.D.S. (sometimes D.M.D.) respectively is reflected by the universal practice of addressing them as "Doc-

tor," but it is not true of druggists except in jocose urban and
perhaps more widely in rustic usage—and even in the country,
when a druggist is called "Doctor" he is called so on quite
another basis in the mind of the speaker than the dentist is.
And he is much more likely to be "Doc" than "Doctor."
"Doc" is used in the same way to pharmacist's mates in the
Navy and medical corps men in the Army. Mr Horwill, again,
says (p. 68) that "the word *class* is not used in America, as it is
in England, to denote the different types of accommodation
provided by the railways. These differences are indicated by
other terms, which do not conflict with the popular theories
that there are no class distinctions in America." This is to some
extent true of colloquial (especially of old-fashioned) usage,
but not of the (at least official) use of the railways themselves.
The colloquial "go coach"—that is, "go by coach"—or "go
Pullman" is roughly equivalent to the British "travel (by) third
or first class," but the American railways themselves officially
use "coach" and "first class." They do not use "third class,"
however, and so, in a characteristically American fashion, we
have it both ways: the opulent are flattered and the penurious
soothed.

British and American colloquial usage not only differ; they
differ sometimes otherwise and for other reasons and with
other implications and overtones than even alert and well-
informed people are likely to think. Professor Wyld (*Hist.
Mod. Colloq. Engl.*, p. 17), in calling *vest* a "shop-walker's
word" for *waistcoat*, says something that is probably quite valid
for England, but not for America (not that he thought it was),
where it is almost everybody's normal, unaffected word—and
where *vest* for *undershirt* would be, to the great majority, quite
unintelligible. But some Americans, wishing not to be supposed to have been shopwalkers (American, "floorwalkers")
before they Made Their Money, painfully learn, not only to
write *waistcoat* but also to say "weskit," and they would be
surprised to discover that the *Shorter Oxford Dictionary* (second
edition, 1936) calls this pronunciation "colloquial *or vulgar*"
and that Professor Daniel Jones (*An English Pronouncing Dictionary*, seventh edition, 1946) calls it "old-fashioned." As usual,

the trouble with keeping up with the Joneses—all of them—is that you are likely not to know how far ahead they have got.

One of the things that Americans are likely to think about their variety of the language is that is is, more than the British, spare and business-like and succinct (which an Educator of my acquaintance, now a college president, used, at least, to pronounce "sukkinct"). This is probably true as a rule, but only as a rule. *Elevator* and *streetcar* (less commonly, *trolley*) for *lift* and *tram*, both of which are universally *understood* in America, are familiar examples of exceptions to the rule. *Lift* is slowly making its way into American usage. *Tram* is having a more complex experience: it is common in newspaper headlines because of its brevity, but is hardly ever found elsewhere either in speech or in writing, and probably now never will be, for the good reason that streetcars are giving way in city after city to busses. A somewhat similar case is that of American *faucet* for British *tap*, though *tap-water* is in universal American use. Again, though in America an advertisement printed on a large sheet of paper and pasted on a wall is almost always called a poster, and practically never a bill, prohibitions against pasting them on a wall almost always read "Post no bills" and are taken as addressed to "bill-stickers." Here the American vocabulary, though "modern" (and perhaps characteristically dissyllabic) in the isolated word, is, in the phrase, just as monosyllabic and archaic—if that is the right expression here—as the British. *Billboard* (British, usually "hoarding") is also in universal American use. (One reason, by the way, for the general American disuse of *bill* in this sense is perhaps its usual substitution for *note* as in "five-dollar bill" as compared with "five-pound note.") A somewhat different kind of occasional British superiority in succinctness is illustrated by *opposite number*, a phrase with regrettably small currency in America, where most people are constrained to say something like "the person holding the corresponding position." On the whole, however, I think that the general impression that American usage tends to surpass British in (sometimes excessive) economy and brevity is supported by the facts.

I have said in an earlier chapter that *temporal changes* in idiom
and syntax are in some ways more important than those in
vocabulary. This is not true in so many ways of *international
differences*, which are likely to be *less* important than those in
vocabulary because, unlike them, they seldom impede mutual
understanding, and are indeed often noticed only by people
who are well enough educated to have learnt more or less to
expect them and to be undisturbed by them. But differences
between British and American idiom and syntax undoubtedly
exist.

They exist in greater number, as one would expect, in the
colloquial than in the literary language, and one of the departments in which the difference most often shows itself is the use
of prepositions. It shows itself here in a number of ways.
(1) British English sometimes omits prepositions where
American English retains them, whereas the reverse is rare: for
instance, (frequent) British "give it me" for (usual) American
"give it to me" or (more rarely) "give me it"; and again,
(almost universal) British" he was promoted colonel" for
American "he was promoted to colonel"—universal except
when some quite different expression is used instead. (2) British:
"off his head"; American: "out of his head." (Here the British
colloquial idiom omits the American *of*, but, what is more
important, has *off* for *out*.) (3) (Frequent) British: "It looked
quite a decent house"; (universal) American: "It looked like
quite a decent house." (Here *like*, though historically an adjective, is practically a preposition.) On the other hand, in at least
one colloquial phrase where the "preposition" is really a final
adverb or separated prefix, British English usually retains a
word always dropped by Americans. This is the British "Just
try it on!" for the American "Just try it!", where *try it (on)*
means "venture audaciously and insolently, if you dare," some
specified action. For an American, *try it on* refers only to a new
hat or the like. There are also a fair number of phrases where,
though both dialects use prepositions, they use different ones;
for example, British "sell by auction" and American "sell at
auction." Another instance is the British "His membership of
the party was discussed" for the American "His membership

in the party was discussed" (though Americans, like Englishmen, use *membership of* collectively for *members of*). But what sounds to an American like the omission of an idiomatically necessary word occurs again with the definite article, which is missing from the usual British variety of certain colloquial phrases; for example, (frequent) British "into hospital" for (universal) American "into the (*or* a) hospital," and (occasional) British "out the window" for (almost universal) American "out (of) the window." I am not suggesting that the American idiom in such phrases is in any way "better" than the British: doubtless "out the window" sounds no odder to an American than "out of the doors" would sound to both him and an Englishman. Another instance of *the*'s presence in American English and absence from British is (*the*) *Government*, but this is complicated by the very important differences in the meaning of the noun. Incidentally, the fact that "the Government" now always means to Americans not only the civil machinery rather than the administration, but specifically the *Federal Government*, as distinct from that of the city or the State or anything else, is in part a sign of the long-increasing importance of the Federal Government in all Americans' daily lives.

Some differences between British and American usage that might be called differences in idiom are more accurately described as differences in morphology. *Whilst*, for example, which is almost as frequent in England (at least in literary use) as *while*, is very seldom either seen or heard in America except in some old-fashioned or rustic speech; *amongst*, on the other hand, is perhaps a little commoner there, though certainly far less common than *among*. Again, such preterites and past participles as *learnt* instead of *learned* are a good deal less often heard in America than in England. I have had both *learnt* and *spelt* edited out of a manuscript (though I was pig-headed enough to restore them); *leapt* is seldom heard or seen, and *leant* never, at least in urban usage.

A few idiomatic differences in colloquial phrases are apparently of recent origin, as are the phrases themselves; thus Mr H. G. Nicholas (in *The American Government*, 1948) follows BBC usage in speaking of Mr Roosevelt's New Deal experts as his "Brains Trust," whereas the form actually *always* used in America was "Brain Trust." A greater number of such differences, however, like some of those of somewhat different kinds discussed earlier, proceed from the sporadic but still unquestionable tendency of American English, like all transplanted languages, to be in some ways archaic. An excellent example is the American past participle *gotten* for British *got*. Many educated Americans follow the British practice, but not by any means all of them, and scarcely any of the uneducated do. Englishmen, by the way, have notorious difficulty in analysing completely and (on occasion) imitating accurately the American idiom here. *No* Americans, even those who say *gotten* everywhere else, *ever* any more than an Englishman say anything but *got* in *I've got* meaning *I possess*, though of course many do say "I've gotten over it" instead of "I've got over it."

This point about *I've got* suggests another striking difference between British and American colloquial idiom. Many Americans under the schoolma'am influence are very careful (when they are above the level of *I got* in the present tense) to say *I have* and to imagine that *I've got* in that sense is inelegant if not "incorrect," a delusion that most Englishmen do not appear to share. But even those Americans that say *I've got* (for *I possess*) without superstitious scruple do not say, as Englishmen very often do, *I'd got* for *I had* (I possessed); to practically all Americans, *I'd got* (or *I'd gotten*) means *I had obtained*, and nothing else. And these two sets of facts about *I've got* have, I suspect, a further and conjoint significance, namely, that *I've got* (for *I possess*) originated in England after *gotten* had become obsolete there, and was then adopted as a whole in America, without being modified by the substitution of the otherwise still general American *gotten* for *got*, but also without *got*'s supplanting *gotten* in other constructions. *I'd got* for *I possessed* was not similarly borrowed by Americans either because it originated later than the present-tense form or because there is less frequent occasion for using the past tense with this idea.

Almost as characteristic as this difference is that shown by "Don't let's do it," common in British speech but seldom heard in American, where "Let's not do it" is much the commoner. This avoidance of *do* is exactly contrary to the common American use of *did* with *have* in phrases where British use usually avoids it (as in the usual American "I didn't have any" for the usual British "I hadn't [*or* hadn't got] any").

Even a brief and sketchy discussion of differences between British and American idiom and syntax must mention the business of *shall* and *will*. In England itself the distinction, or the feeling for it, appears to be breaking down—see, for example, Mr G. M. Young's *Basic* (S. P. E. Tract No. 72, Oxford, 1943, p. 9); and in America, as excited Liberals are forever discovering and proclaiming, the distinction, or rather the subtler part of it, is of late seventeenth-century origin or even later and is not and never has been a part of the vernacular of most Americans (or Scotsmen or Irishmen or Yorkshiremen). I really cannot see that that fact—and of course it is a fact—is very relevant. What does seem to me relevant is that the distinction, like many other subtleties and niceties and elegances of language that are not a part of many or any speakers' vernacular, makes the English language more precisely and delicately expressive and flexible and plastic, and that the majority of the most effective writers of English prose—who also speak—have for a long time, even if not *quite* ever since the immigration of the Angles and Saxons to Britain—and in all places where English is spoken and written, even if less outside of Southern England than there—habitually availed themselves of the principal advantages of the distinction. A form of English from which it is absent is not therefore "bad English"; but any form of English from which it is absent is the poorer. And even in twentieth-century America, however much the New Grammar Boys make it an act of piety and patriotism to discountenance its teaching in the schools, people still pretty generally feel, rightly or wrongly, that an at least partial observance of the distinction is in keeping with any occasion that calls for dignity. I am perfectly sure that the "rules" for *shall* and *will* are not a part of Mr Truman's vernacular, and probably not a part of the vernacular of any of his commission of speechwriters; but I noticed that in his radio address of 1 September

1950 on the Korean war Mr Truman carefully observed the "rules," and I do not think he sounded affected. Neither, I believe, did most of his countrymen.

And yet it cannot be denied that in everyday speech the distinction strikes some Americans as especially if not peculiarly British or Anglophile and as having what Mr Mencken and others have called a "pansy cast" and a "mauve, Episcopalian ring." But to say that certain chiefly or wholly British usages impress some Americans as having those qualities is not the same thing as saying that they really have them. One example, familiar to most Americans in the Army or the Navy in the last war, is British "Most Secret" (as a technical classification of military information) for American "Top Secret." *Most* in the sense "very," being in American English almost exclusively literary, is likely to have for unliterary Americans an affected and "pansy cast." I rather suspect that "pansy cast" was perhaps at least in origin not quite altogether loosely and thoughtlessly used. The pioneer or frontiersman (both words in the American senses) is likely to have, and to indulge as largely as possible, normal appetites, including the sexual; he is likely to be a meek and assiduous conformist in his own immediate society even though in some ways a burly nonconformist relatively to society at large; he is likely to misunderstand and envy and fear and hate other kinds of behavior; he is likely to think that when these differ from his in language, they may very well differ in other respects, including the sexual; he perceives that educated people are often physically weaker and hence physically less daring and less efficient than he, and less primitively and aggressively masculine—in short, effeminate; and he concludes from all this that cultivated or apparently cultivated speech *prima facie* raises a presumption of homosexuality. Hence "pansy cast." I do not mean that this sequence of notions is often prominently or even very consciously operative; but I think it's there.

When we come to differences between British and American usage in spelling and pronunciation, we come to two things that are in a way very closely related, but of which the former is conspicuous and notorious and at the same time rather unimportant, whereas the latter, though somewhat less widely familiar and much less fully understood and analysed, is very important indeed. The differences in spelling are better known for the simple reason that the average Englishman and the average American know each other's usage chiefly from reading. The differences in pronunciation, besides being for the same reason less well known, are less fully understood and analysed because pronunciation generally is a comparatively little understood and ill-understood subject.

The matter of differences in spelling may be quickly dismissed. Everybody knows about *tyre* and *tire*, *kerb* and *curb*, *theatre* and *theater*, *connexion* and *connection*, *travelled* and *traveled*, *defence* and *defense*, *despatch* and *dispatch*, *judgement* and *judgment*, and *labour* and *labor*. The usual and often acrimonious disputes and recriminatory revilings about things like this remind me of a time when a school teacher telephoned an eminent professor of English of my acquaintance, at a moment when he was particularly busy, to ask him whether God preferred *honour* or *honor*. "Madam," he said, "it doesn't matter a damn." (Rejoice not thou, whole Palestina; he was and is exceedingly fussy about his *shall*'s and *will*'s.) I know that *theater* and *honor* set many a British tooth on edge just as "alrite" does mine, but I cannot help thinking that cultivated speakers and writers of English all over the world might better spend their time in forming a united front against the real Philistines. Before going on from spelling to the much more important subject of pronunciation, I will only take time to say that, however unsettling peculiarly American spellings sometimes seem to be to British nerves, most Americans take most peculiarly British spellings in their stride. This may be partly nothing better than colonial humility, but I don't think it's wholly that.

As for pronunciation, of misconceptions and of imperfect analyses and discriminations there are many on both sides, British and American. In the first place, Southern British pronunciation is by no means so uniform as some Americans think, or as I have perhaps so far suggested or seemed to suggest. Though all speakers of Southern British English use a pronun-

ciation in some ways uniform and more or less distinctive, there
are at least as many differences between Limehouse and May-
fair (or, in a sometimes different way, Bloomsbury) as between
Lower Third Avenue and Upper Fifth (or, again in a sometimes different way, Morningside Heights), though there is
such a thing as Eastern (and especially New York City)
American English which may often be usefully considered as
a unit. When I have, earlier in this book, spoken of Southern
British pronunciation, I have usually meant *general* Southern
British, regardless of class and education, or, when I have
meant something narrower, I have meant the Southern
British of the educated or of the upper class or both. But social
and educational differences within Southern British certainly
exist—perhaps, indeed, more glaring ones than within any
American dialect. The best-known example is lower-class
"eye" for standard "ay," where, by overcompensation, we get
the London shop-girl's "refained" pronunciation, just as we
have the New York shop-girl's "modom" for *madam*, to say
nothing of her "ahnts" for *ants* as well as for *aunts*. Cockney
also shows a certain amount of glottal stop (see Chapter Four)
as well as of "ah oo-wuh(r)" for "*ah* oo-uh(r)" (*our*) and "ah
ee yuh(r)" for "*ah*-ee-uh(r)" (*ire*), and the like, just as lower-
class New York speech does (again, see Chapter Four). But
still, just as there is such an entity as Eastern American pronunciation, so there is such an entity as Southern British, and
for the very good reason that "Public School Standard" or
"Received Standard" or "Received Pronunciation" originated
as a *class* modification of a *regional* pronunciation of South-
Eastern England—and the two are hence still in many fundamental ways indentical and identically unique.

Even when Americans understand this, they sometimes do
not understand correctly the incidence of certain sounds in
Southern British. I have already remarked incidentally on
"ahnts" for *ants*, which sometimes, I regret to say, gets extended among American social climbers of whom by no means
all are New York shop-girls to "pahnts" for *pants* (when, that
is, a Reel Lady can bring herself to use the word at all). The
fact is that, except for *can't* and perhaps one or two other words,

educated Southern Englishmen say "ah" before a nasal (usually *n*) only in words of French origin, and, as a rule, only in syllables normally stressed, particularly if they are monosyllabic words. A perfect example of the latter is to be found in the admirable Mr Martyn Green's singing of Koko's first song in the HMV recording of *The Mikado*. In this song, as all Savoyards will remember, Mr Green says "chahnces," "trahnces," and "dahnces," but in *recognizances* and *circumstances* he uses the "flat *a*" that most Americans use in all the other words as well. The *rationale* of this distinction, apparently so lawless and arbitrary, is that in ordinary speech, as apart from singing, the Southern Englishman usually pronounces no clear vowel at all in (as he departs from American usage in ordinarily giving no secondary stress to) the penultimate syllable of *recognizances* and *circumstances*, which he makes instead into "reco(g)niz'nces" and "*circumst'nces*." Mr Green's "flat *a*" in *romances* would seem to be a sort of exception to an exception; the fact remains that this is the only pronunciation given in Professor Jones's *English Pronouncing Dictionary*, and I suppose it must have something to do with the fact that though the second syllable of *romances* is stressed (in educated Southern British speech), the word (even in the singular) is not one of a single syllable. Incidentally, I suspect, though I cannot of course prove, that all six words rimed exactly in Gilbert's speech.

Some Americans who would like to say "cahn't," but don't quite dare, use instead a sound about half-way between that in the noun *cant* (and normal Western American *can't*) and that in "cahn't." This sound does naturally occur in some Northern British dialects, but its occurrence in the speech of most Americans that use it is a genteel affectation (or the innocent imitation of it), and what is more, a timid one. I believe it is somewhat less common than it was twenty years ago, but I may be wrong, though I should like to think not.

Educated Southern British pronunciation certainly has unique prestige throughout the English-speaking world, though this prestige is qualified in various ways. *The New York Times* in September 1950 printed a dispatch from Wellington (N.Z.) to the effect that listeners to the New Zealand radio, though they found the accents of announcers who were their fellow-countrymen to be surprisingly a little jarring, were even more irritated by imports from the BBC. In America, the attitude toward educated Southern British pronunciation is in the strict sense ambivalent. It is hardly an exaggeration to say that *all* Americans envy the educated Southern Englishman his pronunciation. The envy expresses itself in various degrees and very various ways, sometimes by the appearance of loath-ing, but it is envy still. Many of us do not *consciously* wish we spoke or dared speak like a user of "Received Standard," but none of us imagines that any user of Received Standard ever wished, consciously or unconsciously, to speak like us. We are colonial still (I say this with a full realization that some of my countrymen will probably say, "*You* may be, but *most* Ameri-cans," etc., etc.), and I rather suspect that the situation in New Zealand is not very different. And in certain special situations this envy, even as it is felt by the uneducated, appears as frank and open admiration instead of in its more usual guise. I am thinking here particularly of two detective-story radio series broadcast over national networks and listened to every week by a great many people—their Hooper rating, though not among the few highest, is pretty high. In each of them, the detective-protagonist's part is read in a reasonably good imita-tion of educated Southern British speech, emphasized in one case by a clearly deliberate contrast with the exaggeratedly vulgar Western American speech of the stooge, a subordinate detective. Further, the British-speaking protagonist is bright, and his American-speaking assistant is not, and still further, despite the British speech, neither this program nor the other has ever so far as I know contained any express statement that the detective was meant to be thought of as an Englishman; it is just taken for granted. A partial explanation is perhaps to be found in the stage tradition of Sherlock Holmes, established in America years ago by William Faversham, and reinforced not long since by another radio series drawn from or modelled on Doyle's stories, in which a Britisher (Mr Basil Rathbone) played Holmes; but another Britisher, Mr Nigel Bruce, played Dr Watson, and the setting of these was naturally

British, whereas that of the later series is American; and, all in all, the explanation is probably not sufficient. Perhaps Americans admire competence—competence, that is, in anything they think important—so much that they honor it, and honor it gladly, even when it has a British accent. That accent is not, of course, simulated in these broadcasts to perfection, but the imperfection usually takes the form of excess, not of defect. Certain British vowels tend to be what is technically called higher, or at any rate tenser—produced, that is, with the tip of the tongue, or at any rate the top of the tip, closer to the palate —than the corresponding American ones. One of our American radio sleuths o'erleaps himself here, and speaks of the victim of this week's murder as having been "stebbed to dith." Mr Mantalini made much the same exaggeration for much the same reason.

Clearly, most Americans at least recognize educated Southern British pronunciation, native or imitated, when they hear it; many of them, in fact, are likely to mistake for an Englishman a continental European taught English by British teachers, when the trained ear hears clearly the French or German or Danish harmonics above the Southern British fundamental. And certainly most Americans more or less consciously and willingly regard educated Southern British speech with humble respect; and the feeling of superiority they enjoy when they hear a speaker of that variety of English pronounce *ate* as "et" —a pronunciation restricted among Americans (outside of the South) to those from the backwoods—is all the keener for its rarity and none the less keen for being the result of a misconception.

As for American speech itself, I think I can assure Englishmen that it does not seem to Americans to be contemptuous of its consonants, over-fond of its unstressed vowels, slow, shrill, nasal, and monotonous. To Englishmen, however, it certainly does; and as compared with educated Southern British English, it certainly is. Some of these qualities (notably the quadrisyllabic *secretary* and the like) probably owe something to the American preservation of certain features of general seventeenth-century English, but I don't think that this explains all the facts. Possibly all the facts can't be explained, but I have a theory of sorts, and, with due diffidence, I will offer it. When one speaks in any tone of voice, but especially when one shouts from a distance, one tends naturally to labor to be heard, but concomitantly and as it were in compensation one also tries to save effort. Accordingly one shouting a sentence from a distance tends to emphasize the most sonorous sounds (the vowels); to fail, even if he tries, to emphasize the less sonorous ones (the consonants, especially the "voiceless" ones); to use a high pitch, which carries better (other things being equal) than a low one; to speak slowly; to reinforce oral resonance with nasal (as Chaucer's Prioress "entuned in hir nose" the Divine Office—because it was easier on the vocal cords); and to utter everything at about the same (high) pitch. That is to say, a sentence shouted from a distance is likely to have exactly the same qualities as are attributed to American speech. Early English immigrants to America usually lived at greater distances from each other, and were more likely to have frequent and urgent occasion to communicate with each other, than had been true at home. Q.E.D.

A number of scattered observations about American speech are appended.

1. I have already remarked on the comparative slackness of American consonants generally, and especially on the tendency of *t* between vowels to develop into a "glottal stop" or even into practically nothing at all. This is indeed what tends to happen to an American *t* before an unstressed syllable (as in *bottle* and *pretty*), but, especially before a stressed one, it sometimes does not so much disappear as become almost indistinguishable from a *d*; in technical language, the voiceless stop (not only *t*, but also *p* and *k*) becomes or seems to become at least partly voiced (to *d*, *b*, and "hard *g*" respectively), as in something like "buhdayduhz" for *potatoes*. The reason for this is that voiceless stops (*t*, *p*, *k*) normally tend, in English, to be uttered with a greater expenditure of breath than their voiced correlatives (*d*, *b*, "hard *g*"), and that consequently, when less breath than is normal is expended, the hearer is likely to apprehend *t*, *p*, and *k* as closer to *d*, *b*, and "hard *g*."

2. If we classify English vowels in the syllables of ordinary speech as stressed, half-stressed, and unstressed, we may say that speakers of English differ as to whether they commonly use one unstressed vowel or two—"uh" and "ih" or only "uh." In general, the single vowel is heard, I think, rather higher up the social and educational scale in America than it commonly is in (at least Southern) England. For example, *corrected:* Usual British and sophisticated American, "cuhrecti(h)d"; occasional British and unsophisticated American, "cuhrectu(h)d." There is also some geographical variation in America, the "ih" being perhaps more common in the area of the Eastern dialect than elsewhere.

3. A point connected with the preceding one is that in a few words, British pronunciation tends more than American to use a different vowel sound when the word is stressed from what is used when it is unstressed. The best example is *were*. Many more Englishmen than Americans distinguish "weh-uh(r)" stressed from "wuh(r)" unstressed; most Americans say "wuh(r)" (Western "wuhrr") in both places. Many Englishmen, that is, and few Americans, make exactly the same distinction with *were* that both usually make with *there*. *Where*, finally, has only the vowel of the *stressed* form in either kind of syllable in the speech of most English-speaking people.

4. The tendency of American speech to sound vowels fully, even if not always clearly, is seen not only in giving a secondary stress and a full vowel to such syllables as the third of *secretary*; it is seen also in at least two other classes, exemplified respectively by *adult* and *combat*. (a) When *adult* is stressed on the second syllable, as originally it always was, the first vowel becomes obscure—"uh*dult*"; but when the stress is shifted to the first syllable, the second vowel does *not* become obscure— we get "*add*ult," not "*add*'lt," though "*add*'lt" is what the native genius of the language would make one expect. This is partly a consequence of the recency of the form with shifted stress, and partly of spelling pronunciation. This particular word happens to have been treated in the same way in England, but the general phenomenon is more characteristically American. (b) What I believe to be the most frequent American pronunci-

ation of *combat* differs at least from old-fashioned British in two characteristic ways: (i) The noun, instead of the old and still common British "*comeb't*," is often "calmbat," with practically even stress. (ii) The verb is often and perhaps even usually "c'm*bat*," on the model of *desert*—noun, "*dehzuh*(rr)t," verb, "dih*zuh*(rr)*t*". In the instance of this particular word, this pronunciation has even affected the American spelling of the secondary forms of the verb, which are sometimes "combatting" and "combatted." Here again, the phenomenon is not in all ways exclusively American, but, also again, it is characteristically so. The causes, once more, are partly spelling pronunciation, partly schoolm'am analogy, and partly archaism.

5. There is an ancient and general tendency in English to put the stress as early as possible in a word, but this is carried further in American English than in British and further in unsophisticated American English than in sophisticated: "*re*source," "*re*search," and even "*U*nited States." Here again the formerly stressed vowels do not lose their clear quality along with their stress.

6. The almost universal American pronunciation of *holiday* gives the last syllable a strong secondary stress and a clear vowel; the usual British pronunciation is "*holid'y*." At first sight this looks like another case of archaism pure and simple; but, considering *Saturday*, which is almost as universally "*Saturd'y*" in America as in England, and which has exactly the same pattern, I think that the explanation is rather entirely one of spelling pronunciation, the word itself having been comparatively uncommon in America, or at any rate in New England, in the first century or so of British settlement there. The American pronunciation, in other words, is connected with the narrow American meaning (see the section on vocabulary earlier in this chapter).

7. In English family names ending in *-el*, that syllable is usually stressed and given a clear vowel in America; "Alice's" surname is there commonly "Lih-*dell*" rather than "*Liddle*," even among people who use her father's Greek lexicon. I don't know how to explain this unhistorical development (for that is what it is) except on the assumption of an analogy with such

French family names as *Bodel*—an analogy not unwelcome to Americans who think French names romantic. Some other classes of names sometimes get the same treatment—for example, *Hazzard* pronounced "huh*zard*," and *Padelford* "puh*del*fuh(rr)d."

8. American place names do not present such constant surprises in pronunciation as English do (even to Englishmen), but there are enough to trip the foreigner. Chillicothe is not "Chillicoath," but "Chillicahthy"; *Barre* in *Wilkes-Barre* is not "bar," but "Barry"; and a village in Minnesota, *Wayzata*, is not "way*zay*ta" or even "way*zat*ta," but "wye*zet*ta"—why, I do not know, unless it is that, of two white men's hearings of an American Indian name, one got on to the maps and the other into people's mouths. The case of *Chicago*, which is, contrary to all reason, "shih*cah*go" or "shih*caw*go," is generally familiar.

*   *   *   *

"Mr Dooley" said some decades ago that "when the American people get through with [*sic*] the English language, it will look as if it had been run over by a musical comedy." It has been—and by a good many other juggernauts. Doubtless it looks and sounds so, too, to Englishmen, and I am disposed to sympathize in part with some of their deprecations. But if we Americans do not speak the tongue that Shakespeare spoke, neither do Englishmen, of whom also it is true that "in forme of speche is chaunge"; indeed, in England, some of the things that have happened to the language would make Shakespeare and Chaucer open their wise and humorous eyes even wider than some that have happened in America. I think Chaucer and Shakespeare would own us, at our best (and we *have* a best); and I am at any rate sure that it will be a long time before Englishmen and Americans blessed with sense and breeding and goodwill will speak of, or even speak, the English and the American languages.

ACKNOWLEDGEMENTS

Mr Clark makes grateful acknowledgement to the respective publishers and copyright-holders for permission to reprint brief passages from the following works: H. C. Wyld, *A History of Modern Colloquial English*, third edition, 1936, Basil Blackwell, Oxford; A. J. A. Symons, *The Quest for Corvo* (quoting Sholto Douglas), 1940, Penguin Books; H. G. Nicholas, *The American Union*, 1950, Penguin Books; and H. W. Horwill, *A Dictionary of Modern American Usage*, 1944, Oxford University Press.

A Supplementary Article upon Australian English

By a series of mishaps and delays, the following article arrived too late for inclusion in its proper place. To fill the gap, I wrote the article that appears in the body of the book: but I felt unhappy about it, for I wanted all the varieties of Dominions English to be handled by men on the spot. Now that Mr Thomson's contribution has at last arrived, I owe it to him, and to the readers, to print it; I ask them to regard his as the principal and mine as the subsidiary article upon Australian English.

E.P.

AUSTRALIAN ENGLISH

AUSTRALIAN English differs from ordinary English both in vocabulary and in pronunciation, so that the term 'Australian English' is useful and legitimate; but it is necessary to guard against exaggerating the differences between the two. Australian English is still English, and the vocabulary, even of colloquial conversation, is not very different from that of educated Southern English. In that section of the vocabulary dealing with specifically Australian things and conditions, however, a wide difference exists, and there are also subtle changes taking place as the use of Australian phrases widens and as old words take on new meanings.

In 1900 this differentiation had already taken place. A distinctive accent had developed, and a specialised section of the Australian vocabulary existed, though in this section words were constantly in process of creation, some ephemeral, disappearing when the need that called them into being disappeared, and others, enduring.

It might be well to cast a brief glance at these earlier developments before 1900. The speakers of English who came to

Australia were confronted by a new climate, a new landscape, new plants, and engaged in new occupations, or in old occupations under conditions so strange that the old words no longer seemed to fit them. Inevitably the language changed also, and there was loss as well as gain. Words like *glen, valley, meadow, wood, dale,* do not appear in the Australian vocabulary, and the Australian words *bush, scrub, paddock,* and *creek,* have wide and varied meanings. Moreover, these migrants were from different British classes and from different British regions, and their mixing in the new land had its results in the linguistic atmosphere. There are traces of Northern and Southern pronunciations, and many words, believed to be distinctively Australian, have their origins in local dialects, e.g. *larrikin, barrack, cobber.*

Many of the new words and the new usages could be traced to specific circumstances and events in colonial life. The aborigines gave *kangaroo, corroboree, boomerang.* Convictism gave *emancipist, expiree, assignee.* Gold, discovered in 1850, gave *diggings, mullock, fossick.* Bushranging, closely connected with gold, gave *cattle duffing, clearskin,* an unbranded animal, *stick up.* The processes of land settlement, especially the Act of 1867, gave many new words: *selection, selector, squatter.* By 1900 a fair number of words had been well established in Australian English, both in colloquial writings and in speech.

The new century brought a change in the attitude of Australians towards their land. The Commonwealth, proclaimed in 1901, quickened Australian patriotism. *The Bulletin,* founded in 1880, fostered a native-born school of short story writers and bush balladists. Writers like Lawson and Paterson embedded Australian words in their writings and gave them wide currency and permanence. *The Bulletin* was at the peak of its influence in the 1900's.

The 1914-18 war gave rise to many words, most of them ephemeral. More important, perhaps, was the recognition of the fact that Australia was a country in its own right; Australian poetry began to be studied in the schools. *The Oxford Book of Australian Verse* appeared in 1918, and the best known school anthology of Australian and English verse appeared in 1924. This meant that the distinctively Australian vocabulary of the

Australian poets passed into educated Australian speech. The study of Australian history in the schools soon followed and many terms that, dealing with convictism and the like, had tended to fall into disuse, again became current in the educated Australian vocabulary.

The second World War gave rise to a crop of words taken from the 1914-18 War and to a crop of new words, most of them ephemeral. The war years, and the years immediately preceding them and following them, have seen a heightened interest of Australians in Australia. It is significant that most of the Australian novels being written are Australian historical novels. Speech and vocabulary show an Australian point of view. The islands and the region to the north of Australia are now referred to as 'the Near North'. Expressions common twenty years ago like *laughing jackass* and *native bear* have been displaced by *kookaburra* and *koala*. A greater interest is being taken in the aborigines: and aboriginal terms are being adopted freely by the educated vocabulary.

The most important difference between English and Australian English is more subtle and more important, and the difference is widening. When an Australian fisherman says that he is *baited* he means that the fish has taken the bait from the hook. There are many extensions of the word *bush*. A person lost or unable to find his way anywhere can be said to be *bushed*. *Ropeable*, often heard in Australia, means 'angry'. The term derives from an animal so exicted or wild that it had to be roped. *Stock* usually means cattle: the Australian speaks of *stockyards* and *sheepyards*. *Offsider* is commonly used for an intimate or an assistant. Hundreds of such examples could be mentioned.

Because the population of Australia is something like 98 per cent British, the foreign element has contributed little, if anything, to the Australian vocabulary. It has been observed in Queensland, where there are some Italian communities in the North, that Italian children frequently commence school unable to speak English. Once the children learn to speak English, the parents also learn. It would seem that the parent is unwilling that his child should be able to speak English and Italian while he himself can speak only Italian. Even in those communities where the language is connected with religion, the language dies out in two generations. This can be seen in German communities and in Welsh communities.

Differences in a language spoken are much more striking than differences in a language written, and many people feel that Australian is different from English because Australians speak differently from Englishmen. Australia is not a country, it is a continent, and the most noteworthy feature about Australian speech is its uniformity. There are historical reasons for this uniformity. Speech in an old country is both regional and class. The ruling class usually comes from the most important region and the speech of that class gains prestige. Regional speech can arise only where communities have been isolated and have had little or no communication with their neighbours. Australia has been settled within a short space of time, during a period when means of communication were relatively efficient, and no part of Australia has been isolated, and, therefore, there is no regional speech in Australia.

Australia has no clearly stratified society. There is, in Australia, no class which has enough prestige to give its manner of speaking prestige. There are, of course, class differences in Australia and there are differences of pronunciation. Thus a certain type of speech seems typical of the less educated, i.e. the working class, and a different type typical of the more educated, i.e. the business and professional class. But there is no clear division into the two: and features of both types of speech may be found in the speech of any Australian irrespective of his social standard. The two types of Australian speech are termed Broad Australian and Educated Australian.

It is frequently said and written that Broad Australian is Cockney. This is not so. The word 'Cockney' has been probably used loosely as a derogatory term by those who find Broad Australian unpleasant. It is even more frequently said that Australians say *die* for *day*. This also is incorrect. The first element in the Broad Australian pronunciation of *day* is the vowel sound heard in *hut*. Many Australians also tend to avoid the use of the broad *a* in such words as *dance*, and in both

Educated and Broad Australian the sound of *i* in *it* is seldom used in unstressed syllables.

There is much confusion in Australia as to what constitutes 'good' Australian speech. Southern English is in England undoubtedly a widely accepted speech, and is the normal speech for drama and broadcasting. Australian society has its origins in England, and Australia is closely linked with England both economically and culturally. Many people, therefore, feel that to be 'good', Australian speech should be like English speech. This is, in fact, impossible. Australian pronunciation has become, by a spontaneous and natural development, other than English pronunciation. It is not so much wrong as futile to wish to make Australians speak Southern English. In Australia there is still a strong tendency to think that speech which approaches most closely to Southern English is the best. On the stage and in broadcasts we hear speakers who use some such version of English: Broad Australian sounds are avoided, but in the pronunciation of individual words there is little uniformity. Within the last few years there have been some competent studies of Australian speech, free from any bias, and it is inevitable that before very long some form of Educated Australian will become standard Australian speech.

In 1900, it can broadly be said, the majority of educated Australians tried to write and speak like Englishmen. *Colonial* meant to many 'inferior'. In 1950 *colonial* does not exist in the Australian vocabulary. There has grown up a considerable body of literature which is Australian both in outlook and in idiom. It is inevitable that Australian English will become a branch of English in the sense that American is a branch of English.

A. K. THOMSON,
Senior Lecturer in English, University of Queensland.

GENERAL INDEX*

* Predominantly a subject-index with merely cursory references excluded.

Some other works by Eric Partridge

ENGLISH: A COURSE FOR HUMAN BEINGS

Comprehensive, original and stimulating. One-volume edition: 18s. 6d. 3-volume edition; I, Elementary, 7s.; II, Middle School, 6s.; III, Higher, 6s. (Winchester Publications). (U.S.A.: Macdonald, 37 Madison Ave. at 26th, N.Y.C.: $3.50.)

USAGE AND ABUSAGE:
A GUIDE TO GOOD ENGLISH

This modern 'Fowler' has sold over 50,000 copies; now in its 4th edition, 15s. (Hamish Hamilton). (U.S.A.: Harpers: $3.75.)

· A DICTIONARY OF SLANG
AND UNCONVENTIONAL ENGLISH

A vast work (1200 pages in Crn 4to) covering the entire British Empire, from the 16th Century to the present day; 3rd edition, revised and enlarged, £3 3s. od. (Routledge & Kegan Paul). (U.S.A.: Macmillan: $11.50.)

A DICTIONARY OF THE BRITISH AND
AMERICAN UNDERWORLD

In 804 pages (Crn 4to) it covers the English-speaking world of the 16th-20th Centuries, 50s. (Routledge). (U.S.A.: Macmillan: $9.50.)

NAME INTO WORD

A Dictionary of Proper Names become Common Property Demy 8vo, 640 pages; 2nd edition, revised and enlarged, 25s. (Secker & Warburg). (U.S.A.: Macmillan: $4.50.)

EIGHTEENTH-CENTURY ENGLISH
ROMANTIC POETRY

An Historical Study
(Champion, quai Malaquais, Paris 6e, frs 600).

All prices net

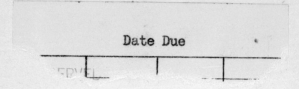

Date Due